ALEXANDER THE GREAT

Each book in the series GREAT LIVES OF THE ANCIENT WORLD succinctly explores the life, culture and lasting legacy of outstanding figures across the ancient world, including China, the Indian subcontinent, the Middle East, and ancient Greece and Rome.

SERIES EDITOR: Paul Cartledge

Alexander the Great: Lives and Legacies   STEPHEN HARRISON
Archimedes: Fulcrum of Science   NICHOLAS NICASTRO
Plato: A Civic Life   CAROL ATACK

ALEXANDER THE GREAT

Lives and Legacies

STEPHEN HARRISON

REAKTION BOOKS

This book is dedicated to the memory of my grandparents.
One who I never met, but who I think of whenever my job feels
like anything other than a privilege. One who taught me the true
meaning of kindness, one the power of curiosity. And one who showed
me the value of doing things with a twinkle in your eye and your
tongue in your cheek – readers may detect a hint of the latter here.

Published by
REAKTION BOOKS LTD
Unit 32, Waterside
44–48 Wharf Road
London N1 7UX, UK
www.reaktionbooks.co.uk

First published 2025
Copyright © Stephen Harrison 2025

EU GPSR Authorised Representative
Logos Europe, 9 rue Nicolas Poussin, 17000, La Rochelle, France
email: contact@logoseurope.eu

Printed and bound in Great Britain by Bell & Bain, Glasgow

A catalogue record for this book is available from the British Library

ISBN 978 1 78914 997 5

CONTENTS

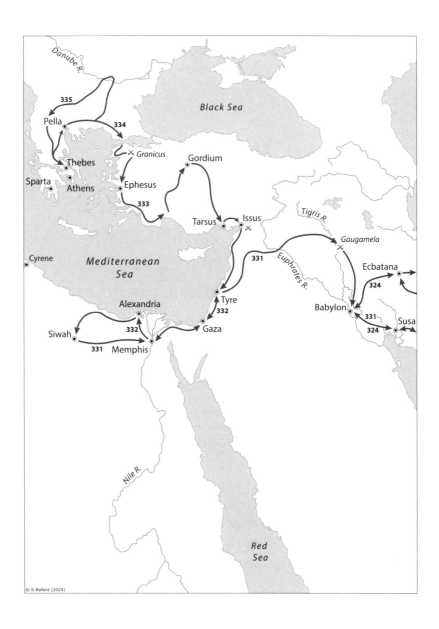

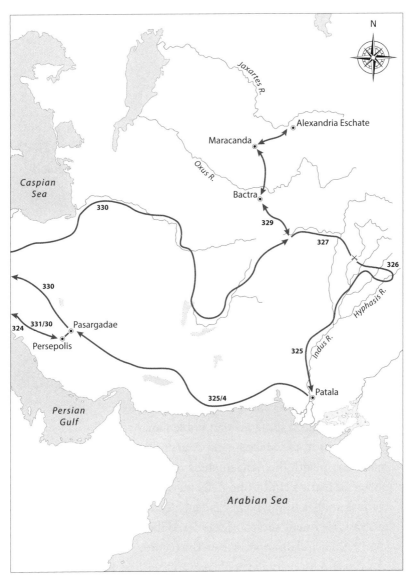

Route of Alexander's campaigns in Greece and the Near East, 335–323.

Key Figures

The nature of Alexander's reign means that this book is full of references to people with similar – occasionally identical – names. This list provides a brief description of the figures who are particularly important or appear most often in the narrative.

ABOULITES: A Persian nobleman and the satrap of Susa under Darius III. He surrendered the city to Alexander and retained his position but was later executed.

ANTIPATER: A Macedonian nobleman and one of the key advisors to Philip II. During Alexander's campaign, he remained in Macedonia to govern. He later played a pivotal role in the years after Alexander's death.

ARISTOBOULOS: Participated in Alexander's campaign, but not in a particularly prominent role. He later wrote an account of events, which Arrian used as one of his principal sources.

ARTABAZUS: A leading Persian nobleman, Artabazus had spent time in exile at the Macedonian court in the 350s and 340s. His relationship with the Achaemenids restored, he was a loyal supporter of Darius III, but he defected to the Macedonians after Darius's murder. By this point, his daughter, Barsine, was Alexander's mistress. He briefly served Alexander as the satrap of Bactria, but soon retired and disappears from the record.

ATTALUS: A Macedonian nobleman and close relation of Philip II's last wife, Cleopatra. Championing his own dynastic ambitions, he was apparently an outspoken opponent of Alexander at Philip's court. He was swiftly assassinated once Alexander came to power.

BAGOAS: A name shared by two eunuchs. The first Bagoas rose to prominence under Artaxerxes III and was allegedly responsible for a string of assassinations in the early 330s that plunged the Achaemenid court into chaos and brought Darius III to power. The second Bagoas was a favourite of Darius III and later passed into Alexander's possession. The infamously good-looking man allegedly had a sexual relationship with both kings.

BARSINE: A Persian noblewoman and the daughter of Artabazus. At the start of the campaign, she was married to Memnon, a military commander from Rhodes who served Darius with distinction. After his death in 333, she was captured by the Macedonians and became Alexander's mistress, allegedly giving birth to a son named Heracles. She was probably murdered during the wars that followed Alexander's death at the same time as her son was killed.

BESSUS: A high-ranking Persian nobleman, possibly related to the royal family, Bessus was the satrap of Bactria, in Central Asia, and held a cavalry command during the Battle of Gaugamela. He subsequently led a coup against Darius III and attempted to establish himself as king, taking the throne name Artaxerxes. He was betrayed to Alexander by some of his supporters and executed in 329.

CALLISTHENES: From Olynthus in northern Greece, Callisthenes was a pupil – and possibly a relation – of Aristotle. He accompanied the campaign as Alexander's official historian but fell from favour and was executed in 327.

CHARES: A Greek from Mytilene, Chares became the *eisangeleus* (chamberlain or usher) at Alexander's court. This gave him oversight of major court events. He wrote an account of Alexander's reign, which does not survive, but which is occasionally referenced by later writers.

CLITUS: A leading Macedonian nobleman, Clitus held an important cavalry command and was responsible for saving Alexander's life during the Battle of the Granicus. He co-commanded the Companion Cavalry with Hephaestion after Philotas' death and was then appointed as the satrap of Bactria. Before he could take up this position, he was killed by Alexander during a drunken banquet in 328.

CRATERUS: A leading Macedonian nobleman, Craterus held a succession of important military commands during Alexander's reign. When Alexander died, Craterus was on his way to Macedonia, where he had been instructed to assume Antipater's position. He was one of the most prominent early casualties of the wars that sprang up between Alexander's generals after the king's death.

DARIUS III: A Persian nobleman and distant relative of Artaxerxes III, whom he served with distinction, Darius became king of Persia in 338. He was Alexander's principal antagonist until he was murdered in a coup led by Bessus.

HEPHAESTION: A Macedonian nobleman, Hephaestion was Alexander's closest friend and possibly his lover. Through Alexander's patronage, he gradually climbed the military ladder, eventually becoming the co-commander of the Companion Cavalry. He died in 324 of illness and was much mourned by Alexander.

LYSIMACHUS: A military commander who served Alexander with distinction and eventually became one of the prestigious bodyguards (*somatophylakes*), Lysimachus was given control of Thrace after Alexander's death. He used this to carve out a kingdom that straddled Europe and Asia Minor, but, in 281, he died in battle against Seleucus, who absorbed Lysimachus' kingdom into his own.

NEARCHUS: A Cretan whose family had moved to Amphipolis while Philip II was king, Nearchus held a variety of commands during Alexander's campaign. Most notably, he served as the admiral of the fleet that was constructed in India and explored the southern coast of the Persian Empire. He later wrote an account of this voyage, which was used heavily by Arrian.

OLYMPIAS: Daughter of Neoptolemus, the king of Epirus, one of the kingdoms that bordered Macedonia. She married Philip II in 357, giving birth to Alexander the Great and a daughter named Cleopatra. She advocated for Alexander's interests throughout the campaign and, after his death, championed her grandson, Alexander IV. Responsible for the execution of Philip III Arrhidaeus and Adea-Eurydice, Olympias was herself killed by Cassander during the wars that followed Alexander's death.

OXYARTES: A Bactrian or Sogdian nobleman, Oxyartes likely served in the Achaemenid army since he appears among the initial supporters of Bessus. He later surrendered and Alexander married his daughter, Roxane. He served as a satrap for Alexander, using this to create a power base, which survived Alexander's death and endured into the 310s. His eventual fate is unknown.

PARMENION: A leading Macedonian nobleman and one of Philip II's principal military advisors. He retained this status during the opening years of Alexander's campaign, commanding one wing of the Macedonian army during all of the major battles against the Persians. He fell from grace in 330, when his son Philotas was executed for plotting against Alexander. Deemed too much of a threat to the king due to his experience and popularity with the troops, Parmenion was swiftly murdered on Alexander's orders.

PERDICCAS: Born into a prominent family from Orestis in Upper Macedonia, Perdiccas held military commands from the end of Philip's life and throughout Alexander's reign. When Alexander died in Babylon in 323, Perdiccas was the most senior commander in the city, so he was responsible for the initial succession arrangements. Ultimately, he took up the regency himself but was unable to prevent splits within the Macedonian command. He was murdered by his own subordinates in 321/20 while leading an invasion of Egypt.

PEUCESTAS: A Macedonian nobleman credited with saving Alexander's life during the siege of a Malloi city in India. He was admitted into the elite unit of bodyguards and then made the satrap of Persia, a position he retained after Alexander's death until his removal by Antigonus.

PHILIP II: The youngest son of Amyntas III and Eurydice, Philip became the king of Macedonia in 359 after the deaths of his elder brothers. He subsequently led a series of remarkable conquests that brought Macedonia to new prominence and created the conditions required for his son, Alexander, to launch an invasion of Persia.

PHILOTAS: The son of Parmenion and thus a leading Macedonian nobleman. He may have held a high-ranking position at Philip's court, and certainly held military commands from the start of Alexander's reign. He was soon the commander of the prestigious Companion Cavalry, a position he held until 330 when he was accused of complicity in a plot against Alexander's life and executed.

PTOLEMY: A Macedonian nobleman and a childhood friend of Alexander. He became increasingly prominent during the second half of Alexander's campaign, holding a succession of military commands. After Alexander's death, he was appointed satrap of Egypt. He used this position to establish himself as king, founding a dynasty which lasted until the suicide of Cleopatra VII.

ROXANE: The daughter of Oxyartes, a Bactrian or Sogdian nobleman, Roxane encountered Alexander during a banquet. The Macedonian purportedly fell in love with Roxane at first sight, and the pair were swiftly married. Her pre-eminence may have been challenged when Alexander took two additional wives, both Achaemenid princesses, at Susa in 324, but she was pregnant when Alexander died. Their son, Alexander IV, was born a few months after his father's death and was immediately proclaimed co-king of the empire. Apart from accusations that she murdered his other wives, Roxane's role in the wars that followed her husband's death is largely unknown. She was murdered along with her son in the late 310s or early 300s.

SELEUCUS: A Macedonian nobleman, Seleucus participated in Alexander's campaign, although precise details of his commands are hard to come by. He became one of Perdiccas' chief subordinates after Alexander's death and likely had a hand in his superior's death because, in the administrative reshuffle that followed this pivotal event, he was appointed to govern the plum satrapy of Babylon. He used this as a base to carve out the largest of the 'Successor' kingdoms, stretching from the borders of India to Europe. He was assassinated when he was on the verge of returning to Macedonia and reuniting the fragments of Alexander's empire.

SISYGAMBIS: The mother of Darius III, she was captured by Alexander along with the rest of Darius' immediate family after the Battle of Issus in 333. She interceded with Alexander on behalf of various groups of subjects, and allegedly starved herself to death after learning of Alexander's own demise.

SPITAMENES: A Bactrian or Sogdian nobleman who had likely served in the Achaemenid army, Spitamenes was one of Bessus' chief supporters after the murder of Darius III. He then betrayed Bessus to Alexander and led his own resistance movement. He was eventually killed by his allies, the Massagetae. His daughter, Apama, was married to Seleucus during the Susa weddings.

Alexander the Great, marble bust, *c.* fourth century BCE, allegedly from Egypt.

Introduction

A genius, a tyrant. A dreamer, a killer. A visionary, a maniac.
Greek, not Greek; gay, not gay; a god, not a god.
Paranoid. Destructive. Delusional. Drunk.
Virtuous. Chivalrous. Magnanimous. Titanic.
Great?

Most opinions of Alexander III of Macedonia are as reductive as these.[1] He is cut down to a two-dimensional figure, driven towards world conquest by one supposedly defining feature: a deep-seated yearning to surpass all known human achievements; an insatiable desire for more and more power; the fantasy of uniting humanity; rivalry with his father; alcoholism; love. How else to explain his accomplishments and understand how he – and so also, we – could change the world? But not here. Not in this book. This book will do things differently.

All treatments of Alexander open with grandiose promises like this. He has been written about so many times that with every new iteration, authors feel the need to justify tackling the subject – to explain what more there is to say about a man examined so often that, surely, there is nothing new left to discover about him. In fact, merely pointing out this pattern is so clichéd that the seasoned

Alexander reader will be rolling their eyes. I'd count myself among those. My scholarly life has been defined by Alexander: reading as much as I could, writing dissertations with his name in the title, publishing, teaching. But I never imagined that I'd write this book. It just seemed so . . . unnecessary. Everything that could be written, had been written.

Then the world changed. The Alexander I was reading about seemed so outdated, the product of a different time. But, for me, Alexander does not really belong in the past; he is a creature of the present. This book is self-consciously informed by the political, social and cultural upheaval of the last two decades. I am interested less in the man himself and more in those around him, the people who facilitated his campaigns and suffered under his rule. I am less concerned by what drove Alexander forward and more worried about what he left in his wake. Rather than seeing things in black and white – Macedonians versus Persians, a 'good' or 'evil' Alexander – this book aims to bring the grey to life: the Sogdian woman whose life was uprooted by Alexander's arrival but became queen of an empire; the Indian ruler who tried to use an alliance with Alexander to achieve his own militaristic goals. Naturally, Alexander will dominate this story, but he will not be the only character who matters. 'Lives' rather than 'life', as the subtitle of this book puts it.

It is important to emphasize that this is a story. What Alexander did is obviously important, but we will see that the sources are so problematic that even the bare facts often elude us: we usually do not know exactly where he went, why he went there or what he did, except in the broadest terms. This makes studying Alexander much more than an exercise in sorting fact from fiction. Instead, it involves examining layers of interpretations developed through the ages as historians have sought to reconstruct his reign. 'Legacies' as opposed to 'legacy'.

I will give my take on the key moments and set out new arguments, but I also want to convey a sense of the difficulties involved in reaching these conclusions and the frustrations that emerge. Historians are supposed to explain what happened in the past, but what do we do when this is largely impossible? This is a book about Alexander the Great. But it is also a book about how and why historians do history – and that means it is also a book about me. That might sound self-indulgent, but being upfront about why I am more interested in some aspects of his life than others, as I have tried to do throughout this book, hopefully shows how Alexander is not only a historical figure but a means to evaluate the changing preoccupations and values of the modern world. It is a reminder too that there is no such thing as a neutral commentator.

Edgar Degas, *Alexander and Bucephalus*, 1861/2, oil on canvas. Alexander's life was full of incidents that have captured the attention of artists through the centuries. In Degas' painting Alexander is depicted taming Bucephalus. The youthful Alexander contrasts with the ageing Philip, but Alexander looks towards his father, perhaps nervously seeking his approval.

1

Macedonia and Greece, 356–334

July 356. It was a good day to be Philip II, king of Macedonia. First came news that his general Parmenion had won a major victory against his Illyrian neighbours, and second came reports that his horses had won victory at the Olympics. Philip then heard that his wife, Olympias, had given birth to a son, whom he would name Alexander.[1] It was an auspicious time to be born, so much so that the Temple of Artemis in Ephesus allegedly burned down on the same day – the goddess apparently too busy overseeing the child's birth. There is just one problem with these claims: they are not true. Parmenion *may* have been victorious against the Illyrians, Philip *may* have won the Olympics, the temple *may* have suffered a fire and Alexander was *certainly* born. But not on the same day. The story is true-ish – is that enough? This will be a recurring theme.

However, Alexander's childhood is especially shrouded in mystery. Given what he subsequently achieved, this is unsurprising: legends grew up around his birth and subsequent generations sought to foreshadow his later achievements in their descriptions of his formative years. This problem is compounded by how few sources there are for this period. As we will see, studies of Alexander are based primarily on just five main narrative accounts from antiquity, but only Plutarch, writing in the first and second centuries CE, discusses Alexander's youth in any depth. Some of the details are well-attested – for instance, Alexander was tutored by the philosopher Aristotle – but other stories seem far-fetched. One good example of this concerns Bucephalus, who would eventually become famous as Alexander's war horse.[2] Plutarch describes how a horse trainer offered to sell the horse to Philip, but Bucephalus refused to allow anybody to mount him; Philip, thinking the horse untrained, declined to buy him. Alexander, watching nearby, muttered something under his breath about this being a wasted opportunity. Hearing this, his father asked if Alexander thought he knew better than him. Yes, Alexander replied, so Philip asked what he would bet to prove it – the price of the horse, Alexander countered. The men with Philip laughed at his impetuousness, but the boy had noticed something they had missed: Bucephalus was afraid of his own shadow. He turned the horse away from the sun, calming him, and Alexander was soon cantering around the field. Philip was aghast and then proud: 'find a kingdom worthy of you,' he told his son. 'Macedonia is too small for you.' This incident displays Alexander's perceptiveness – able to see in Bucephalus something his father had missed – and his confidence in challenging his elders. This mix of vision and self-belief would play an important role in later events. The anecdote builds towards Philip's final remark, which alludes to those future achievements. Alexander's successes, the story suggests, reflect innate qualities.

This is indicative of Plutarch's wider approach. His account of Alexander forms part of a series known as the *Parallel Lives*, in which Plutarch compared famous Greeks and Romans. He aimed to give readers positive or negative role models, whose examples could be emulated or learnt from.[3] In introducing his *Life of Alexander*, Plutarch asks his readers not to complain if he omits key moments or discusses important events only briefly.[4] He explains that he is not writing history, but 'lives', which meant drawing attention to the little things, like the odd phrase or joke that could shed light on his subject's character. This is the central aim of modern biographies. The problem, of course, is that anecdotal material like this is the most prone to exaggeration, distortion and invention. Like Plutarch, I must stress that it has been impossible to discuss every single moment of Alexander's life here, but there is a crucial distinction between this book and those which have followed in Plutarch's footsteps: I do not believe that we can get a sense of Alexander's real personality.

Philip's Macedonia (359–336)

Although the details of Alexander's first two decades of life are largely a mystery to us, we are better informed about the time in which he lived.[5] This was a transformative period for Macedonia, which previously had been nothing more than a second-tier power on the northern peripheries of the Greek world. We know very little about what went on in the kingdom before the reign of Philip II. There was a clearly established royal dynasty, which we call the Argeads because they traced their ancestry from Temenus of Argos, who was in turn descended from Heracles. The throne seems to have remained within this family from the end of the sixth century BCE, but individuals did not necessarily have a firm grip on power. At least four of the kings before Philip were assassinated, another died in battle and another was deposed. Part of the reason for this instability is that Macedonia itself was divided. Lower Macedonia was centred on the lowland territories, which open out onto the Thermaic Gulf in the Aegean Sea, whereas Upper Macedonia rises thousands of metres above sea level, its peaks including Mount Olympus itself.[6] Communication with outlying settlements in the latter region was difficult, so powerful hereditary nobilities emerged and the influence of the Argeads waxed and waned. Macedonia was also surrounded by rivals who were always happy to destabilize the kingdom by supporting challengers to the throne.

Things began to change after Philip II came to power in 359. Philip was the third son of Amyntas III and Eurydice, and he had three half-brothers too. When Amyntas died in 370, Philip's eldest brother, Alexander II, succeeded his father. A few years later, however, he was assassinated by Ptolemy of Alorus, who had an obscure connection to the Argead family. Ptolemy either set himself up as regent for Amyntas' second son, Perdiccas III, who was still a minor, or perhaps seized the throne for himself. Whichever route he took, Ptolemy appears to have been supported by Eurydice, Amyntas' widow, but her motivations and the precise nature of their relationship are unclear. However, by 365, Perdiccas had come of age and taken the throne, killing Ptolemy in the process. This drama played out against a backdrop of interference by Thebes, the dominant power in central Greece. As part of one peace settlement, the teenage Philip was sent to the city as a hostage, but he was back in Macedonia by the end of the 360s in time to see his brother and 4,000 of his countrymen killed in battle against the invading Illyrians in 360/59.[7] Perdiccas' son Amyntas, who had been born in the mid-360s, was next in line to the throne but clearly could not rule. Instead, Philip – still only in his early twenties himself – was the obvious Argead candidate. Some historians imagine that he initially acted as regent for his nephew, but others think that he became king immediately. Either way, he controlled Macedonian affairs.

His nascent reign faced plenty of challenges. The relationship between Macedonia and Athens had been tense for decades. The Athenians had founded a colony called Amphipolis in Thrace, close to Macedonia. Amphipolis had been independent since the 420s, but the Athenians were keen to recapture it and always suspected that the Macedonians had designs on the city. They now offered military assistance to a pretender called Argaeus, presumably in exchange for promises about Amphipolis. Another challenger, Pausanias, had secured the backing of the Thracians. Meanwhile, the Paeonians in the northwest launched a series of booty raids, and the Illyrians to the west were expected to capitalize on their victory over Perdiccas by invading.

Facing war on multiple fronts, Philip showed his diplomatic savvy. He persuaded the Athenians that he had no interest in seizing Amphipolis, so they dropped their support for Argaeus, who was swiftly defeated. The Thracian ruler was bribed to abandon Pausanias, and the Paeonians were also paid off. This let Philip concentrate his forces against the Illyrians, against whom he won a crushing victory – the Illyrians apparently suffered 7,000 casualties and were expelled from Macedonia.[8] To cement the ensuing peace, Philip married the Illyrian princess Audata. Marriage as a diplomatic strategy was a common tactic for Macedonian kings, but it became a particular hallmark of Philip. By the end of the 350s, he had married six times, all to women from places on the periphery of his kingdom. For instance, Alexander's mother, Olympias, came from Epirus, to the west of Macedonia. These marriages helped protect Philip's borders and paved the way for expansion.

Philip's reign was full of accomplishments that would have garnered much more attention were they not overshadowed by the achievements of his son. In brief, through the 350s and 340s, Philip transformed Macedonia's fortunes. Military successes were obviously pivotal in this. For instance, there were victories in Thrace

Tetradrachm of Alexander the Great. The Macedonian kings claimed to be descended from Heracles to legitimate their rule. Alexander celebrated this connection by featuring a portrait of Heracles on his coinage. Some have suggested that Heracles' features increasingly became reminiscent of Alexander's own.

to the west and Thessaly in the south. The latter saw Philip become the leader of the Thessalian League and gave him a platform to interfere in Greek affairs. Most notably, in 346, Philip played the decisive role in ending the Third Sacred War, which had rumbled on in Greece for a decade. Perhaps the most striking sign of what was to come happened in 348, when the Macedonians captured Olynthus, in the Chalcidice in northern Greece. After forces besieged the city, it was razed to the ground and its inhabitants sold into slavery. These victories came at significant personal cost: Philip lost an eye in one siege and walked with a limp after suffering a serious leg wound.

What happened on the battlefield does not tell the whole story, because Philip introduced several significant reforms. The one that gets the most attention is the development of a new weapon, the sarissa. This was an extremely long spear carried by the infantry phalanx, its extra reach offering an advantage on the battlefield. People can be cynical about this: if it were so important, why wasn't it copied by Philip's enemies?[9] But that misses the point. Adopting the sarissa demanded major changes to the way that the infantry operated. Its length and weight meant that it had to be gripped with both hands, so, apart from a small shield slung over one shoulder, individual soldiers had little protection. Safety came only in numbers, which meant endlessly drilling the phalanx so that gaps did not open up in the line. This training required men to be under arms for longer, so they needed to be paid by the state. Philip was able to do this by developing Macedonia's mining industry to take advantage of the natural resources of the region, something that was enhanced through the conquest of resource-rich places like Thrace. This is a bit of an oversimplification, but it captures the essence of the virtuous circle created by Philip: military victories increased his resource base, which funded further conquests and won additional resources. This let him maintain an army for long periods of time and his men duly became extremely experienced soldiers.

One consistent thread through all of this was enmity with Athens. Philip may have persuaded the Athenians that he had no interest in Amphipolis when he first came to power, but he quickly proved false to his word, capturing the city in 357 and taking Pydna and Methone, two other Athenian possessions on the peripheries of Macedonia, for good measure. Athens and Macedonia backed opposing sides in the Third Sacred War, and through the 340s Athens became increasingly belligerent. In 340 Philip seized the Athenian grain supplies as they were being brought down from the Black Sea. This act of war made a major confrontation inevitable, and in 338, at Chaeronea in Boeotia, Philip fought an alliance of Greek city-states led by Athens and Thebes. The Macedonians won a significant victory, with more than 1,000 Athenians killed and another 2,000 captured. According to one source, the pivotal moment came when the left wing of the Macedonian forces, inspired by the heroics of their commander, broke through the allied lines.[10] That leader? An eighteen-year-old Alexander. There is no reason to doubt Alexander's participation in the battle, but it is unlikely that he was anything more than a figurehead, with the experienced generals alongside him responsible for making key decisions. The victory at Chaeronea confirmed Philip's dominance of the Greek peninsula, but a more powerful enemy lay just across the Aegean Sea.

The Persian Empire and the Greeks (550–336)

Persia, in the south of modern-day Iran, was a relatively minor power for much of the first half of the first millennium. This changed in the middle of the sixth century when Cyrus II – known to us now as Cyrus the Great – came to power.[11] In little more than a decade, he defeated the Medes, Lydians and Babylonians, giving him an empire that stretched from the Mediterranean and Aegean coasts to the borders of India. After his death in 530, his son,

Cambyses, extended Persian control into Egypt. The revolutionary impact of these events cannot be overstated. For much of the previous two millennia, the ancient Near East had been divided between several, roughly equal, powers. Individual dynasties had come and gone, and different regions had prospered at different times, but a multipolar world had endured. Now, that had been swept away and the world's first genuine superpower had arrived.

Cambyses died in the late 520s, and, after a vicious power struggle, he was succeeded by Darius I, who may have murdered the rightful heir and seized the throne. In a famous inscription at Bisitun in Iran that tried to justify his accession, Darius claimed to be part of a long royal line established by somebody called Achaemenes.[12] For that reason, we refer to the dynasty as the Achaemenids. Darius founded a new city, Persepolis, in the heart of Persia and developed the empire's administrative structure. For instance, the kingdom was broken down into administrative units known as satrapies, which were governed by a satrap, usually a high-ranking member of the Persian aristocracy. Darius also expanded the empire, campaigning in India and leading an expedition into Europe to attack the Scythians who lived around the edge of the Black Sea. This brought the Persians to Macedonia's doorstep.

From a Greek perspective, Darius' reign is most notable for the beginnings of a serious conflict with the Persians.[13] The region of Ionia along the Aegean coast of modern-day Turkey was home to several Greek cities. It had been part of the Persian Empire since the days of Cyrus, but, in the 490s, the Ionians rebelled. Their revolt was eventually suppressed, but during the uprising the Ionians sought assistance from their fellow Greeks on the mainland; Eretria and Athens agreed to send aid. The Persians could hardly stand for what they saw as external interference in their affairs, so, with Ionia secure, they prepared to send reprisals against the two cities. An initial attempt in 492 was scuppered when a storm wrecked the Persian fleet, but a second force was sent in 490. The island of Naxos was captured, then Eretria was destroyed. Athens was supposed to be next, but the Persians were defeated at the Battle of Marathon and forced to withdraw.

A decade later, the Persians were back. In the meantime, Darius had died and been succeeded by his son, Xerxes. The earlier expeditions had been commanded by Persian noblemen, but this time the king led the invasion personally. A bridge was constructed across the Hellespont, the narrow stretch of water that separates Europe and Asia, and the army marched through Macedonia into Greece. The Persians defeated a Spartan-led force at Thermopylae, which gave them control of central Greece and left Athens defenceless. The Athenians withdrew to the nearby island of Salamis, watching on as their city was ransacked and set alight. However, the Athenians were victorious in a naval battle in the straits around Salamis and Greece thus gained control of the sea. Worried that his communication lines might now be cut, Xerxes returned to Asia. He left a significant force behind under the command of Mardonius, but this army was defeated at Plataea in 479. The invasion was over.

These were crucial events, but they probably meant more to the Greeks than to Xerxes, who could present the spoils captured as evidence of victory. The Greeks, though, had faced down what they considered an existential threat. This had a significant long-term effect on the way that they constructed their identity. Persia became the 'other' against whom Greeks self-defined: if Greeks were to be free, then Persians must be slaves; if Greeks were brave, Persians were cowards.[14] Moreover, several Greek communities had put traditional inter-state rivalries aside and joined forces to fight the Persians. This political alliance had a short shelf-life – Sparta left soon after the invasion was repulsed, and the league eventually morphed into an Athenian Empire – but the notion of Greeks uniting against a common foe had an important legacy. Sparta's military supremacy on land was entrenched by its leadership of the Greeks at Plataea, while Athens' naval domination was established by victory at Salamis. Both cities could also point to major sacrifices to keep Greece free: three hundred Spartans had fought to the death at Thermopylae, while the Athenians had abandoned their city rather than betray the Greek cause.

Not all Greek communities could boast of such proud heritage. Herodotus reports a marriage alliance between the Macedonian royal family and a Persian nobleman in the late 510s.[15] This close relationship may have played a part in Xerxes' planning for the invasion since he marched through Macedonia to reach Greece and encountered no resistance. Indeed, the Macedonian king, Alexander I, was apparently sent to Athens to persuade the Greeks to surrender.[16] Interestingly, several stories survive that seem to indicate an attempt to rewrite this history. For instance, Alexander is supposed to have sneaked out of the Persian camp the night before Plataea to leak their battleplans to the Greeks.[17]

Perhaps the best example is Herodotus' description of the origins of the marriage alliance between the Macedonians and the Persians.[18] After his Scythian campaign, Darius is said to have sent seven ambassadors to Macedonia to demand that the king, Amyntas, acknowledge Persian superiority. Amyntas did so and invited the ambassadors to dinner. During this banquet, the Persians demanded that women be brought in to entertain them. Drunken hands soon wandered, much to the disgust of the watching Macedonians. Now Amyntas' son, the future Alexander I, intervened. He sent his father to bed and told the Persians that the women would withdraw briefly to freshen up. In their place, he sent beardless youths, disguised as women, who quickly killed the Persians. Soon, a Persian force came looking for the missing ambassadors, but Alexander paid off the search party and married his sister to the Persian general overseeing the investigation. This is clearly nonsense – there was no need to resort to such an elaborate ruse to kill seven ambassadors – but Herodotus may be parroting a tale put out by the Macedonians to defend their conduct during the Persian Wars lest any contemporaries suggest they had been willing allies of the Persians.

Given their experiences of the 490s and 480s, Greeks were hardly sympathetic narrators of Persian affairs. From Xerxes onwards, kings are routinely condemned as effeminate and corrupted by a love of luxury, their empire in a state of perpetual decline from the heady days of Cyrus. For much of the nineteenth and twentieth centuries, Western historians followed suit. Their interpretations of the Persians were affected by contemporary attitudes towards the Ottomans and by what Edward Said famously termed 'orientalism' – the notion of the 'East' as homogenous, unchanging, decadent and immoral, the antithesis of the West and its values.[19] This perspective was exploded as a fallacy in the 1980s by a group of scholars known as the 'Achaemenid Workshop', led particularly by Heleen Sancisi-Weerdenburg and Amélie Kuhrt. In place of a weak and decaying realm, a new image emerged, one that emphasized the vitality of the Persian kingdom into the fourth century: the administrative system remained robust, the army effective and the monarchs able rulers.

From Philip to Alexander (338–336)

Philip was all too aware of the power of the Persians and their antagonistic historical relationship with the Greeks. This is reflected in the treaty that he drew up after the Battle of Chaeronea.[20] Rather than attempt to incorporate the Greek city-states into his own kingdom or appoint rulers to govern each *polis* on his behalf, Philip invited the Greeks to enter into an alliance with the Macedonians and with one another. This was to be a military alliance and a common peace, with participants prohibited from making war on each other. It was modelled on the Hellenic alliance that had seen off Xerxes, but it tends to be called the League of Corinth after the location of its first meeting. The League was governed by a council,

with every state having an equal vote. Its first job was to elect a
hegemon, a leader. The council chose Philip. This was an ingenious
solution to the problem of how to govern Greece. A fiction of free
choice had been maintained, even if the Greeks realistically had no
option other than to elect Philip. There was, however, one notable
absentee from the League – the Spartans, who refused to join.

The League of Corinth was created as a means of managing
Greece, but it was also explicitly outward-looking: its stated goal
was a campaign against the Persians.[21] Preparations were soon
underway and by 336 an advance force, commanded by Attalus
and Parmenion, had been sent into Asia Minor to prepare the
ground for a major attack.[22] Philip, though, would not live to lead
this invasion.[23] In the autumn of 336, he organized a major festival
at Aegae in Macedonia to celebrate the marriage of his daughter
Cleopatra to Alexander of Epirus. Dignitaries were invited from
all over the Greek-speaking world – this was also an opportunity
for Philip to advertise his successes. A magnificent new palace had
recently been constructed, and a theatre too. Athletic contests were
organized, and the games opened with a procession into the theatre. The parade included busts of the twelve Olympian deities, but
the gods had a new companion – a statue of Philip carried among
them.

But Philip was no immortal. As he entered the theatre, one of
his own bodyguards, a man called Pausanias, rushed forward and
stabbed the king to death. Pausanias fled but was killed while trying
to escape. Sources suggest that his motivation was deeply personal.
He had been Philip's lover but had been dropped for a younger man
who even shared the same name. The elder Pausanias had virulently
abused his namesake, causing the younger man such shame that he
deliberately sacrificed himself in battle while protecting Philip. He
had, however, confided in the nobleman Attalus, who quickly sought
revenge: the older Pausanias was invited to dinner, plied with alco-
hol and then handed over to Attalus' slaves, who sexually assaulted

him. Pausanias immediately complained about this treatment to Philip and demanded that Attalus be punished, but Philip refused. This explanation is perfectly plausible and similar incidents had happened previously – for instance, the death of Archelaus, an earlier king, discussed in Chapter Seven. However, since Pausanias was killed in the act of escaping, it is unclear how this motive came to light. If this were a wider conspiracy, it served the interests of the others involved to present this as an entirely personal affair. In antiquity, suspicion fell particularly on Olympias, Alexander's mother, while some ancient authors accuse the Persian king, Darius III, of bribing Pausanias to act. Some, however, have posited that Alexander himself was involved in his father's assassination, or was at least aware of Pausanias' plans.[24]

This is typical of the strand of scholarship that accentuates Alexander's flaws, but there is no hard evidence to support this accusation. Instead, these suspicions are based on indications that the relationship between father and son had become strained. The chief cause of this was Philip's polygamy. Having successfully used marriage as a diplomatic tool, in the 330s Philip married again; this time his wife, Cleopatra, was Macedonian and his motivation was love. Attalus – the man responsible for Pausanias' rape – was related to Cleopatra and he made much of his newfound kinship with the king. According to Plutarch, not long after the wedding, a drunken argument broke out at a banquet.[25] Attalus allegedly raised a toast, praying that the new marriage would bring the Macedonians a legitimate successor. Alexander demanded to know what he was supposed to be and threw a cup at Attalus; Philip now rose, drawing his sword against his own son. Fortunately, he was so drunk that he fell over before he could deliver a blow. Alexander now crowed over his father: 'here is the man who was about to cross from Europe into Asia, but who cannot cross from one couch to another.' This is a good line, but it cannot be true, since nobody at the banquet had any incentive to publicize this story.

Donato Creti, *Alexander the Great Threatened by His Father*, *c.* 1700–1705 (?), oil on canvas. Whereas Plutarch's account of the argument between Alexander and his father builds towards Philip's drunken stumble, here Creti focuses on the dramatic moment when Philip drew his sword at Alexander.

Nevertheless, the anecdote plays on the fact that having multiple wives created the potential for several heirs. Ancient courts did not necessarily follow the rules of primogeniture, where the first-born son succeeds his father, which meant that different factions could grow around various children and competition between these cliques was common. However, any challenge was evidently still a long way off. Philip's own rise to power demonstrated that a proven, adult Argead would win support over an untested infant, and Alexander had already undertaken significant public duties. His prominent role at Chaeronea was the most important of these, but he had apparently acted as regent for Philip during another campaign.[26] It is unlikely that he exercised any real power in these roles, but merely acting as a figurehead meant that he was firmly established in the public consciousness as Philip's self-appointed successor. There was, therefore, little reason for Alexander to support an assassination attempt on his father; but an irrational or paranoid Alexander may have seen things differently.

Irrespective of any forewarning, Alexander and the Macedonian nobility acted quickly when Philip was struck down.[27] Antipater, one of Philip's leading advisors, is usually understood to have presented Alexander to the assembled soldiers, inviting them to acclaim him as their king. Potential challengers were swiftly removed. Amyntas, Philip's nephew, could have succeeded to the throne as an infant in the 350s. This made him a potential threat and he was executed. Cleopatra, Philip's latest wife, was another obvious target, particularly as she had supposedly given birth to a son. The blame for her killing often devolves onto Olympias, but misogynistic tropes regarding the cruelty of royal women abound here – in one version, she is said to have burned Cleopatra and her son alive.[28] Alexander reportedly upbraided his mother for this, but ruthlessness was necessary, and it is unlikely that deaths like this occurred without his agreement. Other members of the nobility with tangential links to the Argead family or who were perceived as potential challengers were also done away with. The most important of these was Attalus. When Philip died, he was in Asia Minor with the army. Given the obvious factions within the court, his co-commander Parmenion essentially had to choose between supporting Attalus or throwing his weight behind Alexander: he picked the latter and stood by as Attalus was killed. Thanks to Antipater and Parmenion, Alexander had secured power, but to keep it he would have to prove himself a worthy heir of Philip.

The Balkans and Greece (335)

Transitions of power are moments of potential crisis for all states, especially when an unprecedentedly successful ruler is replaced with somebody so young and inexperienced. New Macedonian regimes were often tested by their neighbours, so Alexander was quick to assert his authority.[29] In the spring of 335, he led his troops north through Thrace against the Triballi, and then advanced to the Danube. There was a brief foray across the river to attack the Getae and plunder their city, and an alliance, perhaps best understood as a non-aggression pact, was agreed with the Celts living in the region. There was no real interest in conquering these territories, but this created a buffer zone that would ensure Macedonia's security during the planned invasion of Persia. Alexander then looped through the Balkans, sweeping down into Illyria against the Macedonians' old enemy. There was fighting in this period, but on the scale of skirmishes rather than anything more major.

While Alexander was occupied with his northern and western frontiers, trouble was brewing to the south. A group of Thebans encouraged their compatriots to break with Alexander, aided by rumours that he had died in Illyria. Learning of this, Alexander swiftly tied up affairs in Illyria and marched south, his sudden appearance taking the Thebans by surprise. Rather than take advantage of this by attacking immediately, Alexander preferred to wait, hoping the Thebans would back down. The Thebans, however, were recalcitrant, and even sent out a lightly armed force that killed some of the Macedonians in the most advanced positions. Alexander moved the army closer but still did not attack, hoping that confrontation could be averted. However, matters were taken out of his hands. Perdiccas, who commanded one of the battalions stationed nearest the Theban positions, assaulted the palisade wall without orders, and advanced against the Thebans; seeing this, the neighbouring unit followed. This forced Alexander's hand: fearing that these units would be isolated and destroyed, he sent in the rest of the army. The Thebans were quickly forced back, and the Macedonians fought their way into the city. A massacre followed, with women, children and even those who sought protection within the temples killed. This slaughter was driven primarily by some of Alexander's Greek allies who had long been hostile to Thebes and saw this as an opportunity to destroy their rival. With Thebes captured, Alexander asked these same allies what should be done with it. They elected to raze the city and sell the survivors into slavery, except those with ties to the Macedonians. Alexander offered mitigation of sorts: the house of the poet Pindar was saved.

This account is based on the report of Arrian.[30] Born in Nicomedia towards the end of the first century CE, Arrian was a Greek who rose through the administrative ranks of the Roman Empire, eventually being appointed governor of Cappadocia by Hadrian. At some point – probably close to his death around the middle of the second century – he composed a history of Alexander. Arrian had a heady opinion of this work, stating that anybody wondering why he would follow so many others in writing about Alexander should read the other accounts, read his own and then declare themselves surprised.[31] He also explained why Alexander's exploits paled into insignificance compared to lesser figures: Achilles had Homer to commemorate his deeds, Cyrus the Younger had

Route of Alexander's campaigns in the Balkans and Greece, 335.

Xenophon, but Alexander had only second-rate writers – until now.[32] In the nineteenth and twentieth centuries Arrian's work was generally regarded as the most accurate source to survive. His style was admired, but this reputation primarily rested on the authority of the two men he names as his principal sources, Ptolemy and Aristoboulos.[33] Both had participated in Alexander's campaign so had first-hand knowledge of events; Ptolemy especially was often held up as an unimpeachable source. He was one of Alexander's closest friends and held important positions at his court. After Alexander's death he became king of Egypt, establishing a dynasty that survived until the suicide of Cleopatra VII. If anybody knew what had happened during Alexander's reign, it was Ptolemy. Sometimes it was thought that Ptolemy even had access to the 'royal journals', a daily log of events supposedly maintained by Alexander's secretary for administrative purposes. A straight line could be drawn from Arrian to these journals and thus to the truth.

Over the last forty years or so, however, Arrian's standing has been challenged; episodes like his description of the fall of Thebes reveal why.[34] Arrian explains that he preferred Ptolemy and Aristoboulos over other contemporary reports because both men wrote after Alexander's death when neither could benefit from lying. But is this true? Diodorus offers a very different picture of what happened at Thebes.[35] Alexander plays a much more prominent role in his account, dictating events and ultimately deciding to destroy the city as a warning to the rest of Greece. Perdiccas is never mentioned. Diodorus does report that the final destruction of Thebes was done in accordance with the decree of the council and notes that the Greek allies had participated in the slaughter, but this strikes a different tone to Arrian's account, where it is the Greeks who lead the massacre and are given sole responsibility for the decision to destroy the city.

We might dismiss Diodorus because his account seems less detailed. He evidently knew what happened at Thebes, but this was common knowledge, and he perhaps simply assumed that Alexander was in complete control. But one important piece of context should make us hesitate: when Ptolemy was writing, Alexander's generals were fighting one another for control of his empire. As we will see, Ptolemy and Perdiccas became bitter enemies in this period, and Ptolemy probably had a hand in his rival's murder. Consequently, we should surely be sceptical of an account that paints Perdiccas as impetuous and disobedient, an incapable military leader whose recklessness risked disaster. These traits hardly made him the right person to succeed Alexander. The destruction of Thebes was also a lightning rod for criticism in Greece, so pinning this on Perdiccas and the Greek allies was also a way to defend Alexander's reputation. Given that Ptolemy owed his position to his relationship with Alexander, this was important in protecting his own future.

Eyewitnesses were far from impartial observers, and first-hand sources had their own aims and motivations. There are no disinterested accounts, a problem we will encounter repeatedly as we explore Alexander's life.

So, should we prefer Diodorus' account of the fall of Thebes? Not necessarily. Like Arrian, Diodorus was writing hundreds of years after Alexander's death – in his case in the first century BCE – which meant that he too was reliant on earlier reports. For Alexander, his main source was Cleitarchus. Cleitarchus is usually understood to have written within a Ptolemaic environment, but it is unclear whether he was attached to the Ptolemaic court and the date when he was writing is debated. Some scholars situate him within a generation or so of Alexander's death, but others have him pegged later in the third century.[36] Either way, he was not an eyewitness himself and his sources are unknown. Ptolemy may have misrepresented events at Thebes to suit his own agenda, but we have no idea how the ultimate source of the alternative version got his information.

Diodorus is often grouped with Curtius and Justin, who also created accounts based on Cleitarchus. Collectively, these authors are known as the 'Vulgate' (a pejorative term reflecting old attitudes about their perceived unreliability), but historians are now more prepared to take them seriously. Curtius is usually understood to have been active in the first or second century CE, but Justin may have been working as late as the fourth century. His account actually summarizes a work written by Trogus during the reign of Augustus, and we cannot be sure what he left out or how faithful he was to Trogus' original. Justin's account is at least four removes from eyewitness testimony, yet it remains one of the five most important sources for studying Alexander. This gives a clear sense of the problems we face.

Behind these surviving reports lie a plethora of additional eyewitness and second-hand descriptions. This creates an incredibly complicated source tradition and significant effort has been put into trying to assign bits of the extant accounts to earlier writers. This is obviously important, but ancient authors rarely cite their sources, so this inevitably involves a degree of guesswork. It also underrates how far the Roman-era writers shaped the texts that come down to us. Arrian did not just copy Ptolemy, and Ptolemy did not merely duplicate the royal journals (if these even existed, which is doubtful). Instead, these writers made choices about what to include, what to leave out and how to tell the story: every word they chose is an exercise in characterization. When details are attributed to an early source, authors might be quoting directly, but they might be paraphrasing, perhaps quite loosely based on a passage they half-remembered reading some time earlier.

There is a deeper issue too: the surviving sources did not operate in a vacuum. Alexander became a vehicle for exploring ideals of rulership, which was perhaps particularly important in the first century or so after the transition from republic to empire in Rome, as the senatorial elite struggled to come to terms with the new political situation. For some critical voices, Alexander was a means of examining the dangers of one-man rule, or to point the finger at the corrupting influence of flatterers around the edges of a royal court. Leaving aside conscious efforts to present Alexander in a particular light to serve a specific purpose, all historians are affected by contemporary attitudes and their writing is a product of their time. Even if the surviving authors had tried to be entirely faithful to their sources, this would have been impossible.

What does this mean for our discussion of Thebes? Well, we can be confident that the city was brutally sacked and that this ruthless display made it clear to the Greeks that Macedonian military might had not died with Philip. More generally, the victories that Alexander won in 335 demonstrated that he was a worthy successor to his father, which was important in shoring up support in Macedonia, and secured the borders of his homeland. He could pursue Philip's unfinished business – the invasion of Persia – safe in the knowledge that the home front was stable. But if we want to say more about the fall of Thebes and examine Alexander's own role in this we run into problems. There is a wider warning here which is important to remember as we move into the campaign that made Alexander famous. We often do not know exactly what happened and we can never truly understand the motivations of anybody who was involved.

2

Asia Minor, the Levant and Egypt, 334–331

In the spring of 334, Alexander led his troops to the Hellespont, where they boarded transport ships bound for the Persian Empire. As the ships approached the shore, Alexander allegedly cast his spear into the sand, claiming Asia as spear-won land.[1] The mythologizing continued as he headed to Troy, where he sacrificed to Athena and exchanged his own armour for some of the weapons in her temple – which supposedly dated from the Trojan War.[2] Stories like this wrote Alexander into mythic history, drawing a parallel between a famous Greek victory over an Asian power and what Alexander hoped to achieve. Whether or not these events happened, it seems plausible that tales like these were told to the Greeks during the campaign. From Troy, Alexander secured the coast and then turned inland, where the Persians were waiting.

The Battle of the Granicus and the Conquest of Asia Minor (334–333)

The Persians knew that the Macedonians were coming and had gathered an army, led by members of the Persian nobility. As Alexander advanced, they apparently considered retreating, implementing a scorched-earth policy to leave Alexander short of supplies, and playing for time. In the end, they decided to make a stand at the river Granicus. Arrian claims that as the Macedonians approached, Parmenion advised Alexander to make camp, hoping

Route of Alexander's campaigns in Asia Minor, the Levant and Egypt, 334–331.

that the Persians would not occupy the riverbanks overnight and the Macedonians could cross unopposed the following morning.[3] Alexander refused, saying this was not befitting of Macedonians and would only give the Persians confidence; instead, he launched an immediate attack. Diodorus, however, suggests that the Macedonians did camp until dawn.[4] Again, we see the difficulty of working out what actually happened. Arrian had access to the eye-witness testimony of Ptolemy, which is a point in his favour, but his account heroizes Alexander, which might seem suspicious. Either way, the Macedonians had to fight their way across the Granicus.

Alexander personally led a thunderous cavalry charge into the rushing waters, his warriors spurred on by the fervour of their

young commander. As they advanced, Alexander cunningly positioned the front of his column beyond the reach of direct assault,
yet the towering banks granted the Persians a strategic advantage,
leading to an intense initial exchange that exacted its toll on both
sides. Amid the chaos, the air resounded with the clash of steel
and the scene erupted into a swirling melee, with Alexander at
its heart. Alexander's blade found its mark time and again, claiming the lives of Mithridates, son-in-law to the Persian king, and
Rhoesaces, a nobleman of great renown. Yet, as victory seemed
within grasp, danger lurked in the form of Spithridates, who sought
to strike Alexander from behind until the swift intervention of
Clitus severed his arm, halting the blow before it could find its
target. With the tide turning in their favour, the Macedonian cavalry surged forward, driving the Persians back in a frenzied retreat
that bordered on chaos. Though the pursuit was not extensive, the
fate of the Greek mercenaries in the Persian ranks was sealed, as
they found themselves surrounded and dispatched.

A confession: I had artificial intelligence write that paragraph.[5]
Why? Partly it is because I promised that this book would reflect
the time it was written and there is nothing more zeitgeisty than
experimenting with AI. Mainly, though, it's because I despise battle
narratives. Visions suddenly fleet; spears glint and glisten; shields
clash; dreams are dashed – phrases historians would never normally
use, enlivened with gratuitous half-rhymes and needless alliteration.
Partly this is the result of mimicking the style of what we read our-
selves, so the genre creates expectations. Battles also seem a chance
to add a dash of excitement to our narratives, and playing on the
senses creates a phenomenological experience, which draws readers in: we hear the war cries, always 'fearsome', and the pounding
of horses' hooves – on the rare occasion when the screams are
mentioned, they are 'piercing' or, God forbid, 'bloodcurdling'.

But should battles be exciting? Should we try to write so evoc-
atively that a reader can almost imagine themselves alongside

Alexander straining every sinew to keep up with him as he charges, beads of sweat forming on furrowed brows? We are talking about the deaths of thousands of people. Perhaps this all happened so long ago that it is easier to be detached, to forgo the personal cost of battle and simply enjoy the ride. But where do we draw the line? If we glorify battles in the ancient world, then we are complicit in the celebration of war. In Alexander's case, this is a very particular kind of conflict: unprovoked, expansionist, imperialist. We can point to the different values of his era as mitigation and argue that we cannot judge Alexander against the standards of today. That much is obvious. But irrespective of context, whenever we seek to paint a vivid picture of a daring cavalry charge, or a heroic death in single combat, we imply that there is nobility in this, that this is somehow a model to emulate.

There is more to this than my snowflakeish wokery. My other great objection is that portraits of ancient battles often offer an entirely unrealistic picture of how things worked. Maps are drawn, arrows show how different units moved and various stages of a battle are marked out. At the centre of things, generals push troops around like chess pieces, always in control. Here is one example, written about the Battle of Issus, which took place a year after events at the Granicus:

> As Alexander watched the distant seashore speechless, he saw the fate of his great bid to conquer Persia dangle by a thread. With more than a mile between them, Alexander knew that the only help he could provide to Parmenion's doomed men was to set his masterstroke into motion without a moment's delay.[6]

This passage has all the hallmarks of the style I criticized above, but this depiction is especially unrealistic. As we will see, Issus was fought on a narrow coastal strip, with part of the cavalry battle taking place along the shoreline. Hundreds of horses on terrain like this kick up big clouds of dust: Alexander could not have meditated on the impending doom of Parmenion because he probably could not see what was happening on the other side of the battlefield. Generalship was important in the ancient world, but its greatest impact came with initial troop deployments and in inspiring men to fight. After that, leaders had very little control and were reliant on their subordinates and the qualities of the ordinary soldiers.

Here, the experience accrued under Philip gave the Macedonians a distinct advantage: troops were well trained and confident. The Persians had professional soldiers too, many of them mercenaries hired from Greece. Particularly in later battles, however, most of the men in Achaemenid armies were irregulars, called up to service from across the empire. They had rudimentary training and some of them would have fought before, but they were not battle-hardened in the same way as the Macedonians. Alexander's leadership, then, was crucial, but if we focus exclusively on his personal heroics, the danger is that we overlook more important factors. But narratives that pay due attention to these factors risk a fate even worse than inaccuracy – being boring. So, when we come to Alexander's later battles, I'll turn my hand to the sort of description that I despise. Swords will twirl and body parts will be lopped off, though readers may detect a hint of irony. For now, I will just say that the Macedonians won the Battle of the Granicus, and that Alexander was almost killed. This is undoubtedly too reductive, but at least it is truthful.

The battle was fought in the spring of 334 and Alexander spent the rest of the year in Asia Minor exploiting his victory.[7] In general, he accepted the surrender of the cities that offered submission and attacked those that hesitated. For instance, Mithrenes, the Persian commander of Sardis, gave up the old Lydian capital without a fight and was welcomed into Alexander's retinue. At Ephesus, the oligarchic regime which had been sympathetic to the Persian cause was replaced with a democracy, a time-honoured tactic pioneered by the Persians themselves. Miletus, however, wavered, first offering to surrender but then attempting to negotiate a neutral position. This was unacceptable, and the city was captured after a brief siege. The most significant resistance came at Halicarnassus, where the Persians had stationed a major force. After a prolonged siege, which seriously damaged the city, the Persians were forced to take refuge in two fortresses. Recognizing that capturing these sites would result in an unnecessary delay, Alexander left a small force to keep the defenders bottled up and moved on.

By winter, the Macedonians had made serious inroads into Asia Minor, securing Lydia, Ionia and Caria. In the spring of 333,

Gordius en nodus: quem si dissolueret arte
Quispiam, huic sceptrum terris fatale regendis

II

Numina spondebant, ueterumque oracula uatum:
Credit Alexander, strictoque praeoccupat ense.

Antonio Tempesta, 'Alexander Cutting the Gordian Knot', 1608, one of several prints from the series *The Deeds of Alexander the Great*.

Alexander reached Gordium in Phrygia where, in the royal palace, he supposedly found a wagon with a particularly complex knot; local folklore had it that whoever could untie this knot was fated to rule Asia. According to Aristoboulos, Alexander successfully unfastened it, but other versions say that he drew his sword and cut through the ropes claiming that this fulfilled the prophecy.[8] With tales like this, which play so much on his characterization, readers may choose their own Alexander.

The Battle of Issus (333)

While Alexander was occupying Asia Minor, the Persians were gathering a major army. Levies from across the empire were summoned to Babylon and this new force would be commanded in person by the king, Darius III.[9] Darius was probably born around 380 and, like Alexander, came to power in 336. However, he had not been directly in line to the throne. Greek authors paint a chaotic picture of the Achaemenid court in the 330s.[10] The drama centres on Bagoas, a eunuch. In 338, Bagoas allegedly murdered Artaxerxes III and his oldest children, enthroning the youngest son, Arses, as Artaxerxes IV. Two years later, Bagoas discovered that Artaxerxes planned to punish him, so struck first. He chose Darius, previously a courtier, as the next monarch, but quickly soured on him and prepared to do away with another king. Darius, however, was wise to Bagoas' scheming and forced him to drink his own poison. We should be suspicious of stories like this, which reflect so many Greek tropes about Persians. However, a Babylonian document seems to suggest that Artaxerxes IV was killed by a eunuch and that power was taken by somebody else, so Darius may have murdered his way to power.[11]

There was also a more flattering portrayal circulating in antiquity, which describes Darius winning renown during one of Artaxerxes III's military campaigns.[12] A Cadusian, famed for his strength and bravery, challenged any of the Persians to face him in single combat. Only Darius was prepared to accept, and he was rewarded with significant honours after emerging victorious. When Artaxerxes IV was murdered and his line extinguished, Darius' prowess as a warrior meant he was widely considered the best candidate to take over. Irrespective of his personal bravery or previous military experience, Darius was still new to the throne when the Macedonians invaded. This was a different challenge, and he needed to prove himself a capable ruler.

By late summer or early autumn 333, the Persian force was assembled, and Darius led his troops to Sochoi in Assyria, with his family accompanying the army.[13] He intended to choose one of the open plains of Assyria as a battleground as this would allow him to utilize his numerical advantage. Meanwhile, Alexander was making his way through Cilicia, accepting the surrender of various cities. His progress was stalled, however, when he fell ill, either from exhaustion or after catching a chill from swimming in one of the rivers. Keen to find signs of heroism in even the most human of moments, several sources claim that while his doctor, Philip, was preparing medicine for him, Alexander received a letter from Parmenion warning that Philip had been bribed to administer poison.[14] Alexander was nonplussed. He handed Philip the note and drank the medicine fearlessly, emphasizing that he trusted his men. The medication eventually worked, but Alexander was still laid low for a couple of weeks.

Once he was on the move, Alexander occupied Soloi, Tarsus and Mallos. Upon reaching the last of these, he learned Darius was at Sochoi and so he pressed on quickly, passing through Issus and reaching Myriandros. In doing so, the Macedonians stuck to the coastal plains west of the Amanus Mountains. However, east of the mountains, Darius was moving in the other direction. With Alexander apparently hesitating, he had abandoned his original plan to fight in Assyria and elected to force the issue. The two armies slipped past one another on opposite sides of the mountain range, each apparently unaware of the other's presence. Darius' decision meant that the battle would be fought on a narrower coastal strip where he could not make full use of his numerical superiority. This meant giving up a tactical advantage, but it allowed him to spring a strategic surprise on the Macedonians. The Persians suddenly emerged from the mountains and recaptured Issus, where Alexander had left some of his wounded soldiers; these men were apparently mutilated and killed. Darius then marched south towards Alexander, halting behind the Pinarus River. Alexander was forced to recalibrate quickly and reverse his course. He secured the passes leading onto the plain where Darius' army was assembling and rested his men overnight. The following morning, he led his men down onto the battlefield, his line stretching from the foothills of the mountains to the sea.

Darius set up his main army behind the Pinarus, positioning a screening force in front of the river to hide his deployments.[15] His Greek mercenaries held the centre of the line, flanked by the elite Persian infantry. Behind the Greeks, Darius established a second infantry line and sent lightly armed troops to occupy the foothills to his extreme left. Darius himself took up a central position. The Macedonians lined up in their usual formation: the phalanx in the centre, allied cavalry on the left and the Companion Cavalry, the army's elite cavalry unit, on the right. As Darius withdrew his screening force, he sent the cavalry to his right flank, massing them against the allied cavalry; Alexander reacted by sending the Thessalian horsemen to reinforce his left wing. As the Macedonians began a slow advance, the Persians stayed behind the stream, which they had made more impregnable by constructing a palisade where the banks were least steep.

During the final stages of his preparation, Alexander rode behind his line, encouraging his men until they were urging the king to let them attack. But the advance remained gentle until the

Macedonians came into range of the Persian archers – then Alexander led the Companion Cavalry at full speed across the river. The assault hit the Persian left wing hard, and it quickly fell backwards. In the centre, however, the Macedonians struggled to cross the river. Some units made it, but others were held in the water and gaps began to open in the line. The strength of the phalanx lay in its ability to present the enemy with an impenetrable wall of spears, but the sarissa was an unwieldy weapon and any gaps in the Macedonian line could be exploited by more mobile infantry units like Greek hoplites, some 30,000 of whom were serving as mercenaries in Darius' army. Things were worse on the right. The Persian cavalry had attacked across the Pinarus and were putting the Thessalians under serious pressure.

As it was, however, Alexander's opening charge was enough to win the day. The Companion Cavalry was able to turn inwards against the Greek mercenaries, attacking them from their unprotected flank. Even more importantly, Alexander's breakthrough left Darius exposed. Arrian has him flee as soon as he recognized this, but others describe vicious fighting around his chariot. It was only once his own horses were wounded and threatening to throw him from his chariot that Darius' thoughts turned to escape. Those around him followed and, seeing the centre of their army in retreat, the Persian cavalry broke off their attack. Like other ancient battles, it was probably at this stage, as cohesion broke down and individuals prioritized their own safety, that most casualties were inflicted. Inevitably, the sources exaggerate: Ptolemy apparently claimed that during their pursuit of Darius, the Macedonians crossed one ditch by riding across the bodies of Persians who had been cut down as they fled.[16] Persian losses allegedly totalled 100,000 dead. These details are hyperbolic, but this was certainly a significant victory for the Macedonians.

Discussing Darius' role in battle is tricky. His initial deployments seem sound, but what should we make of his flight? For

This floor mosaic from Pompeii depicts one of Alexander's battles with Darius. As Alexander charges, Darius' charioteer is already spurring the horses on to pull Darius to safety. Meanwhile, a Persian has thrown himself in front of the king – ideas of heroism during Alexander's campaign were less black and white than we might imagine.

ancient authors, this was a clear sign of cowardice and proof that Darius was unfit to rule. In Darius' actions, they found confirmation of their existing biases about the Achaemenid kings. But they also use Darius as a mirror to illuminate Alexander's character, juxtaposing his role in the front line with Darius' craven attitude to emphasize his heroic leadership.[17] Their perspective may also be affected by the Macedonian model of kingship, which demanded that the king fight in the front line. There is surprisingly little stress on this in Achaemenid inscriptions, and Persian kings are often portrayed as observing battles rather than participating.[18] This evidence is Greek, which is obviously problematic, but the death of a king can easily throw a kingdom into chaos so there were good reasons for minimizing his exposure on the battlefield. The Achaemenid king's first duty in war, it seems, was to survive, so we should not necessarily impugn Darius' character due to his behaviour at Issus.

However, Darius' flight allowed Alexander to seize the Persian ruler's royal robe, chariot and bow, which were cast aside to make escape easier. These were important royal symbols and capturing them let Alexander emphasize his victory. Retreating also meant that Darius abandoned his family: Sisygambis, his mother; Stateira, his wife; his infant son; and two daughters. On the evening of the battle, the Macedonians partied in the Persian camp, Alexander taking over Darius' tent for the occasion.[19] Their celebrations were interrupted, however, by the sound of wailing from a nearby tent belonging to the Achaemenid royal women. Hearing that Alexander had captured Darius' clothing and weaponry, they assumed Darius had been killed. Alexander sent Leonnatus to explain what had happened and to inform the women that they would be treated in accordance with their royal status. This much, Arrian says, was recorded by Ptolemy and Aristoboulos, but he notes an additional story, which appears elsewhere too. The next day, Alexander visited the Persian women accompanied by Hephaestion. When the pair entered the tent, Sisygambis moved to perform *proskynesis* – a gesture involving kissing and bowing that the Persians used to acknowledge the king's authority. But Hephaestion was the taller of the two men, so Sisygambis assumed he was the king and bowed in his direction. This mistake was swiftly pointed out and Sisygambis was mortified, but Alexander gently raised her up, telling her not to worry because 'Hephaestion, too, is Alexander.'

This is a nice line, but it is unlikely that Alexander ever said it. We will come to Hephaestion properly later, but here he is cast almost as the alter ego of the king, and the way that the episode builds towards Alexander's final remark suggests it has been invented. Similarly, Alexander's treatment of Darius' family is routinely held up by the ancient authors as a sign of his generosity and noble spirit. The daughters were treated like his sisters and promised significant dowries, while Stateira was protected from the endemic sexual violence. Some sources, however, record her later death in childbirth or after a miscarriage; their timeline is hazy, but this might suggest a very different story.[20] In any case, the positive characterization of Alexander that emerges from the tale regarding Sisygambis and Hephaestion, and the fact that Arrian did not get it from Ptolemy or Aristoboulos, suggests that it was a later creation.

But let us suppose that this really did happen and add one more counterfactual: what if this was deliberate? Imagine the moment when Sisygambis prostrated herself before Hephaestion. What would Alexander have thought? What about Hephaestion? The briefest of seconds an awkward eternity, Hephaestion shifting uncomfortably, looking nervously towards Alexander. The dynamics of the situation were changed completely, Alexander's control of the encounter was undercut and his authority as a king questioned. This demeaned Alexander not only in front of his friend, but before Sisygambis' own court, sending a very clear message:

Charles Le Brun, *The Family of Darius before Alexander*, 1661, oil on canvas. Le Brun was Louis xiv's court painter and played a major role in the artistic programme at Louis' palace at Versailles. Here, he portrays Sisygambis performing *proskynesis* to Hephaestion, who is depicted as Alexander's 'other', his dress mirroring the clothing of the king.

there is nothing special about this man. And what happened after the Macedonians left? How long before somebody let out a nervous giggle or made a joke: 'Did you see the look on his face? The other bloke looked like he'd seen a ghost!' Suddenly, the act of submission is transformed into a moment of subversion, with the foreign conqueror reduced from an object of fear to a laughing stock. And what if Sisygambis let slip – with a quiet word, a slight nod of the head or the Persian equivalent of a knowing wink – that this had all been deliberate? The resultant shared notion of complicity in a small act of resistance would have brought those present closer together, giving them a sense of collective identity as people who possessed a secret. This would have emboldened them with the knowledge that, together, they could survive interactions with Alexander and the Macedonians. In the very moment of surrender, the seeds of resistance are born.

This is all based on several hypothetical questions that take us well beyond what the sources say. It is important to emphasize that I do not think this actually happened. Rather than arguing that this is how we should see this episode, my aim in using this sort of *what if?* is to give an indication of what was possible more generally. It is tempting to imagine that military conquerors control interactions with their new subjects. This is true to an extent, but exploring this story from a different perspective helps us appreciate that we should not imagine these people as having no agency at all. Even little acts of 'everyday resistance' were a means of shifting the balance of power and grasping a modicum of agency, however briefly.[21] There are also clearer signs of Sisygambis exerting influence. For instance, she later interceded with Alexander on behalf of the Uxians, who lived in the mountains near Susa.[22] In doing this, she was fulfilling a role traditionally played by women within a royal court, offering petitioners another route to the king's ear.

As the dust settled after Issus, Darius apparently requested the safe return of his family and proposed peace in return.[23] However, he does not appear to have offered any major concessions and his proposition was dismissed out of hand. A time for negotiation might come, but the Macedonians' position of strength in the weeks after Issus meant compromise was unlikely at this stage.

Phoenicia (332–331)

Alexander now had to make a crucial strategic decision: head inland after Darius or continue down the coast. He chose the latter. Old and powerful cities were dotted along the coastline: Aradus, Marathos, Tripolis, Byblos, Sidon and especially Tyre. These cities had long been part of the Persian Empire, and their local elites had well-established links with the Achaemenids. If Alexander immediately left the region, these key decision-makers would have little incentive to change sides and could wait to see how things played out. Furthermore, the Phoenicians were renowned sailors and contributed significantly to the Persian fleet. Dominating the seas would allow the Persians to interrupt Alexander's supply lines and communications with Macedonia – if he was to go after Darius now and suffer a defeat, it might prove impossible for the Macedonians to get home. So, while giving Darius the opportunity to regroup might seem like a missed opportunity, we get a sense here of Alexander's strategic acumen.

Aradus, Marathos, Byblos and Sidon swiftly surrendered, and the Tyrians appeared ready to do the same, sending envoys who promised to do whatever they were told.[24] Alexander presumably issued a list of demands, but the sources focus on his request to enter Tyre and sacrifice to Melqart, an important local god whom the Macedonians identified with Heracles. The Tyrians refused, declaring that they would admit neither the Macedonians nor the Persians. Arrian offers a perceptive remark here: for the Tyrians, neutrality seemed the best way to secure their future safety when the war remained undecided.[25] Alexander could hardly accept this. Doing so would leave an unreliable city in his rear and would weaken his bargaining position with other communities who might expect the same treatment as the Tyrians. Alexander may have wanted to sacrifice to Melqart, but I suspect that this story is part of an attempt to pin the blame for the breakdown of negotiations entirely on the Tyrians. With neither side prepared to compromise, both began preparations for a siege.

The Tyrians' confidence in their ability to hold out against Alexander was boosted by their city's position on a heavily fortified island a little way off the mainland. Their naval supremacy meant that the city could be supplied from the sea. Alexander opted to build a causeway across the strait, but the Tyrians consistently harried the Macedonians, slowing progress. When the causeway eventually started to come close to Tyre, its defenders were able to shoot at the Macedonians from their own walls and ships. Alexander responded by building two enormous siege towers as a base for counterattacks; the Tyrians then launched a fire ship against these towers. Punch, counterpunch, and the offensive began to stall. Weeks turned into months, and even Alexander apparently began to wonder whether persevering with the siege was worth it.

The turning point came the better part of a year later, early in the summer of 332. The rulers of Aradus and Byblos were serving in the Persian fleet when their cities were captured by Alexander. Learning of this, these men now abandoned the Persian cause, bringing with them the eighty ships that they controlled. Shortly afterwards, the kings of Cyprus arrived with another 120 ships, having decided that now was the time to weigh in on Alexander's side. This shifted the naval balance of power in the Macedonians' favour and the Tyrian fleet was blockaded in its home harbours. At some point in July or early August a major attack began, with the Macedonians able to assault Tyre from multiple directions. The decisive breach came from the sea, where ships had been adapted to carry siege engines up to the city's walls. The Macedonians flooded in and massacred the Tyrians. Some 8,000 were killed in the fighting, another 2,000 were purportedly crucified and perhaps as many as 30,000 sold into slavery.[26] Finally, Alexander sacrificed to Heracles.

During the siege, Darius made a more serious peace over-ture.[27] He offered to surrender the territory west of the Euphrates and marry his daughter to Alexander. Parmenion, apparently, was eager to accept these terms, which prompted Alexander to deliver one of his more memorable lines: 'I would accept this offer – if I were Parmenion; but I am Alexander.' Perhaps Parmenion did offer this advice, but anecdotes like this are impossible to prove. Instead, this episode is one of many where Parmenion is cast as a dramatic foil, his suggestions witheringly rejected so that Alexander's heroism can shine even more brightly. They may also reflect later attempts to undermine Parmenion's reputation in light of his eventual fate. Either way, agreeing terms now risked allowing Darius to rebuild Persian forces in preparation for a future counterattack.

Instead, Alexander headed south. Syria quickly submitted, but Gaza held out.[28] The siege engines were brought up and began pounding away at the walls, while tunnels were dug to undermine the fortifications. The Macedonians forced their way in, and Gaza's defenders were slaughtered; the women and children who survived were enslaved. Curtius reports an especially brutal scene involving Batis, the Persian commander of the city, who was captured by the Macedonians.[29] In imitation of Achilles' treatment of the corpse of Hector at Troy, Alexander dragged Batis around Gaza's perimeter. But there was a crucial twist – Batis was still alive when this torture began. No other source reports this, while the parody of the *Iliad* seems designed to heighten the impression of Alexander's cruelty, so we might doubt whether this happened, but it is not entirely implausible.

Reading the ancient accounts of what happened at Gaza has been a sobering experience. When news bulletins in the present day are headlined by bombed-out buildings and displaced civilians in the same place that you are researching, it is hard to push those images aside and remain detached. Originally, I had described the defenders being 'hacked to pieces in their thousands'. This probably captures reality, but it seemed to go too far. Among the ancient sources only Curtius gives a figure for the total casualties: 10,000, he says, but it is hard to know how seriously to take this. Writing this book has helped me appreciate how contemporary experiences shape the way we see the past, so perhaps I am hyperaware of this issue here. It turns out that in Alexander's treatment of Gaza the ancient and modern worlds are more intertwined than ever.

One might argue that passages like this, which ground this work so explicitly in the time that it was written, will make it age more quickly than would otherwise be the case. But it feels more intellectually honest to be upfront about these issues, and to explain some of the thought processes that have shaped the composition of the book, especially since the contemporary influences that affect the way we see the past will eventually fade from view. How I wish Arrian and Curtius had outlined the pressures that prompted them to present episodes in a particular light instead of leaving us to guess.

Egypt (332–331)

After its initial conquest in the 520s, Egypt had been ruled by the Persians for more than a century. However, the Egyptians had regained independence at the end of the fifth century and were not reconquered until the 340s. Consequently, the Persian aristocracy had fewer ties with their local counterparts here than elsewhere, and fewer of the movers and shakers in Egypt had reason to defend Persian rule. With Phoenicia lost, Darius unable to help and with Egypt apparently lacking significant military resources of its own, Mazaces, the satrap, recognized that his position was hopeless and surrendered. Entering Egypt, Alexander sailed up the Nile to Heliopolis and Memphis, two of the country's major cities.[30] He venerated the local gods appropriately – part of an attempt to ensure that his rule was accepted – and held an athletic and artistic competition before returning to the coast. On the western edge of the Nile Delta, he founded a new city, which he named after himself. This Alexandria is one of the most tangible aspects of Alexander's legacy, its very name still memorializing its founder, just as was intended. Arrian suggests that Alexander played an active role in planning the city, marking out the sites for key buildings and so forth, but Alexandria was really a Ptolemaic creation, its most iconic features – the lighthouse and library – developed only after Alexander's death.

Alexander now headed for the oasis at Siwah on Egypt's western periphery, home to the oracle of Ammon, whom Greeks equated with Zeus. His visit to the oracle is shrouded in mystery. Diodorus claims that one of the priests addressed Alexander as 'son'.[31] Alexander then asked whether he was destined to rule the world, which the priest confirmed, and he inquired whether his father's murderers had been brought to justice. The priest responded angrily, declaring that Alexander's father could not be harmed by humans but that Philip's killers had all been punished. Curtius offers a similar account, clearly based on the same source, but frames the visit in slightly different terms.[32] He suggests that Alexander visited Siwah with the intention of claiming to be the son of Ammon, either because he thought this was true or wanted others to believe it, and then demanded to be addressed with this title. Justin goes even further, claiming that the priests had been bribed.[33] Alexander is more egotistical in Justin and Curtius than in Diodorus, driven by a desire to arrogate divine honours. This discrepancy emphasizes that the ancient authors shaped their narratives to affect our interpretations. Plutarch knew of this story too but adds an alternative explanation: the priest tried to address

Alexander as 'my son' but confused two similar Greek terms and accidentally said 'son of Zeus'.[34]

Some historians are also adamant that Alexander pursued divine recognition, and this episode is central in their arguments. Usually, it is connected to other incidents, such as a debate we will come to about whether *proskynesis* should be introduced to Alexander's court. A danger of this approach is that we imagine that Alexander was driven by just one or two overarching motivations, so we remove moments like this from their context and miss alternative explanations. Alexander may, for instance, have visited Siwah because it represented the western borders of Egypt: going here was a way of constructing the frontier of his kingdom, just as he seems to have done in the east by traversing the Indus. Consequently, his reasons for visiting Siwah may have been oversimplified. This is especially clear in how Arrian's account has been handled. He makes three statements about what happened.[35]

1   Perseus and Heracles were understood to have visited Siwah; Alexander claimed descent from both heroes and was keen to surpass them.

2   Alexander wanted to attribute his own birth to Ammon just as Perseus and Heracles were recognized as the sons of Zeus. He went to Siwah to discover more about this or, at least, so he could say that this relationship had been clarified.

3   Alexander took the coastal route to Paraetonium, then travelled across the desert to Siwah.

Arrian explicitly acknowledges Aristoboulos as his source for the final statement. For Ian Worthington, one of the main proponents of the view that Alexander wanted to be recognized as divine, this evidence is pivotal:

It is significant that we hear from a contemporary source that he went there to learn 'his own origin more certainly, or at least that he might be able to say that he had learned it'. In other words, it did not really matter what the priest told him. Alexander believed he was Zeus's son, and that was what he told everyone.[36]

Worthington cites Aristoboulos as his source here, which means assuming that Arrian based his second statement on the same source used for his third. However, Arrian's account is more complicated than this. To appreciate this, we need to consider Strabo's account of the episode.[37] Like Arrian, he claims that Alexander went to Siwah to follow in the footsteps of Perseus and Heracles, but he names Callisthenes as his source. As Alexander's court historian, Callisthenes provides an official version of events. Strabo describes the route to Siwah in very similar terms to Arrian, which suggests that Callisthenes also lay behind Aristoboulos' report, or that a little bit of Aristoboulos has found its way into Strabo's account without acknowledgement.[38] So, Arrian's first and third points are repeated by Strabo and grounded explicitly in contemporary accounts: if Callisthenes or Aristoboulos were also the source of Arrian's second statement, we might reasonably expect Strabo to mention this too, but he does not.

Arrian goes on to describe the route to the oracle and notes a disagreement between Aristoboulos and Ptolemy: the former declares that two birds led the army across the desert, whereas the latter claims it was two snakes. Arrian suggests that Alexander clearly benefitted from some divine assistance but says that he cannot ascertain precisely what happened. Here, Arrian weaves between different sources and adds his own personal take. This, I think, had happened earlier too: Arrian's first and third statements are grounded in the evidence, whereas the second is his own opinion. Instead of going to Siwah to prove that he was the son of

Ammon, the official explanation was that Alexander wanted to emulate his heroic forebears.

One challenge for historians is ridding oneself of one's own preconceptions. I should admit that I find it hard to accept that Alexander genuinely thought of himself as the son of Zeus because I find it difficult to imagine anybody thinking this of themselves. There was, of course, a clear division between humans and gods for the Greeks too, but there were ways of blurring the lines. Heracles is the most obvious example, but there were more recent precedents too. The Spartan general Brasidas liberated Amphipolis from the Athenians in 422 but was killed in the action. The Amphipolitans gave him the title of 'founder' of the city.[39] In line with Greek traditions, this status came with a cult in his name and religious veneration. Twenty years later, a series of victories won by another Spartan commander, Lysander, ended the Peloponnesian War. This enabled an oligarchic government to return to power on the island of Samos. They set up altars and sang paeans (songs of praise) to Lysander and even renamed a religious festival after him. This appears to have taken place when Lysander was still alive and so attests to the lifetime worship of a mortal.[40] We have already seen how Philip II also associated himself with the gods by having his bust carried alongside the Olympians in the procession that preceded his assassination. Honours like these did not necessarily mean divine parentage, but this does mean that the notion of achieving divine recognition was not entirely alien to Alexander. The Egyptian context is important too. Pharaohs were traditionally regarded as the offspring of Amun-Re and therefore divine, if not immortal: ruling Egypt meant occupying a liminal position between the human and divine worlds. It is striking, however, that these precedents were ground-up rather than top-down: the citizens of Samos and Amphipolis awarded divine honours to individuals, the Egyptian priesthood inscribed Alexander into local religious traditions. Agency did not lie exclusively with the king.

However, the visit to the oracle certainly had an important long-term impact. The best evidence of this comes from coins produced by Ptolemy and Lysimachus after Alexander's death that show him wearing the horns of a ram, one of Ammon's main symbols. Having served in his campaigns, both men knew Alexander well, understood the contemporary significance of Ammon and were fighting to control Alexander's legacy. If the association with Ammon was ahistorical or problematic, they would not have referred to it; that they did so indicates that Alexander advertised a link with Ammon. If Alexander eventually claimed a relationship with the god, does it matter why he first visited his sanctuary? However, there is scope for the significance of this connection to have changed over time and for the episode to have been recast, even during Alexander's lifetime.

To appreciate this, we need to return to the passage from Strabo. Callisthenes apparently declared that oracular communication at Siwah was wordless, but that the priest told Alexander he was the son of Ammon. This seems to discredit my suggestion that the official explanation for the visit was rivalry with Alexander's heroic predecessors, but it is part of a series of tales that Strabo dismisses

The best indication that Alexander cultivated an association with Ammon comes from coins like this, which show Alexander wearing the horns of Ammon. This coin, from 297–281 BCE, was produced by Lysimachus, one of Alexander's successors, after Alexander's death.

as flattery. Most notably, the oracle of Apollo at Didyma in Ionia had apparently been silent for years; after Alexander's arrival, it supposedly regained its voice. Oracles were allegedly brought to Alexander at Memphis, confirming his divine descent; they also predicted his victory at Gaugamela, the death of Darius III and the Spartan revolt in Greece – episodes which occurred after Alexander left Egypt. Either the prophecies were genuine, or the account was written later. We do not know much about how Callisthenes operated. He may have circulated regular updates to keep Greek audiences informed about events, but the material discussed by Strabo must have been composed between the summer of 330, when Darius died, and 327, when Callisthenes himself came to a sticky end. In his reporting on Siwah, Callisthenes was evidently operating with hindsight, and the surviving fragments of his account may suggest that the visit to the oracle had begun to take on new meanings within Alexander's court by the time he was writing. Alexander may not have gone to Siwah to be proclaimed the son of a god, but, by the time one of our principal primary sources described the episode, this may have become one of the key messages.

I have often criticized attempts to reach judgements about Alexander's character and explain his behaviour through the narrow lens of one or two characteristics. But the historical Alexander certainly had a personality. However, rather than fixate on a particular trait we are perhaps better off thinking about how Alexander was affected by his experiences. Of course, the evidence means that there is a limit to how far this is possible, but nonetheless we should take a broader view of how character develops and acknowledge the potential for change over time. Alexander may have eventually presented himself as the son of Ammon, and he may even have come to believe it himself, but that is not necessarily why he went to Siwah in the first place. When we recognize this nuance, the visit to the oracle of Ammon and its subsequent impact may give us a sense of his personal journey. Ironically, it is in thinking about Alexander as a god that we perhaps get the best glimpse of Alexander as a man.

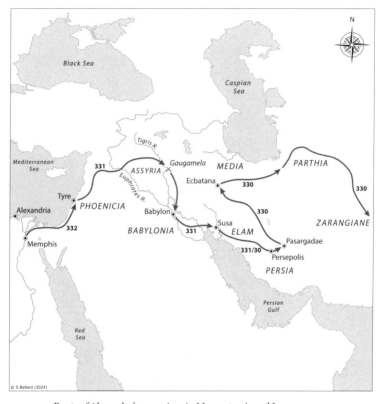

Route of Alexander's campaigns in Mesopotamia and Iran, 331–330.

3

Mesopotamia and Iran,
331–330

Adding Egypt to Phoenicia and Asia Minor meant that Alexander had secured the periphery of the Persian Empire, and he could head into Asia with a degree of security. In the spring of 331, the Macedonians left Egypt, retracing their steps through Phoenicia, before moving inland towards the Euphrates and the Tigris, the two great waterways of Mesopotamia.[1] Alexander crossed both rivers unopposed and advanced into Assyria. Darius had not been idle while Alexander was in Egypt, but had assembled a large force, drawing on men from across his empire: Indians, Bactrians, Sogdians, Scythians, Parthians, Medes, Babylonians and more besides. By demonstrating the diversity of his peoples, the army indicated the huge, almost universal, reach of the king. Consequently, some of these units may have been included more for their representational value than any expected military contribution, but Arrian claims that the army included 1 million infantry, 40,000 cavalry and hundreds of chariots too. Figures like these reflect a problem of the Greeks' own making. After centuries of rhetoric belittling the Persians' military abilities, there was a risk of Alexander's achievements being undercut. One solution was to exaggerate the scale of the forces that he faced: Alexander may only have defeated Persians, but there were, at least, a lot of them. Nevertheless, Darius' army was undoubtedly larger than Alexander's. The stage was set for a major battle.

The Battle of Gaugamela (1 October 331)

Having been tempted onto an unfavourable battlefield at Issus, Darius had learned his lesson.[2] He had carefully chosen a site near the village of Gaugamela, north of today's Erbil in the Kurdistan Region of Iraq. Here, the plain was completely wide open, so Darius could make use of his full force. The Persians had even levelled the ground where they expected the battle to be fought to aid their chariots and cavalry.

As the Macedonians drew near, a celebrated strategic discussion is said to have taken place. Parmenion allegedly went to Alexander's tent and urged him to attack the Persians at night when they might be taken by surprise and their numerical superiority negated. Alexander's response was already the stuff of legend by the time it was recorded by our sources: 'I will not steal victory,' he supposedly declared. But it was not just the later authors who sought to emphasize Alexander's heroic qualities. According to Plutarch, Callisthenes' report of Alexander's pre-battle exhortation to his Greek troops included a prayer to the gods to deliver victory if he was, indeed, the son of Zeus.[3] As we saw earlier, Callisthenes was writing after these events, though still within Alexander's lifetime; if Plutarch represents his report accurately, we again see that divine associations were growing during the course of the campaign. By chance, Aristander, Alexander's seer, was then able to point to an eagle flying overhead: with the bird of Zeus present, the Macedonians could not lose.

The support of the gods was one thing, but the Persians' significant numerical advantage created a tactical problem for Alexander. Without a shoreline or mountain foothills to protect his flanks, as had been the case at Issus, the danger was that his smaller force would be encircled by the Persians and annihilated. The only solution was to win victory before the Persians could bring their weight of numbers to bear. I have expressed scepticism about battlefield accounts that focus on generalship to the detriment of other factors, but it is only fair to acknowledge how important Alexander's initial decisions were in determining the course of this battle.

Darius arranged his troops in an orthodox fashion. Cavalry held the wings, while Darius stationed himself in the middle of the Persian line behind the infantry. Again, the centre was occupied by the most elite Persian units and mercenaries hired from Greece. (There is an irony in this. For all that Alexander purported to be leading a war of revenge on behalf of all Greeks, the Greeks in Darius' army may still have outnumbered those fighting with the Macedonians.) Alexander too adopted his typical tactics: the phalanx in the centre of the line, Parmenion commanding the allied cavalry to the left, and Alexander himself leading the Companion Cavalry on the right. There was one defensive wrinkle to the usual plan with a second phalanx deployed behind the main line, ready to turn around in the event that the Macedonians were encircled.

The real innovation came in the opening moments of the battle. Alexander did not advance straight at the enemy but led his troops at an oblique angle, marching to the right. This took him towards ground that was unsuitable for Darius' chariots, which were launched against the Macedonians but made little impact. From the Persian perspective, this appeared to be an outflanking manoeuvre, so the left wing moved left, keeping step with Alexander's movement. However, the Persians' mixture of cavalry and infantry units shifted at slightly different speeds and gradually a gap began to open up in the Persian line. Recognizing this, Alexander turned and led the cavalry at full speed through the opening – straight for the centre of the Persian line and Darius himself. As the cavalry cut through the line, the phalanx attacked too. As at Issus, the fighting around Darius was intense, but he was eventually forced to flee the battlefield.

Alexander raced after him in hot pursuit while the battle raged behind him. The Persian right had attacked and was threatening to envelop the Macedonian left. Some Persians even managed to break through the Macedonian line and made for the baggage train. Parmenion recognized the danger and apparently sent a messenger after Alexander, calling him to break off the pursuit. It is tricky to know what to make of this. It is a plausible reconstruction of events, but the way that Parmenion is often characterized means that it is tempting to be suspicious of passages that seem to cast doubt on his abilities or make him responsible for Darius again escaping.

Arrian reports that as Alexander was returning to the battlefield, he encountered the Persian right, who were already fleeing. Darius' flight may have prompted a collapse in Persian morale, but the Macedonian and allied troops may have already won the day despite the challenges they were facing – again, we must emphasize their skill and experience. Alexander's tactics created the opportunity to win the battle, but this plan still needed to be executed and the difficulty of doing this should not be underestimated. With the battlefield secure, Alexander was able to resume his pursuit of Darius. Again, he captured the king's treasure and royal insignia, but Darius himself vanished into Media.

Babylon and Susa (331)

Rather than pursue Darius further, Alexander headed south into the heartlands of Mesopotamia, where the jewels in the Persian crown lay waiting to be seized. As the Macedonians approached Babylon, the townspeople poured out of their city to welcome Alexander.[4] Curtius paints a vivid picture of the Babylonians lining the road, with musicians playing, flowers strewn across the street and Babylon's leaders bestowing fine gifts upon Alexander. He gives the impression of a joyous celebration as the delighted Babylonians rejoiced in the presence of their new king; it is, almost, a liberation.

Charles Le Brun, *Alexander Entering Babylon*, 1665, oil on canvas. Le Brun portrays Alexander as a conquering hero, serenely entering Babylon, resplendent in his chariot. The scene plays on orientalizing tropes like the elephant, while the Hanging Gardens are pictured in the background. The inhabitants of Babylon look on, and there are signs that looting is beginning.

Occasionally alternative sources open up different perspectives on Alexander's reign. The Esagila – the temple of Marduk, chief god of the Babylonian pantheon – was at the heart of religious and cultural life in Babylon. For centuries, the priests of the temple kept detailed records of their activity. Every night, they tracked the movements of the stars and the planets, noting their observations down on tablets we call 'Astronomical Diaries'. Though focused on the heavens, we occasionally get a glimpse of more earthly pursuits. For instance, a scribe might write 'I did not watch' or explain that measurements were taken 'despite clouds'.[5] There is something unmistakably human about the sudden appearance of this personal touch, which gives us a rare sense of intimacy with these often-forgotten voices from the past.

Sometimes, the priests reported on the news of the day. One of these references lets us date the Battle of Gaugamela to 1 October 331 – it is unusual for precise details like this to have survived from antiquity.[6] The same document describes Alexander's approach to Babylon in the weeks that followed. The text is fragmentary, but Alexander appears to have sent a message to the Babylonians declaring that he would not enter their homes.[7] There are perhaps also signs that the status and property of the Esagila were discussed.

This clay tablet from Babylon records astronomical observations made by the priests at the Esagila temple in 331 and 330. Amid remarks about the planets, the tablet records the date of the Battle of Gaugamela and notes Alexander's arrival in Babylon.

This gives a sense of how negotiations played out, helping us see Curtius' account in a new light. Rather than the spontaneous rejoicing of liberated people, the royal welcome afforded to Alexander was likely a product of discussions that involved assurances on both sides: Alexander would be acknowledged as king, provided he agreed to take on the traditional obligations of Babylonian kingship. This sort of back-and-forth is to be expected as the Babylonians weighed up their options, but it is largely absent from the literary sources – even just a glimpse of the Babylonian viewpoint is extremely valuable.

Alexander was in dialogue not only with the Babylonian elite, but with the Persian leadership of the city. Mazaeus, the satrap of Babylonia, had commanded the Persian right wing at Gaugamela but had returned to Babylon rather than fleeing with Darius. He had not been the satrap for long, but two of his children had Babylonian names, so he may have had a familial connection with the city.[8] Perhaps this affected his motivation for further fighting or perhaps he calculated that Darius would be unable to rally the Persian forces. Either way, he surrendered. In a politically astute move, Alexander reappointed Mazaeus as satrap and he also made Mithrenes, who had earlier surrendered Sardis, the satrap of Armenia.[9] Mazaeus was surrounded by Macedonians who controlled key military and financial institutions, but Alexander was evidently keen to demonstrate to leading Persians that there was a place for them if they switched sides.

The same pattern played out as Alexander approached Susa.[10] The satrap, Aboulites, welcomed Alexander into the city and retained his position, though Macedonians commanded the garrison. Susa was a significant administrative centre, the site of a major palace built by Darius I, and a royal storehouse. The Macedonians found almost unimaginable wealth there, including some 50,000 silver talents. (A talent was an ancient weight measurement. Its value differed from place to place but in Athens it was more than

25 kilograms (55 lb), so 50,000 talents was an awful lot of money.) There were also symbolic goods aplenty. Like their Near-Eastern predecessors, the Achaemenids had seized statues of gods and other treasured items from the communities they conquered as victory symbols. Among these, the Macedonians apparently discovered the statues of Harmodius and Aristogeiton, the famous 'tyrannicides' feted in Athens for their role in ending the Peisistratid tyranny and thus paving the way for democracy. Alexander swiftly repatriated these statues, conscious of their propagandistic value: there could be no better signal that, like his father before him, he took his role as hegemon of the League of Corinth seriously.

Persepolis (331–330)

Alexander now headed for the heartlands of the Achaemenid Empire. The cities of Mesopotamia had essentially been left defenceless after Gaugamela, but Persia itself was afforded some protection by the terrain since the Macedonians had to cross the Zagros Mountains to reach Persepolis. Ariobarzanes, the satrap of Persia, took up a defensive position with 40,000 infantry and seven hundred cavalry at a mountain pass known as the Persian Gates, whose narrowness favoured the defenders and prevented Alexander from utilizing the mobility of his cavalry as he had elsewhere.[11] A wall had been built across the pass to aid the Persians even further and an initial frontal assault proved fruitless. The Macedonians were forced to rethink. Fortunately, a prisoner offered to lead Alexander around the pass via a hidden track to attack the Persians from the rear.[12] Caught between two forces, they were massacred. However, this story sounds suspiciously like accounts of the Battle of Thermopylae, so it looks like creative licence has been taken to generate another link between Alexander's campaign and the invasion he was avenging. Whether this reflects the official version of events is impossible to say.

As things transpired, this battle became the final act of organized resistance by Persian imperial forces. Lots more fighting lay ahead, but this was the last time that Alexander faced a major Persian army in battle. Victory meant that Persepolis, the symbolic centre of the realm, lay defenceless. Tiridates, apparently the highest-ranking official left in the city, wrote to Alexander promising to surrender if the Macedonians arrived before any loyalist forces sent by Darius.[13] A series of forced marches ensured that they did: the main capital of the Achaemenid Empire was now in Macedonian hands. But what to do with it?

The way that Babylon and Susa had escaped relatively unscathed from the initial Macedonian occupation perhaps gave the inhabitants of Persepolis some hope that they would be spared. They were not. Curtius and Diodorus offer a brutal account of what happened when Alexander handed the city over to his soldiers to plunder.[14] Men were killed indiscriminately, women dragged off into slavery – the sources do not explicitly say that they were sexually assaulted, but this will have been rife. To escape the indignities, some families climbed to the roofs of their houses, dressed in their finest clothes, and threw themselves to their deaths; others burned themselves alive in their homes to prevent the Macedonians from seizing their possessions. Gold, silver, jewellery, rich robes and embroidery poured from the Persians' houses. The best loot was fought over. Valuables were cut apart as greedy hands sought out a piece each; limbs were lost in the struggle, cut off by those desperate to get hold of a particular piece of treasure. In extreme cases, soldiers killed one another in the frenzy. After a day of unbridled carnage, Alexander called a halt to the plundering.

We can hardly be shocked at the fate that befell Persepolis. There are lots of similar examples from antiquity and the Macedonians had form here, as the inhabitants of Olynthus, Thebes and Tyre knew only too well. Furthermore, the Macedonians and Greeks in Alexander's army had been brought up to see the

Persians as the epitome of evil, while the war had been fed by tales of Persian hubris and promises that victory would bring riches the likes of which had not been seen before. The ordinary soldiers had been conditioned to dehumanize the enemy, and their behaviour unsurprisingly reflected this.

More interesting is Alexander's own treatment of the city. He spent several months in Persepolis while the surrounding area was pacified and the royal treasury emptied, its contents transferred to Susa. Then, according to one prominent tradition, he held a raucous banquet.[15] The drinking got out of hand and one of the courtesans present, an Athenian woman named Thais, jumped up and shouted that Alexander would truly punish the Persians if he burned down the royal palace. Swept along by the excitement, the Macedonians rushed to set the buildings alight. Arrian, however, reports that this was a calculated decision to avenge the Greeks for earlier Persian atrocities.[16] This was, he says, not a prudent decision. And that's it – a few sentences. He wrote more about how the Romans built pontoon bridges to illustrate one way that Alexander might have crossed the Indus, only to admit that this did not really matter![17] But burning the palaces at Persepolis really was important, and the fact that Arrian deals with it so briefly seems suspicious. Was he hiding something? There was, perhaps, some scandal lurking beneath the surface: Thais was Ptolemy's mistress and later gave birth to his children.[18] Did Ptolemy – presumably Arrian's source here – cover up his lover's role in events? It was hardly in Ptolemy's interests, writing while trying to establish himself on the throne of Egypt, to admit that he was so closely tied to a woman with a history of leading kings astray. If Alexander did come to regret this decision, as the sources suggest, this would have been further incentive to suppress the story.[19] But the alternative version still seems a bit far-fetched.

When the site was excavated in the twentieth century, remarkably few valuable objects were found, which supports the claims that the royal treasury had been systematically emptied.[20] Alexander clearly intended to treat Persepolis differently from Susa and Babylon since the removal of the treasury from the city would have downgraded its status. Consequently, historians now tend to agree that the destruction was pre-planned, but they dispute Alexander's motivations.[21] For some, Alexander wanted to send a message to the Greeks. To explain this, I must admit to having done the very thing I had intended to avoid – I have been so fixated on what Alexander was doing that I have neglected important wider context. While Alexander was preparing for Gaugamela, the Spartan king, Agis III, launched a war he had been planning for several years.[22] Communications with Greece will not have been straightforward, but Alexander was probably receiving reports sporadically and Agis' war will have been concerning. There was little point in conquering an empire only to lose his homeland; should things go badly in Greece, Alexander would be forced to return. The Spartans were backed by other cities in the Peloponnese, but they suffered a significant defeat at Megalopolis, with Agis dying in the fighting. This occurred before the Achaemenid palaces were burned, but whether Alexander knew about it when instigating the arson is debated. I suspect that he did, but either way his actions could benefit the Macedonians at home. They could be spun as evidence that Alexander was indeed avenging the Greeks, but they were also a veiled threat: if Alexander could destroy Persepolis, what could he do to Greece?

There are archaeological hints that support revenge as the principal motivation. Heleen Sancisi-Weerdenburg noticed that the buildings that suffered the most damage were those associated with Xerxes.[23] After the Persian invasion of Greece, Xerxes was the chief villain in Greek eyes, so targeting the structures he had built was perhaps seen as a way of exercising some retribution. We might wonder, however, whether Alexander would be quite so discerning – Darius I had sent a fleet against Athens, and other Persian rulers had Greek blood on their hands. Sancisi-Weerdenburg also emphasizes that gift-giving played an important role in Achaemenid monar-chical culture. Kings rewarded their supporters with not only money, but fine robes and precious objects. Persepolis was one of the places where this material was stored, and Sancisi-Weerdenburg suggests that these objects were as much the targets as the build-ings themselves. Alexander knew he had to leave Persepolis, so he destroyed these goods to prevent anybody else seizing control of the royal storehouse and taking up the mantle of Achaemenid kingship.

I am not entirely convinced by this argument, but crucially it recognizes that there was a Persian audience for the burning of the palaces. Others have also acknowledged this too, suggesting it emphasized the Macedonian victory and would demoralize those Persians who still supported Darius. We should not imagine that an episode like this had only one motivation or intended audience, and we should also accept that the same event could be presented in different ways to different audiences.[24] However, seeing this episode within the ongoing war with Darius seems to me to be the most con-vincing approach; the Persians were the principal targets and the Greeks a secondary audience.

On that score, another factor may have been important.[25] From the city's earliest days, Achaemenid rulers had put up inscriptions at Persepolis as part of their strategy for legitimizing their rule. Several texts celebrate the construction activity commissioned by the kings, and such documents often included a prayer to the gods to preserve these structures. Xerxes, for instance, declared: 'what (has been) built by my father, that too may Ahuramazda protect.'[26] In another text, Darius I prayed to the Persians' chief god: 'may Ahuramazda protect this country from the army (of the enemy).'[27] By setting the palaces alight, Alexander sent the Persians a clear message: Darius had been abandoned by his gods. In doing so, he used the legitimizing strategies of the Achaemenids themselves to undermine Darius III.

Alexander's actions at Persepolis saw him vilified in later Persian sources, particularly in Zoroastrian circles. The *Ardā Wirāz Nāmag*, a Middle Persian text written in the ninth–tenth centuries CE, describes Alexander's conquest as bringing misery and devastation to Iran. He is accused of burning the Avesta, the Zoroastrian holy text, and killing religious leaders, which allowed wickedness to emerge and sowed the seeds for future chaos and impiety.[28] The *Greater Bundahišn*, written a century or so earlier, gives a similar account, but adds that religious fires were extinguished.[29] Historians, too, have painted a bleak picture of this episode, with one going so far as to write of a 'holocaust'.[30] This exaggerates the scale of the destruction and the extent to which Alexander sought to attack Persian culture. Behind these modern interpretations lies the belief that Alexander had no interest in legitimizing his rule in Iran: he was a conqueror and nothing more. This partly rests on the assumption that destroying Persepolis confirmed to Persians that they could

Despite the fire set by Alexander, significant remains
of the Persian royal palaces at Persepolis have survived.

never accept him as king and thus strengthened their resolve to resist. In the short term, this does not seem to have been the case. Instead, as he left Persepolis in pursuit of Darius, Alexander continued to welcome Persian defectors.[31] Unhappy though they may have been, and likely motivated by self-interest, leading Persians were still prepared to abandon Darius in the hope of finding favour with Alexander, choosing desertion over defending an Achaemenid king. Burning Persepolis, it seems, changed nothing in this regard.

The Death of Darius III (330)

If one of Alexander's aims was to increase the pressure on Darius, then it seems to have worked. Darius had retreated to Ecbatana (modern Hamadan), a major city in Media, to muster troops for another battle; Alexander left Persepolis ready for a final confrontation.[32] As he approached Ecbatana, however, he learned that Darius had failed to recruit a large enough force to risk battle and had fled. His authority began to collapse as it became increasingly obvious to his remaining supporters that he was unable to stem the Macedonian tide. Knowing that Alexander was hot on their heels, intent on capturing their king, a small group of nobles arrested Darius. Quite what they planned to do is unclear. Was Darius a bargaining chip designed to win them favour in negotiations with Alexander? Or was this one last effort to inject some life into the Persian resistance? Perhaps it was both – Arrian suggests that handing Darius over was a last resort if Alexander continued his pursuit and resistance proved impossible. However, it transpired that only the figure of Darius III was holding the Persian elite together, and his removal led to further fragmentation. Several Persians chose to defect to Alexander rather than serve the usurpers, among them Artabazus, a leading nobleman and father of Barsine, by now Alexander's mistress. Hearing news of the coup, Alexander increased the pace of his pursuit still further, marching overnight to cut the gap. As he closed in, the conspirators took the only action left open to them: they killed Darius and fled. Bessus, the satrap of Bactria, had emerged as the leader of the plotters. He now took the royal title and adopted the throne name Artaxerxes.

In some accounts, as he lay dying, Darius was found by some of Alexander's soldiers, who had with them a Persian captive. Darius spoke his final words to his countryman, urging Alexander to take vengeance on his behalf to protect the sanctity of kingship, and entrusting Alexander with his family.[33] In one version, Alexander himself finds Darius, who dies in his arms after a brief conversation.[34] Arrian, however, is clear that Darius was dead before Alexander arrived, and there is no reason to doubt this. But this prompted a switch of approach from Alexander; having pursued Darius relentlessly and ultimately driven him to his death, Alexander now posed as his avenger. He sent Darius' body back to Persia for burial in the royal tombs alongside his predecessors.[35] This was evidently an attempt to present himself as Darius' legitimate successor and to establish a contrast with Bessus: one had killed Darius, the other buried him with appropriate honours.

Northern Iran (330)

Another significant development took place in this crucial transitional period: Alexander began wearing Persian clothing.[36] Given the Greek antipathy to all things Persian, this must have been a difficult decision. At the same time, making some visible concessions to the Persians' way of life was a means of making it more difficult for Bessus to suggest that he was the last hope for protecting Persian culture. Alexander's wardrobe seems to have been constructed with these considerations in mind since some of the most egregiously Persian garments, like trousers, were avoided.[37] Instead, he took up items that were the preserve of royalty, such as a purple tunic that had a white stripe down the middle.[38] He did not, however, wear the distinctive headgear of the Achaemenid kings, which was apparently seen by Greeks as being too emblematic of Persian excess.[39] Here, Alexander was trying to make it clear to Persians that he claimed to be their legitimate ruler without alienating his own men.

Modern historians talk about this as the adoption of 'mixed dress'. They tend to agree that Alexander aimed to appeal to the Persians, but they disagree about how meaningful this was.[40] Was this a long-term strategy for integrating the defeated Persians into his new empire or was this simply a short-term ruse to tackle the threat of Bessus? Ultimately, we cannot possibly know what Alexander was thinking, so debates like this are impossible to resolve. Persian clothes did become a permanent feature of Alexander's display, but this may not have been the original intention. We should also credit him with the imagination to experiment: some strategies will have worked and survived, while others were dropped.

This discussion rests on the assumption that Persians would respond positively to mixed dress; but would they? Alexander's perseverance with the attire suggests it was thought to be effective, but there are reasons to wonder just how far this was true. Some Persians might see his choice of clothing as a sign of assimilation or proof that he respected Achaemenid traditions; others, though, might have seen this as appropriation or as a painful reminder of his victories. Some might imagine that this reflected a genuine commitment to engage with Persian culture, others may have been more suspicious. We should not presume that the Persian response would have been homogenous.

One item especially highlights this: the diadem.[41] Xenophon reports that Cyrus the Great appeared in public with a diadem wrapped around what he calls an 'upright tiara'.[42] The latter was donned only by the king, but the diadem was apparently also worn by Cyrus' courtiers. Xenophon claims that the Persian nobility continued to sport the headwear during his own lifetime; given that he had seen Persian nobles up close, there is no reason to doubt this. Alexander did not adopt the tiara, but he did begin to wear the diadem. In the decades after his death, this became the most important symbol of royalty. Kings across the Mediterranean world were depicted wearing one on their coins and 'taking the diadem' was understood to represent a claim to kingship: this can only have happened if it was worn exclusively by kings. Given Alexander's influence on the royal image in this period, it seems sensible to conclude that the diadem developed this connotation for his successors because of how it was used by him. In other words, the diadem was almost certainly Alexander's sole prerogative. What happened to the diadems traditionally worn by the Persian elite? Alexander's diadem may have been distinguished from these somehow, but were the Persians forced to give up their diadems?[43] This would explain how they became markers of royalty, but how would the Persians have felt about this? The diadem had been one marker of their status, so removing it could be seen as an attack on their standing. The nature of the evidence makes this line of thinking speculative, but this point emphasizes that we should not take Alexander's adoption of Persian clothing only at face value. There are complexities at play here which will have affected how this was received by the Persian aristocracy.

While Alexander was considering how to treat the Persian elite, a crucial event occurred that prompted a fundamental reshaping of the Macedonian high command. For obscure reasons, an otherwise unknown figure called Dymnus became involved in a conspiracy to kill Alexander.[44] The ancient authors show remarkably little interest in his motivations but delight in the details of what they see as a sordid plot. Dymnus attempted to recruit his lover, Nicomachus, to the conspiracy. He refused. But when Dymnus became hysterical and threatened to kill both of them, Nicomachus relented and was told that a host of notable figures were part of the plot, including Demetrius, one of the seven-strong bodyguards, the most prestigious rank at the Macedonian court. Nicomachus forced a smile and feigned enthusiasm, but quickly revealed everything to his brother, Cebalinus. Hoping to avoid attracting the attention of the plotters, the brothers decided that Cebalinus should be the one to inform Alexander. He went to the royal quarters and waited by the entrance – his status meant he could not enter uninvited. Instead, he stopped Philotas as he was going into Alexander's tent, told him what had happened and begged him to pass on the message. Philotas was a hugely influential figure. He was the commander of the Companion Cavalry, and he was the son of Parmenion, who had so often been Alexander's second-in-command. Both men had served Philip with distinction.

When Philotas emerged, Cebalinus asked him whether he had informed Alexander; the king had been preoccupied by other matters, he was told. Cebalinus tried again the next day with the same results, but still he waited by the entrance to the king's quarters, pestering Philotas as he came and went. Two days passed with no action and Cebalinus became suspicious. He stopped another courtier, Metron, who immediately took him to Alexander. Soldiers were sent to arrest Dymnus, who killed himself to avoid capture. His suicide was interpreted as confirmation that the plot was real.

Meanwhile, Alexander was interrogating Cebalinus. When he discovered the two-day delay in reporting the information, he ordered Cebalinus' arrest, thinking that this was indicative of some ill intent. But he had told Philotas, Cebalinus protested. Alexander was at first disbelieving, then aghast. He summoned Philotas, who confirmed Cebalinus' story. To him, the whole affair had sounded like nothing more than a lovers' tiff, and Cebalinus had provided no hard evidence of a conspiracy. It was not worth mentioning, he had decided, though he now realized that this was an oversight. Alexander accepted this explanation, but he called a council meeting and did not invite Philotas. In his absence, his peers turned on him. Craterus especially was allegedly particularly outspoken:

Philotas cannot have thought the information unsubstantiated, he argued, or he would have sent Cebalinus away – the only explanation for his inaction was his own involvement in the plot. Alexander demurred and the decision was taken to arrest Philotas.

The army was assembled for a show trial at which Alexander himself accused Philotas of involvement in the plot, and also levied charges against Parmenion. Philotas spoke in his own defence but was unable to sway the crowd: he was led out of the assembly and either tortured to death or executed by javelins. There was remarkably little evidence against Philotas to justify this treatment. Some ancient accounts claim that he confessed under torture, but any such testimony can carry only minimal weight. According to Arrian, both Ptolemy and Aristoboulos claimed that Philotas' conspiracy had first been reported to Alexander back in Egypt, but it had been dismissed. If Ptolemy did record this it must have been part of the official explanation, but that is no proof of a genuine plot.

When this happened, Parmenion was commanding forces in Media. Irrespective of his potential involvement in the plot, Alexander could hardly execute Parmenion's son and risk leaving the wily commander in control of an army of his own. Polydamus, a close friend of Parmenion, was sent to Media to instruct Parmenion's subordinates Cleander, Sitalces and Menidas to murder the general. They passed this test of loyalty with flying colours, butchering Parmenion as he took a leisurely stroll through a grove. This was just the beginning of the bloodletting. Others named as conspirators were executed, so too some of the close associates of Philotas and Parmenion. Alexander also decided this was the moment to get rid of another supposed traitor, Alexander of Lyncestis. He had been imprisoned since 334/3 on treason charges but had not been brought to trial, perhaps because he was Antipater's son-in-law. After a faltering defence, which left witnesses in no doubt about his guilt, he too was executed.

As is so often the case, the most important question cannot be answered: did Alexander genuinely believe that Philotas was conspiring against him? History taught Argead kings to fear assassination, and the spectre of Philip II's murder surely loomed large for Alexander. One can construct the bare bones of a theory that implicates Philotas and Parmenion. Perhaps they thought that Alexander's death so far from home would encourage the army to turn to Parmenion for leadership; since Alexander was still childless this could be the vehicle for elevating Parmenion to the throne. Involving nobodies on the peripheries of the court may have seemed a way to ensure that blame would not fall on the perpetrators. Against this, we must acknowledge that Parmenion had served the Argeads faithfully, Philotas too. The only evidence against Philotas is his failure to report information. One wonders, too, why he would act when Parmenion was away from the main camp.

Consequently, cynics might wonder whether Alexander seized the opportunity to remove a powerful noble family and increase his own authority (Ernst Badian even went so far as to suggest that Alexander perhaps orchestrated the whole affair).[45] When Alexander first came to power, his youth and inexperience meant he was forced to lean heavily on the magnates who had been his father's principal advisors. Together, men like Antipater, Attalus and Parmenion could restrict Alexander's freedom of action. But Attalus was dead, and Antipater left behind in Macedonia – only Parmenion remained. We have seen how Parmenion was often portrayed as a dramatic foil to Alexander, his advice rejected by a king who preferred decisions that advanced his own heroism. This is a literary technique designed to draw out the options open to Alexander by presenting a parallel course of action, but stories like these do give a sense of how Parmenion was in a position to advocate for alternative strategies. Moreover, there are lots of examples of young kings initially relying upon inherited advisors only to turn against them and discover that death is the only way to remove them. This reflects generational divides, the difficulty that experienced advisors have in ceding authority to kings as they come of age and the desire of new rulers to bring in their own appointees to key positions.

Alexander, though, could not sack Parmenion and expect no consequences. His years of service and leadership had won him the loyalty of his troops, who respected his achievements. Moreover, noblemen like him were exceptionally wealthy in their own right. For much of Macedonian history, the collective resources of the Macedonian aristocracy had probably been roughly equitable with those of the king. This meant that they could demand a seat at the table. However, Alexander's victories had changed the balance of power, and his resources now vastly outstripped those of the elite: he had less need to rely on their support and less incentive to make concessions to them. Irrespective of their possible role in a conspiracy, this demonstrates how the downfall of Philotas and Parmenion reflects longer-term concerns about power dynamics at Alexander's court. It also begins to show how this was a test case for the rest of the Macedonian aristocracy. By trying Philotas in public, Alexander effectively put his own reputation on the line: he declared that Philotas was guilty and asked the Macedonians to support him. They did, which issued a stark warning to the Macedonian nobility that the common soldiery would back the king. The timing of this event is instructive. Darius' death, the disintegration of Persian aristocratic unity and Bessus' retreat meant that there was no immediate danger of a major pitched battle in which Parmenion's experience would be especially valuable. If Alexander wanted to reorganize the structure of his army, this was as good a moment as any. After the successes of the previous year, his prestige was at its zenith. If ever there was a time to test the soldiers' loyalty to their immediate commanders, it was now.

There was one other important factor at play in these events – other Macedonian courtiers.[46] Curtius suggests that while Alexander deliberated about how to respond to the accusations against Philotas, Craterus weighed in heavily, arguing that he must be punished. Hephaestion, Coenus, Perdiccas, Leonnatus and others played a key role in what followed. It is impossible to corroborate these details and we cannot be sure that these names are correct, but the picture that Curtius paints rings true. These men represented the next rung down in the Macedonian army and several of them, especially Hephaestion and Perdiccas, belonged to a younger generation. Childhood peers of Alexander, these were his closest confidants and men who owed their positions at least in part to their friendship with the king. With Parmenion and Philotas in place, there was a clear ceiling for their careers. Irrespective of how far they believed in Philotas' guilt, this was a chance for them to create new opportunities for themselves. The results demonstrate this: Philotas' command was split between Clitus, one of the old guard, but with close ties to Alexander, and Hephaestion, one of the new men, whose relationship with the king was even closer. Ptolemy replaced Demetrius as a member of the bodyguard, making him one of the most important players at court. This was a pivotal turning point in Alexander's reign. Moving forwards, the new generation would rise to greater prominence, appointed less by birthright and more due to their ability and their loyalty to Alexander.

The final thought should perhaps go to Philotas. He has been portrayed as a haughty, arrogant man, but his death reveals the dangers that come with a powerful position at court. Rulers cannot take every decision themselves, so courtiers play a vital role in filtering what information reaches the king's ears. Choose incorrectly, as Philotas apparently did, and the consequences can be severe.

4

Bactria and Sogdiana, 330–327

While Alexander was cleaning house, Bessus retreated into Central Asia. This was a natural move for the satrap of Bactria as he could call upon strong ties both there and in neighbouring Sogdiana. Darius appears to have struggled to build a new army during the final months of his life, but Bessus presumably hoped to have better luck in a region where he was already powerful. However, once Alexander crossed the Hindu Kush and entered Bactria early in 329, Bessus withdrew across the Oxus (today's Amu Darya). Key strategic sites, like the capital of the satrapy, Bactra (now Balkh in northern Afghanistan), were captured without much of a fight. Alexander then went after Bessus, whose chief supporters, Spitamenes and Dataphernes, decided that handing over their leader was the safest route to self-preservation.[1] Alexander ordered that Bessus have his nose and ears cut off, and then sent him to Ecbatana to be executed in public.[2] In an inscription written two centuries earlier, Darius I explained how he mutilated two would-be usurpers and paraded them in public before their execution.[3] By aping this, Alexander was posing as a legitimate Achaemenid ruler and communicating this to Persians in language they would recognize.

Recently, some new documents concerning the management of the Achaemenid Empire came to light.[4] They are written in Aramaic, the language of the Persian administrative system, and date from the 350s to the 320s. However, they were acquired on the

Route of Alexander's campaigns in Bactria and Sogdiana, 330–327.

open antiquities market and their provenance is unclear, which is problematic. One of these documents may contain a list of supplies collected by Bessus.[5] It is dated to the first year of 'Artaxerxes the King', which could refer to Artaxerxes IV, who reigned from 338 to 336, or to Artaxerxes III in the 350s; it may, however, come from the year when Bessus was attempting to establish himself as king, with the regnal name Artaxerxes. The literary sources reflect the Macedonians' position that Bessus was a rebel who had seized the throne that rightfully belonged to Alexander. However, if this document does date from 330/329, it would demonstrate that some people in Bactria accepted Bessus' claim to kingship and were prepared to facilitate his struggle with Alexander. This is far from certain, but it reminds us that when we adopt terminology like 'rebel', as we so often do when we talk about this period, we are using words that intrinsically defend the position of the people who hold power; naturally, there were other views.

Another list from a few years later is dated to King Alexander, so his authority was evidently accepted eventually.[6] However, this second document reveals how little the administrative structure seems to have changed. It is often acknowledged that Alexander took over the Achaemenids' satrapal system, but the practicalities of this come through here as we encounter people performing similar roles within a comparable hierarchy to that seen in the earlier evidence. Everybody mentioned has a local name: Vakhshudata, Nafabarzana, Vishtaspa. Obviously, Macedonians could not take over every administrative job or Alexander would soon have run out of men, but this emphasizes how important local people were to the conquest and its aftermath. This helps us peek beneath the imperial surface and understand the impact that Alexander's campaign had on the conquered regions. At the same time, the limitations of this evidence reiterate that we cannot move away from the literary material entirely. Thirty written documents and eighteen inscribed wooden sticks, the entirety of the published collection, gives us at best a handful of isolated and contested snapshots.

Guerrilla Warfare (329–328)

The pursuit of Bessus had taken Alexander beyond the Oxus and he now advanced to the Jaxartes (the Syr Darya). Like the Achaemenids, Alexander seems to have accepted this as an appropriate border for his kingdom since he reached an alliance with the Scythians who inhabited the territory beyond the river.[7] A city, Alexandria Eschate ('the furthest'), was established on the river, close to a settlement allegedly founded by Cyrus the Great. While Alexander was preoccupied with the peripheries of his empire,

Bactria and Sogdiana rose in revolt (if I can use that term, given my note above). The chief culprit was Spitamenes, who avoided pitched battles and took advantage of the mountainous terrain to wage a guerrilla war. The Macedonians found themselves pulled from pillar to post; as soon as they dealt with one threat, another emerged. For instance, while Alexander was subduing the rebellious Sogdian cities, he discovered that his Scythian allies were preparing to attack his new city.[8] A swift display of Macedonian military superiority followed, with the Scythians routed and a thousand or so killed. The sheepish Scythian king claimed that this had been the unauthorized action of outcasts; Alexander was naturally suspicious, but the alliance was later renewed. Nevertheless, this example shows how these relationships were built on shifting sands and the Macedonians could expect little loyalty.

Alexander also faced fierce resistance as he moved into new territory and was forced to find innovative solutions to fresh military challenges. The sources describe the so-called Sogdian Rock as an imposing mountainous stronghold, extremely steep on all sides and sheer in places.[9] Thousands of Sogdians had gathered there, prepared for the type of long siege that simply was not practical for Alexander at this stage of the campaign. Offered the chance to negotiate, the man commanding the Sogdians allegedly taunted Alexander, telling him to come back when he had troops with wings. The next morning the defenders of the rock were shocked to discover Macedonian soldiers occupying the heights above their position; they immediately surrendered. Alexander had rounded up his best climbers and offered them significant financial incentives to reach the summit of the rock. Several died in the attempt, but Alexander had successfully improvised a special forces unit overnight.

He also experimented with different ways to bring the region under control. Although he had founded an Alexandria in Egypt, city-foundation now became a hallmark of his colonizing activity, with several established in this period. Creating new urban centres was a means of developing Macedonian strongholds in strategic locations. These cities were primarily populated with local people who were incentivized or forced to move to them. This disrupted existing regional networks, making resistance harder to maintain, and brought disparate communities together, making them easier for relatively small numbers of Macedonians to control.

Even this proved inadequate. As Alexander was dealing with one hotspot, Spitamenes would pop up somewhere else before melting away again into the hills. Ambushes became commonplace. On one occasion a detachment of Macedonians was attacked as it crossed a river; everybody in the unit was killed.[10] After blazing a trail across the Persian Empire, the Macedonians were becoming bogged down. Losses mounted and tension began to build until, in Maracanda (modern Samarkand), things exploded.

The Death of Clitus (328)

In the autumn of 328, Artabazus, the Persian nobleman whom Alexander had appointed as the satrap of Bactria, requested to retire.[11] His replacement was a Macedonian named Clitus. A generation older than Alexander, Clitus had served under Philip, and he had held a cavalry command from the beginning of the campaign; most notably, during the Battle of the Granicus he had saved Alexander's life. Moreover, Lanice, his sister, had apparently nursed Alexander as an infant. Loyal and battle-hardened, Clitus was the perfect person to tackle the ongoing resistance.

A banquet was organized to celebrate the appointment, but the evening culminated in a drunken dispute between Alexander and Clitus.[12] Precise details differ from source to source, but Clitus seems to have been particularly irked by the discussion of recent Macedonian history. Philip's achievements were apparently downplayed in favour of Alexander's, and Alexander allegedly sought to take sole credit for his victories. This proved especially popular with the younger men who had not participated in Philip's battles, but Clitus spoke up, defending the older generation. Eventually, he is said to have raised his hand, reminded Alexander of the Granicus, and declared, 'this was the hand that saved you!' Alexander became increasingly incensed, until his temper boiled over and he leapt up to attack Clitus. His friends grabbed him, which apparently prompted Alexander to cry out that he was suffering the same fate as Darius. Meanwhile, Clitus was dragged away from the banquet, shouting insults as he went. Moments later, he was dead.

The way that they describe this denouement says much about how the ancient sources present Alexander. Arrian gives two versions. In the first, Alexander wrestles himself free from the clutches of his Companions, grabs a spear from a nearby guard and immediately runs Clitus through. This is certainly murder, but it is a crime committed in the heat of the moment. The second report is explicitly attributed to Aristoboulos.[13] Ptolemy allegedly removed Clitus from the banquet, taking him beyond the wall and ditch of the citadel where the event was taking place. But Clitus was not to be deterred. As Alexander stumbled about shouting Clitus' name, his antagonist suddenly reappeared and was struck down. By highlighting Clitus' refusal to let the matter lie, Aristoboulos evidently sought to defend Alexander's reputation and paint Clitus as the principal aggressor. This apologetic tradition comes through in Arrian's own comments on the episode. He criticizes Clitus not only for his insubordination, but for reprimanding Alexander: courtiers should avoid flattery at all costs, he states, but they should keep their criticisms to themselves.[14] Even so, Arrian's discomfort is clear as he condemns Alexander for his anger and drunkenness. Curtius paints the blackest picture.[15] In his account, Alexander storms out of the banquet first, grabbing a spear from a guard. He stands by the exit as the guests leave, until only Clitus is left. Clitus emerges quietly, apparently trying to diffuse the situation. Alexander, however, cannot be mollified and kills him. In this version, Alexander is more calculating and the murder more intentional.

The portrayal of a drunken brawl certainly rings true: the gradual heightening of the argument; insults turning to threats and violence; Alexander being restrained by his friends but struggling to break free; Clitus being hauled away from the scene, but returning, spoiling for a fight. The sources are consistent in this general outline, which is another reason to think that things broadly happened in this way. We cannot know precisely how events played out and, given the levels of inebriation involved, participants will likely have had very different memories of what occurred. Nevertheless, the surviving reports are a plausible account of a tragedy that shows Alexander to be an all-too-human figure: angry, arrogant, drunken.

But he played the aftermath perfectly. He shut himself up in his tent for three days, refusing to eat or drink, apparently intent on starving himself to death out of remorse.[16] This display of grief, whether genuine or feigned, had an impact. His friends were quick to comfort him, urging him to forgive himself and move on. Curtius even claims that Clitus was posthumously condemned by the Macedonians and Alexander's actions vindicated. Whether or not a legal resolution was ever passed, the Macedonians appear to have openly accepted something they must have known for a long time: thousands of miles from home and surrounded by potentially hostile forces, they needed Alexander. Handling the fallout in this manner was a political masterstroke. Alexander had murdered a leading member of the Macedonian elite in a drunken rage, but he used this to strengthen his own grip on power. The message for the future was clear: dissenters could be punished with impunity.

The Marriage to Roxane (327)

Instead of Clitus, another Macedonian, Amyntas, was made the satrap of Bactria, and Coenus was left to defend the Sogdian frontier. Alexander himself headed towards the Massagetae who had been supporting Spitamenes.[17] Spitamenes soon attacked Coenus. We have no details about this battle, but it was evidently a significant Macedonian victory because Spitamenes' allies swiftly abandoned him. Learning that Alexander was intent on attacking them, the Massagetae killed Spitamenes, sending Alexander his head in the hope of deterring the planned invasion. The fall of one of the principal architects of military resistance was important, but it did not end the fighting. As the recent history of Afghanistan reminds us, the terrain favours the defenders – as soon as the Macedonians captured one mountaintop fortress, another needed to be pacified. Tales of bravado survive, but there was little glory to find here, and few riches either. Alexander, it seems, began to look for an alternative resolution.

After the capture of one rock fortress, a celebratory banquet was reportedly held.[18] The entertainment included dancing by local women, among them the most beautiful woman that Alexander had ever seen: Roxane, the daughter of Oxyartes. Alexander fell head over heels in love, so much so that in Curtius' account they were immediately married. Ancient writers interpreted this differently. For Arrian and Plutarch, this was a sign of Alexander's moral fortitude; he could have treated Roxane as a captive and sexually assaulted her, but he chose marriage.[19] Curtius was less impressed: the marriage was beneath Alexander and his friends knew it, but Clitus' murder had terrified them into silence. However, the ancient authors all suggest that this was a love match and they all seek to paint a romantic picture – if, that is, one can find romance in the tale of a conqueror picking out a beautiful woman from a parade of dancing girls.

Gerard Hoet (1648–1733), *The Marriage of Alexander the Great and Roxane of Bactria*, oil on panel. Given the romantic traditions that surrounded Alexander's marriage to Roxane, it is unsurprising that this became a common subject for later artists. Here, the Dutch painter Gerard Hoet portrays the two sharing bread, adapting a detail mentioned by Curtius.

Historians tend to see things more pragmatically.[20] For many, Alexander was imitating his father and securing his borders by marrying into the local elite.[21] Figures like Spitamenes had proven duplicitous, immediately betraying agreements as soon as the tail of the Macedonian column disappeared over the horizon. Tying a member of the local nobility into a marriage alliance promised longer-term stability, not least because that person might become grandfather to Alexander's heir, with all the status that would bring. If this was Alexander's logic, then he appears to have made a sound choice of wife and father-in-law because Oxyartes seems to have proven a reliable supporter. We soon see him negotiating with other members of the local elite on Alexander's behalf and later the territory that he controlled was extended, which suggests that Alexander was convinced of his loyalty.[22]

The marriage benefited Oxyartes too. He was evidently a nobleman, but he does not appear to have been the most important regional figure before 327. The marriage gave him a new status, and during negotiations with other local leaders he was not only doing Alexander's bidding but advertising his own powerful connections. His last appearance in the historical record came in 316, when Antigonus, one of the Macedonian generals seeking to succeed Alexander, reached Persia.[23] Antigonus was in the habit of appointing his own satraps, but apparently recognized that Oxyartes was too powerful to dislodge. We do not know how or when Oxyartes died, but he is one of the few people to survive the fall of the Achaemenid Empire, the Macedonian conquest and the chaos that followed Alexander's death. The sources offer little by way of insight into his character, but the bare facts suggest a shrewd operator.

As ever, interpretations of what prompted the marriage focus on Alexander himself: he either fell in love or made a rational decision to win over a local ally. There might be another way to see this. A year or so earlier, Scythian ambassadors visited Alexander, pledging their friendship and offering Alexander the chance to cement this alliance through marriage to the king's daughter.[24] Darius III allegedly also offered Alexander his daughter's hand as part of peace negotiations.[25] Both proposals were refused, but they remind us that Alexander was not the only mover in diplomatic exchanges. If others had suggested a marriage alliance as part of negotiations, might Oxyartes have done the same? Unless he was genuinely besotted with her, Alexander would not have married Roxane without a commitment from Oxyartes that this would buy his loyalty. Once we accept this, it is not much of a step to suggest that Oxyartes himself may have raised marriage as his price. We cannot prove this, but if we want to look for explanations beyond love at first sight, then it is important to consider how other people may have behaved. Roxane is unlikely to have had much say in the matter, but we should not necessarily imagine that Oxyartes was only a passive observer.

Passion and politics aside, his marriage to Roxane gives a good insight into the challenges of analysing Alexander's life. Most modern interpretations, including my own, essentially disregard the only explanation given by the ancient sources. Is it fair for historians to do this? There are other problems too. Arrian, Curtius and Strabo place this event at different rock fortresses: three accounts, three locations and three different dates. For good measure, the medieval manuscript that preserves Curtius' text is damaged. The name of the host of the banquet at which Alexander met Roxane has traditionally been restored as Oxyartes, but a now destroyed manuscript from late antiquity known as the *Metz Epitome* names Chorienes.[26] These accounts are so similar in other respects that they are evidently derived from the same source, so scholars now tend to prefer the latter, where the manuscript is clearer.[27] But if Chorienes organized the banquet and Oxyartes was only a guest, this might imply that he was the more high-ranking figure – so why didn't Alexander marry into Chorienes' family? More generally, why choose Oxyartes as his father-in-law? Were there no other potential brides available, or might genuine attraction to Roxane have influenced Alexander's choice after all? Considerations like these are pivotal in understanding how, when and why this marriage took place; unfortunately, the source tradition is so confused that such questions cannot be resolved.[28] Sometimes, studying Alexander is frustrating . . .

The *Proskynesis* Affair (327)

This should have been a time of celebration, but things quickly turned sour. Two incidents took place in quick succession that attest to splits within the Macedonian camp. The first issue emerged at another banquet and centred on a Persian custom known as

This relief from Persepolis gives a sense of how *proskynesis* might have been performed at the Persian court.

proskynesis.[29] This Greek word essentially means 'kissing towards', which gives a sense of what the gesture entailed. Herodotus reports that when two Persians of equivalent rank met, they would kiss one another on the lips, but, if there was a small distinction in their status, they would kiss on the cheeks.[30] If there was a significant difference between the two, the social inferior might blow a kiss towards their superior and prostrate themselves in a show of deference. We get a hint of what this might have looked like on a relief from Persepolis. Here, a courtier approaches the enthroned king and bows gently; his hand is held in front of his mouth as though in the act of blowing a kiss towards the monarch. Originally, this image was the centrepiece of two large reliefs that decorated the stairways up to the Apadana, the building where the king conducted royal audiences. This placement is telling since the image was the final thing that visitors saw before they entered the Apadana, and it reminded them of what was expected inside.

This emphasizes that *proskynesis* was an important part of Achaemenid courtly rituals, and this comes through in the Greek evidence too.[31] The Greeks, however, were uncomfortable with the gesture. In one notable example, Ismenias of Thebes was allegedly told that *proskynesis* was a prerequisite for meeting with the king.[32] Entering the audience hall, he dropped his ring onto the floor and pretended to complete the action as he bent down to pick it up. In Herodotus, the Spartan ambassadors Spethias and Bulis state that it is not customary for them to perform *proskynesis* to a man.[33] This phrasing implies that they considered it acceptable in other situations, and the term does appear in contexts with a religious connotation. In Sophocles' *Electra*, for example, Orestes tells his companion Pylades that they will enter his ancestral home to kill Clytemnestra, but only after making *proskynesis* to his father's gods.[34] In Xenophon's *Anabasis*, it is performed as an instinctive response to a sneeze, which was interpreted as a divine sign.[35] This prompts Xenophon to emphasize that Greeks only directed the gesture towards the gods. Given that this is set as the Greek mercenaries who had served Cyrus the Younger desperately attempted to reach home, this remark becomes a way to differentiate the Greeks from the Persians they were fighting. Thus the Greeks used the word in lots of different contexts to describe a range of actions.[36] They certainly appreciated the role the gesture played at the Persian court, but this background helps us appreciate why *proskynesis* might prove contentious, not just with Alexander's contemporaries but also later writers.

Indeed, *proskynesis* became one of the most controversial moments in Alexander's life. A debate allegedly took place during a banquet.[37] Alexander was not present but one of his acolytes delivered a lengthy speech extolling his achievements. These, the speaker argued, put Alexander on a par with deities like Dionysus and Heracles, and courtiers should recognize this by adopting *proskynesis*. Callisthenes spoke passionately against this, stressing that Alexander deserved every honour given to humans but that anything more would be blasphemous. Alexander, who Curtius depicts as deviously eavesdropping behind a curtain, recognized that the motion had no support and sent word that the idea should be dropped.

He evidently then returned to the room because the leading Persians performed *proskynesis*. One stooped so low that Leonnatus burst out laughing, thinking the man's appearance ridiculous. Alexander exploded at this; according to Curtius, he threw the Macedonian onto the floor, declaring that he was now doing the very thing he had mocked.[38] For ancient critics, this represents the height of Alexander's hubristic arrogance. Even Arrian voices his disapproval, although he later suggests it was merely a way for Alexander to impress his subjects.[39] The logic underpinning these ancient interpretations is clear: Alexander knew what Greeks and Macedonians thought of *proskynesis*, so trying to impose it upon them must have been an attempt to force them to recognize his divinity.

Many modern commentators have followed suit.[40] Often, they connect this moment to events at Siwah, seeing this as an attempt to fulfil a long-held ambition. Teasing out behavioural patterns is an important task for biographers, but, as I have stressed, the evidence renders character judgements about Alexander almost impossible, while removing events from their context leads to overly simplistic interpretations. Historians have certainly gone too far in suggesting that adopting *proskynesis* was a way for Alexander to make all of his subjects acknowledge his divinity.[41] For Persians, certainly, and perhaps other Near-Eastern peoples, it had no such connotation. If Alexander was intent on arrogating divine status, why lay so much store in something that had nothing to do with this for millions of his subjects? Moreover, the whole story of a debate at a banquet is completely implausible. If Alexander wanted his leading courtiers to perform *proskynesis*, would he really have asked a

Greek philosopher to bring up the topic? Leading Macedonians would hardly have set much store by this. In fact, why set things up in a way that actively invited discussion and dissent? If Alexander genuinely wanted the Macedonians to adopt this Persian protocol, there were better ways to do it. Most obviously, he could have told his leading supporters – men like Hephaestion and Ptolemy – to lead the way and hope that everybody else followed suit.

This is exactly what we see in another version of events, recorded by Arrian and Plutarch.[42] During a banquet, Alexander apparently passed a cup around his Companions. Upon receiving it, guests stood up, took a drink and then performed *proskynesis* to Alexander, who kissed them in return. The guest sat back down and handed the cup to the next man. Everybody was doing this, apparently without complaint, until it was Callisthenes' turn. He drank from the cup and made to kiss Alexander – but without doing *proskynesis*. Alexander was too busy chatting to notice, but Demetrius pointed this out and Alexander refused to kiss Callisthenes: 'I'll go away a kiss worse off,' he is said to have replied. There are questions about this variant, not least because it ends with Callisthenes' remark and we are never told how Alexander reacted, but this strikes me as a more plausible explanation of how things may have gone. What is especially important is that Plutarch names Chares as his source. He became Alexander's chamberlain, a role with responsibility for overseeing events at court, so he was extremely familiar with the protocol that governed occasions like this.

A philosophical debate could have taken place around this time. Major court events would not have been held every day so there was scope for figures like Callisthenes to dine and debate with one another around the edges. Perhaps Callisthenes was called upon to explain why he had refused to perform *proskynesis* in a context like this, but it is more likely that the tale of a debate is a later invention. Bowden, for instance, argues that it was created during the Roman imperial period, when contemporaries were forced to reckon with the potential deification of the emperor.[43] In this environment, Alexander became a useful vehicle through which unhappy Romans could explain their dissatisfaction. Alternatively, O'Sullivan suggests that the tale emerged during the two decades after Alexander's death.[44] In this period, the Peripatetic school of philosophy, which had been founded by Aristotle, was attacked by rival thinkers because of its close relationship with the Macedonians. Callisthenes was associated with this movement so making him the central figure in the opposition to Alexander's hubris was a way to protect the reputation of the Peripatetics. Either context would make more sense as the locus for this story than Sogdiana in 327.

If we ignore the noise generated by the alternative tradition, Chares paints a very different picture of the role of *proskynesis* in Alexander's court. Here, the leading Macedonians do not find the practice laughable and do not seem to oppose it. Indeed, Demetrius is happy to police the event and point out that Callisthenes had broken protocol. We might imagine that the Macedonian old guard would be uncomfortable with the notion of bowing before Alexander, but Chares' report suggests that there was no unified opposition to *proskynesis*. In fact, there is no indication that this was the first time the action was performed or that it was abandoned. Should we imagine that *proskynesis* featured at Alexander's court until his death? This probably goes too far, but Chares' account suggests that *proskynesis* was more problematic for later Greek and Roman writers than it was for Alexander's courtiers. Furthermore, the way that Alexander talks to those around him while *proskynesis* is performed hardly works in a religious context – if this was a one-off attempt to claim divine honours, he would surely have been paying closer attention to what was going on. Instead, Chares describes a run-of-the-mill scene made notable only by Callisthenes' misbehaviour. This all sounds very much like the type of activity we associate with the Persian court, where *proskynesis* was a vehicle through which courtiers acknowledged the royal status of the king.

If Alexander was not pursuing divine recognition through *proskynesis*, why introduce it? One possibility is that this was an attempt to emphasize his authority over the Macedonian elite. Despite his treatment of Parmenion and Philotas, men like Clitus had continued to challenge him. *Proskynesis* was a way of establishing greater distance between Alexander and the Macedonians; now, rather than speak their minds, the Macedonians would bow before the king. We should also remember that Persians had now been welcomed into the court and they performed *proskynesis* to Alexander just as they had to Achaemenid monarchs. But this created an uncomfortable situation where some people at court behaved differently to others and Leonnatus could openly mock the Persians. This was hardly tenable in the long term, so several historians see this as an attempt to equalize court protocol.[45] Any Macedonian dissent reflected their objections to being treated like Persians.

We should go further than this, however, because traditional treatments overestimate Alexander's agency. *Proskynesis* was such an integral part of Achaemenid protocol that it was performed by Persians habitually. As they joined Alexander's court, they brought the practice with them. Since it was one of the principal ways in which the Persian nobility demonstrated their acceptance of royal authority, we can imagine that *proskynesis* to Alexander was demanded of defectors. Furthermore, seeing leading members of the nobility publicly acknowledge Alexander's kingship was a means of encouraging those lower down the social ladder to do the same. This may have been going on since the earliest days of the campaign, so there are good reasons for thinking that the gesture had a longer history at Alexander's court than is usually acknowledged. It would also have been performed by the slaves and attendants that Alexander acquired as he captured Persian royal spaces. Their servility may have been taken for granted by the Macedonians, but it would have heightened the visibility of the gesture. Perhaps it is an exaggeration to say that *proskynesis* was everywhere by 327, but it was surely common.

Finally, bowing or prostrating is so visual, and so striking, that it could not be ignored. This was not a minor cultural quirk that could be sidelined or overlooked, and its importance as a marker of royalty meant that Alexander could not ask the Persians to abandon the practice and expect to retain his authority. Regularly seeing this gesture forced Alexander and the Macedonians to confront an alternative model of ruler-subject interaction. So, simply by behaving in the way that they always had, Persians challenged the status quo at the Macedonian court. Of course, only Alexander could order everybody to adopt the practice wholesale, and in that sense his agency was vital. But ultimately, it was the Persians who made *proskynesis* an issue.

The Pages' Conspiracy (327)

How far we imagine that *proskynesis* prompted a challenge to Alexander's power evidently depends on which version of events we prefer, but a more dangerous threat emerged shortly afterwards. The Royal Pages were a group of adolescent boys who helped to look after the king's daily needs and watched over him while he slept. They are sometimes understood to have functioned like bodyguards, but their youth and inexperience means we should not take this too seriously – a group of fifteen-year-olds can hardly have been expected to fend off determined attackers. Instead, I rather imagine that they were there to deal with basic requests if the king stirred during his sleep: fetching a light, getting a cup of water and so on. Regardless, this meant that the Pages had uncontrolled access to Alexander when he was at his most vulnerable, so this was an important role built on mutual trust. The Pages were drawn from the nobility, and spending time together helped build bonds of loyalty between the ruler and people who could be expected to play a prominent role in the kingdom in the future. More cynically, the arrangement meant that the sons of important noblemen became hostages, which perhaps went some way towards guaranteeing the loyalty of their fathers. The system seems to have its roots in Philip's reign as part of his drive to centralize the Macedonian government and bring greater unity to the kingdom.

One of these Pages was called Hermolaus.[46] The story goes that during a hunt he killed a boar before Alexander had an opportunity to attack the animal. The king was furious: Hermolaus was publicly flogged, and his horse was confiscated. Hermolaus was stung by his treatment and complained to his lover, Sostratus, another Page. This indignation turned to thoughts of revenge and the two men plotted to murder Alexander, recruiting several other Pages to their scheme. Naturally, the plan was to kill Alexander while he slept, when the conspirators controlled access to the king. However, the way that the rota was arranged made it difficult to find a night when only those involved in the plot were on duty. Eventually, perhaps as much as a month later, the Pages were ready. However, as so often seems to have been the case, Alexander got lucky – he stayed up all night partying with his friends. Aristoboulos, always keen to downplay Alexander's drinking habits, claimed that he tried to leave early but was stopped by a woman in a state of agitation. Her condition was interpreted as a sign of divine possession so, when she begged Alexander to return to the banquet and prolong festivities until morning, he was only too happy to oblige. For the Pages, this was a catastrophe. They hung about as dawn came, knowing that they were due to be relieved at daybreak. The opportunity had slipped away.

So far, the Pages had shown remarkable solidarity, but now one of them got cold feet. Epimenes either told his brother, Eurylochus, about the conspiracy, or revealed it to his lover, Charicles, who in turn spoke to Eurylochus. Eurylochus went straight to Alexander's tent to raise the alarm. In describing what followed, we again see the primary sources shaping the narrative to their own advantage: Curtius reports that Eurylochus spoke to Ptolemy and Leonnatus, whereas Arrian mentions only Ptolemy. Ptolemy, it seems, omitted Leonnatus from his account so that he could take full credit for bringing the conspiracy to Alexander's attention. Apparently, he burst into Alexander's bedroom and woke him up – a stark contrast, of course, with how Philotas had behaved in an identical situation. The plotters were swiftly rounded up and tortured until they confessed. They were then tried before an assembly of the Macedonian soldiers. According to Curtius, Hermolaus gave an angry speech that denounced Alexander as a tyrant. Arrian alludes to this but presents it as something that neither Ptolemy nor Aristoboulos recorded so it is unclear what, if anything, the Pages said in their own defence. In any case, they were swiftly found guilty of treason and executed – they were not alone.

Apparently, Alexander's anger with Callisthenes had festered. He had reportedly spent lots of time with the Pages, which aroused suspicions that he had encouraged their plans. The sources take a cynical attitude towards this. Curtius, for example, is emphatic that the Pages did not implicate Callisthenes.[47] Given contemporary stories of authoritarian leaders cracking down on academic freedom of expression, it is tempting to see Callisthenes as the archetype of the historian who told truth to power and paid the ultimate penalty. However, if his role in opposing *proskynesis* was exaggerated, there was less reason for Alexander and his adherents to implicate him falsely in the conspiracy. According to Arrian, both Ptolemy and Aristoboulos claimed that the Pages revealed Callisthenes had supported their plotting, so this was clearly part of the official story.

However, accounts of what happened next differ radically: Aristoboulos reported that Callisthenes was imprisoned and died of disease, whereas Ptolemy claimed he was tortured and hanged.[48] Arrian throws his hands up in frustration at this, complaining that even otherwise dependable eyewitnesses who must have known what happened cannot agree on basic details. There were other versions too. According to Plutarch, Chares explained that Alexander wanted to try Callisthenes in Greece with Aristotle present, but he died of obesity and disease before this could happen; conversely, Justin suggests that he was viciously mutilated.[49] Aristoboulos and Chares offer apologetic descriptions designed to persuade Greeks that Alexander was intent on offering Callisthenes a fair trial, whereas Ptolemy had nothing to gain by reporting his torture and execution; we should accept his version.[50]

For the ancient authors, Callisthenes was the most important connection between the *proskynesis* affair and the Pages' Conspiracy, but for me there is a more important link. To appreciate this, we need to return to the trigger for the conspiracy: the boar hunt. Alexander's decision to have Hermolaus beaten for jumping in front of him to kill a boar might feel a tad unnecessary. Even if you think that Alexander had a short fuse, this still seems like an overreaction. Similarly, we can understand why Hermolaus may have felt humiliated by his treatment, but was this really enough to make him decide to kill the king? And why were his fellow Pages so outraged by Alexander's conduct that they plotted with Hermolaus? The close bond between the young men, strengthened through sexual relationships, offers one explanation, but there is more to it than this. According to one ancient source, Macedonians could not recline at banquets until they had killed a boar without a net.[51] Symposia were an integral part of Greek life, and reclining, rather than sitting, was a mark of status. Since success in the hunt translated directly into a status symbol which they carried with them forever, killing a boar was a rite of passage for Macedonian youths. This helps to explain why Hermolaus reacted so strongly, and why his peers joined his conspiracy. Hermolaus thought he had proven himself a man, but he was infantilized and criticized, not congratulated. If Hermolaus was denied the opportunity to become an adult, his friends may have wondered what hope there was for them.

Why did Alexander behave like this? He obviously knew about this custom so he could appreciate why Hermolaus would have been so eager to attack the boar first. The answer lies in Achaemenid monarchical traditions. The Greek writer Ctesias, who was familiar with Persian protocol having spent several years as a doctor at the Achaemenid court, reports a similar incident.[52] The nobleman Megabyzus allegedly killed a lion before the king, Artaxerxes I, could strike. Megabyzus was sentenced to death, though this was subsequently reduced to exile. Hunting was an important royal activity in Macedonia as well as the Near East. It was fun and an opportunity to build bonds with courtiers, but it was also a chance to demonstrate skills with obvious military applications. Furthermore, dangerous animals like lions could wreak havoc among communities and they were sometimes used in art as symbols of chaos. Killing them was a way for rulers to show that they could protect their people and to demonstrate that they were suitable for kingship. By jumping in front of Artaxerxes, Megabyzus acted as though the king was unable to protect himself and needed saving; this meant casting doubt on his abilities.

Alexander's treatment of Hermolaus is clearly reminiscent of this incident and there is no evidence of earlier Macedonian kings behaving in this manner. As with *proskynesis*, historians sometimes argue that Alexander actively chose to adopt this Persian custom.[53] There is merit to this: Alexander gave the order to punish Hermolaus, which meant actively deciding to adhere to a Persian practice. But there is more to it than that. It is hard to imagine Alexander sitting down and working through a list of Achaemenid protocols, choosing to borrow some and discard others. In fact, it is unlikely that there was one single list detailing every courtly regulation that Alexander could consult. It is more likely that individual examples were discussed only when relevant situations occurred, so Alexander's decisions were probably taken with less foresight than is sometimes thought. In this context, the behaviour of the Persians was critical.

As we have seen with *proskynesis*, they had well-established ways of acting, which they brought with them into Alexander's court; seeing something unusual, curious Macedonians could ask, 'why do you do that?' Indeed, words did not need to be exchanged – simply by being present, the Persians offered an alternative image of how courtiers were supposed to behave.

Persians were probably participating in Alexander's hunts by this point, so their behaviour helped cast Hermolaus' actions in a different light: while they deferred to the king, he rushed to take the kill for himself. What may once have been interpreted as youthful impetuousness was now viewed more seriously. Perhaps Alexander was frustrated at missing out on a kill, but this offers another way to understand his anger. Moreover, to any watching Persians, the king's abilities had been slighted by a mere boy – Alexander could not overlook Hermolaus' transgression without undermining his authority in their eyes.

So, while ancient accounts fixate on Callisthenes, these two episodes are revealing of a much bigger issue: the challenge of bringing together two different cultures. Staying true to Macedonian traditions may have meant that Alexander failed to live up to the image of monarchy held by his newly conquered subjects, but making changes risked destabilizing his court and alienating the very people who had won him his empire. As these incidents show, walking this narrow line was all but impossible.

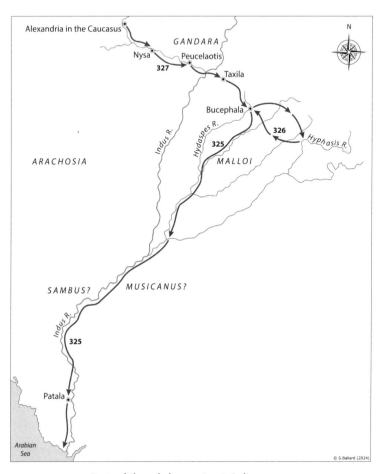

Route of Alexander's campaigns in India, 327–325.

5

India, 327–325

The alliance with Oxyartes gave Alexander the security he needed in Afghanistan, and his eyes shifted to a new target. For Alexander's contemporaries, India included what is now Pakistan and, knowing nothing of China, it was generally a catch-all term for the eastern edge of Asia. The region had long captured Greek imagination. Herodotus, for instance, had described a land of wonders, extremes and contradictions: huge and unusual animals, untold riches, unconventional habits, vegetarianism and cannibalism.[1] Of course, this was not based on observation; any genuine information was transmitted at second or third hand across the Persian Empire, and the rest was invented to suit Greek sensibilities – Dionysus and Heracles were said to have visited India, for instance. Consequently, these accounts tell us more about the Greek world view than about India itself, but they meant that the Macedonians thought of themselves as entering a world of legends.

This came to the fore immediately. Arrian describes how Alexander advanced towards the city of Nysa in Gandara, ready to attack.[2] Rather than resist, the inhabitants sent out an envoy, who explained that the city had been founded by Dionysus to be a free and self-governing community. As proof, the ambassador is said to have pointed out that ivy, which was associated with Dionysus, grew in the region but not anywhere else in India. This apparently proved an effective tactic, and the Macedonians were delighted to see this ivy. There was scepticism about this report even in antiquity – Arrian remarks that Alexander wanted to believe that Dionysus had founded Nysa because it meant that he was about to go even further east than a god. He also mentions that Eratosthenes of Cyrene, the librarian of Alexandria during the third century BCE, had concluded that all of the divine allusions that the Macedonians reported in India had been invented to curry favour with Alexander. The Macedonians were certainly keen to present their campaign in the best possible light, and the mythological associations that India had for audiences at home were an obvious connection to exploit. Alternatively, stories like this might reflect the efforts of enterprising Indians, who quickly learned about Hellenic culture and spotted an opportunity to ingratiate themselves with Alexander. In any case, the sources do shift gears as Alexander moves into India. From competing with his supposed ancestors Heracles and Perseus, Alexander is now presented as following in the footsteps of Dionysus.[3]

Sometimes historians can get sucked in by these tales too. Positive interpretations can present the Indian campaign as an adventure into the unknown and a voyage of exploration. The Macedonians, it is true, were treading on unfamiliar ground, and new encounters were an inevitable part of the expedition. There are tales of Alexander conversing with Indian sages and comparing their wisdom with that of more familiar Greek philosophers.[4] New flora and fauna were discovered. But these interpretations exaggerate the reality, and Alexander can become a precursor to the navigators of the age of discovery or the thinkers of the Enlightenment. Scientific advancement may have been one effect of Alexander's invasion of India, but it cannot have been one of its main motivations – Alexander was hardly risking life and limb to send a few plant cuttings back to Aristotle. In the final decades of the twentieth century, a new strand of thinking emerged that stressed the scale of the destruction that Alexander wrought on India.[5] This is crucial to emphasize, and we will encounter clear examples of the

Macedonians killing for the sake of killing as they moved through the region.

But there is another story too, which I hope comes through in the following pages. Postcolonial thinkers have increasingly recognized that a straightforward juxtaposition between conqueror and conquered is too simplistic in situations like this. Instead, local communities have pre-existing relationships with one another; they are bound by shared pasts that create bonds, mutual obligations, suspicion and enmities. These experiences affect the way that they respond to the arrival of an imperial power. If you saw your hated neighbour agree an alliance with a foreign general, could you imagine reaching a similar accord or would this set you on the path to resistance? In the opening years of Alexander's campaign, the warring parties were well defined, but things become more complicated with the collapse of Achaemenid authority. In the absence of a centralizing force, regional elites jockeyed with one another for status and advantage. We have seen one potential example of this with Oxyartes, but this became a more pronounced feature of the campaign as Alexander entered India, where ties to the Persian Empire were looser or non-existent and local rivalries were even more prominent. In these circumstances, even while experiencing the brutal effects of colonization, some Indian rulers spied opportunities for advancement, while others were drawn – sometimes forced – into Alexander's service and shaped the course of the campaign. We will see that the people of India were not only victims, but people who actively sought to control their own destinies.

Taxiles and Porus (327–326)

Alexander's first encounter with an Indian ruler was with a figure called Taxiles, who promised his loyalty before the Macedonians left Sogdiana.[6] Alexander was keen to cement their relationship, and this decision would have a profound impact on the campaign in

India. We immediately see Taxiles using his new ally to influence local politics. Astis, the ruler of Peucelaotis (modern Charsadda), was said to have revolted: Alexander replaced him with a man called Sangaeus, who had earlier fled from Astis and sought refuge with Taxiles.[7] The sudden elevation of his protégé expanded Taxiles' influence, and we can imagine that he played a role in orchestrating these events. This comes through even more clearly in what happened next. Alexander was told that a neighbouring king, Porus, was preparing to offer resistance.[8] We are never told how Alexander discovered this, but Porus and Taxiles were apparently old enemies. In a cynical reading, Taxiles was attempting to use the Macedonians to settle pre-existing scores. Perhaps Porus really was gathering his forces to oppose Alexander, but was he doing so out of genuine hostility or was he affected by suspicions about Taxiles? If my enemy's enemy is my friend, then my enemy's friend must also be my enemy. This logic is key to understanding what happened in India.

Porus had deployed his forces along the banks of the Hydaspes (Jhelum), aiming to prevent Alexander from crossing.[9] Alexander is usually depicted as a dashing commander, swift to attack and first into the fight himself. We saw this in Arrian's depiction of the Battle of the Granicus at the beginning of the invasion, when Alexander plunged headlong into battle even across a well-defended river. A heroic model underpinned this behaviour, but there was calculation too: delay risked emboldening the Persians. At the Hydaspes, though, a different quality comes to the fore – patience. Contested river crossings are extremely difficult to pull off, and this was compounded at the Hydaspes since the seasonal rains meant that the river was deep and fast-moving. Recognizing the risks, Alexander declared that he would wait it out. We must also acknowledge another aspect of his command that is often overlooked. Keeping men under arms requires significant supplies of food and resources, and the challenges are magnified when an army is stationary because local resources are swiftly exhausted. Alexander was able to delay at the Hydaspes, and thus pull off the stratagem that would win him victory, only because he mastered the logistics of the situation.[10] Carts carrying supplies are less exciting than a cavalry charge, but they are also important.

The lull, however, was a ruse. Scouts were dispatched along the river to search for potential crossing points, though Porus was found to be guarding these too. When night fell, detachments were sent out in different directions, raising a hullabaloo and giving the impression that they were about to attempt a crossing. Porus was forced to shadow the Macedonians. But over time, with nothing happening, Porus became complacent and began to keep his army in their camp. This was Alexander's moment to strike. His scouts had found a bend in the river where the course of the water created a prominent headland, and where there was also an island. Both were heavily wooded, giving the Macedonians the cover they needed to steal across. Alexander divided his army into two: he would lead an advance force across the river and attack Porus. If Porus left camp and marshalled his entire army against Alexander, Craterus was to lead the remaining Macedonians over the Hydaspes to attack him from the rear. Smaller units were posted elsewhere along the riverbank, again with instructions to cross only when the battle was underway. Alexander's crossing proved far from straightforward. His men landed first on a second, unknown, island and the remainder of the river was forded only with difficulty, but, eventually, the Macedonians were across.

One of the challenges of interpreting the works produced by ancient writers is that their practice as historians is usually hidden. Today, historians are expected to highlight disagreements in their sources and to explain why they prefer a particular version of events. This was unusual in antiquity, however, where literary considerations predominated, and we often do not know whether the narratives given by ancient historians reflect a consensus among their sources or whether disagreements have been concealed. In his description of this battle, however, we do get a rare insight into Arrian's way of thinking, because at this crucial moment he encountered contradictory reporting. Aristoboulos, Arrian says, has Porus' son arrive on the scene with almost 60 chariots, whereas Ptolemy claims that he commanded 2,000 cavalrymen and 120 chariots.[11] Arrian argues that Aristoboulos's account makes little sense because the force he describes was too big to act as a scouting unit, but too small to engage in any actual fighting. This seems a sensible conclusion, and we might also add that Ptolemy apparently participated in this crossing himself. Of course, this does not mean that we should imagine that Arrian's judgement was unimpeachable and simply accept what he says elsewhere, but it does demonstrate that Arrian could think critically about his sources.

With Alexander safely across the river, Porus faced a difficult decision: march out against Alexander with his entire force and risk allowing Craterus across the river or stay put and allow Alexander to plan an assault on his position. He chose the former but left some elephants occupying the riverbanks to panic Craterus' horses and disrupt the crossing. Reaching a level, sandy plain, Porus now prepared for battle. According to Arrian, his army comprised some 30,000 infantrymen, 4,000 cavalrymen, 300 chariots and 200 elephants.[12] The elephants were Porus' not-so-secret weapon. These had long been a feature of warfare in India, but this was the first time a Macedonian army had encountered the animal in a major pitched battle.[13] Alexander's men were surely apprehensive of these strange beasts, and they terrified the horses.

The importance of the cavalry in Alexander's major victories to date meant that this was potentially a significant challenge, though local allies like Taxiles, who had their own experience of elephant warfare, will have been able to help Alexander find solutions. Porus certainly appears to have centred his plans for the battle around the elephants as they were placed in the front line. Arrian explains that they were positioned close together – less than 30 metres (100 ft), he reports – so that there were no gaps through which Alexander's cavalry would dare to attack. However, if all of the reported two hundred elephants were stationed here, the battle line would have been almost 6.5 kilometres (4 mi.) long, which is implausible: either the numbers are exaggerated (Curtius has 85 elephants, Diodorus 130), or some of the elephants were held in reserve. In the gaps, but set back behind the elephants, Porus posted his infantry. Curtius and Diodorus, evidently drawing on the same source, give a sense of the visual effect of this, describing the elephants as rising above the rest of the army like towers in a city. More infantry units were posted on each wing, lining up behind the cavalry and the chariots.

Faced with this imposing sight, Alexander . . . waited. For all his tactical genius, Alexander understood that ancient battles were decided first and foremost by the men who fought them. Their conditioning was vital, and Alexander recognized the efforts his men had already expended in fording the river. After this breather, Alexander launched his attack. Infantry were to hold the centre while the cavalry was divided into two groups. Alexander would command one of these himself, with the other led by Coenus; together, they would target Porus' wings so as to avoid the elephants and infantry at the core of his formation. Alexander attacked Porus' left and Coenus was probably sent against the other wing.[14] Threatened by overwhelming numbers on his left, Porus transferred the cavalry from his right wing to counter the threat. But this left Coenus unopposed. He outflanked Porus' army and attacked the cavalry from the rear. Faced with a two-pronged assault, the Indian cavalry were driven back into their own elephants. This gave the Macedonians a decisive advantage as the Indians were surrounded. Bitter fighting ensued as the Macedonian phalanx now advanced against Porus' elephants and infantry. Cornered elephants careered around the battlefield, caring little whether they trampled friend or foe. Finally, the resolve of the Indians gave in, and they fled – straight into the spears of Craterus' men, who had crossed the Hydaspes and were advancing towards the battlefield. Caught between two experienced armies, the slaughter on the Indian side was vast; Arrian reports that more than 20,000 died.[15]

With victory all but certain, the ancient writers focus on Porus himself. Without exception, their admiration shines through. He towers over the other Indians – even Alexander is said to have been impressed by his height – and this was exaggerated when he was mounted on his elephant. Curtius paints a particularly vivid picture of Porus' heroism.[16] As the men around him flee and his enemies swarm around his elephant, Porus soldiers on. He launches javelin after javelin at his attackers, receiving wound upon wound – nine in all – in return. These injuries begin to take their toll. His throws become weaker, weapons start to slip from his hand, until his mahout notices that he has almost passed out and steers the elephant from the battlefield. Recently, Pierre Briant has sought to rehabilitate the reputation of Darius III, highlighting some of his positive qualities and suggesting that he was unfortunate to find himself cast into Alexander's shadow.[17] In many respects, however, it is Porus who proved Darius' dramatic foil and Arrian draws an explicit contrast between the two: whereas Darius had fled at the first sight of trouble, Porus fought to the end.[18]

The impression that Alexander had finally encountered a worthy enemy is emphasized by what followed.[19] As Porus retreated, Alexander allegedly sent Taxiles to negotiate with him. Porus, though, was unimpressed at the appearance of his old foe. He roused himself and launched such a furious attack that Taxiles was forced to flee.[20] Eventually he was persuaded to surrender by Meroes, another Indian. Alexander now met his rival for the first time and asked Porus how he should be treated: 'like a king,' Porus responded.[21] Alexander pushed further as to what that meant, but Porus replied that there was nothing more to say. Mightily impressed at this display of fortitude, Alexander decided that Porus was the sort of character he wanted to work with. He not only let Porus retain control of his kingdom but even extended its boundaries. Pragmatism will have been at work here, since this decision established Porus as a client king, but the way that this interaction is framed in the sources captures the essence of the romantic tradition around Alexander. Here, we see a chivalric figure who is magnanimous in victory and can recognize the inherent nobility of a defeated rival.

Of course, there is no way of knowing what the two men actually said to one another, and we should remember that conversations were presumably conducted through interpreters, but Porus evidently impressed Alexander favourably. Although Alexander had welcomed and rewarded Persian defectors, those who defied him had usually been killed. One thinks of Batis, the governor at Gaza, or the inhabitants of Tyre. Indeed, during the rest of the fighting in India resistance almost invariably meant death. So, Alexander's treatment of Porus is unusual, which suggests that there was something about him that struck a chord.

'Porus coin', minted *c.* 326–323. This silver coin, which depicts a cavalryman attacking two figures on an elephant, is usually interpreted as a representation of Alexander and Porus. Very few of these coins survive – if they were produced by Alexander, they would represent some of the only images of the king from his own lifetime.

This cannot, I think, have been a purely pragmatic consideration, either. His ally Taxiles had encouraged this confrontation and was presumably expecting to be rewarded for his own loyalty in its aftermath. Had Alexander wanted to replace Porus and retain local expertise within his own administration, Taxiles was well-placed to take over. Instead, Taxiles was sent back to his own kingdom while Porus saw his territory expanded. I tend not to set much store by the romantic strands in Alexander's tale, but here I do think that there is scope to imagine that Alexander genuinely admired, or at least respected, Porus. Two cities were founded to commemorate the victory, one named after Nike, the other after one of the notable casualties in the battle, Bucephalus, Alexander's trusty horse.

Mutiny at the Hyphasis (326)

The Macedonians now advanced further into India, negotiating the various tributaries of the Indus. Perhaps the most interesting illustration of how this part of the campaign played out came as they reached another river, the Hydraotes.[22] Around the time of the Battle of the Hydaspes, Alexander had been contacted by a local ruler, confusingly also called Porus, who promised to surrender. Arrian explains that this Porus was motivated by his antagonistic relationship with his namesake; seeing Alexander poised to destroy his rival, he imagined a profitable alliance. But Alexander's sudden change of heart shifted his calculations: his bitter enemy had somehow acquired a powerful patron, so he gathered as many warriors as he could and fled from his kingdom. Alexander pursued, but we do not discover what happened. Instead, Arrian explains that Alexander learned that the Cathaeans were preparing for battle.[23] They had previously been attacked by the first Porus but held out, and now they prepared to resist his ally. Here, as with the second Porus, Alexander was discovering that the peoples of the Indus Valley were connected by a variety of ties and enmities, many of them no doubt deeply rooted. Just as his alliance with Taxiles appears to have prompted battle against Porus, their reconciliation drew the Macedonians further into inter-Indian conflicts. Taxiles may have imagined using Alexander to establish himself as the principal player in the region, but, as it turned out, it was his rival who benefited from Macedonian military power. Arrian reports that 17,000 Cathaeans were killed and another 70,000 captured; thousands more were displaced from their homes when their capital, Sangal, was razed to the ground. These numbers might be inflated, but they give a sense of the scale of annihilation that was beginning to unfold in India.

Slaughter on an almost unimaginable level, but to what end? Darius was dead, the Persians defeated. The wealth of India was already at Alexander's disposal – so why go on? What was the plan? Murmurings of dissent began to spread through the camp. Rumours began to reach the Macedonian soldiers of even more powerful Indian kingdoms on the horizon, populated by even braver warriors and more fearsome elephants. Gradually, whispers turned to open chatter, and, as the army came to the banks of yet another river, the Hyphasis (Beas), they reached such a pitch that Alexander could ignore it no longer. He gathered his army together and addressed his men.

As Arrian tells it, Alexander listed the places he had conquered for the Macedonians and then outlined his future ambitions.[24] Further conquest in India would bring the Macedonians to the Outer Ocean, which Greeks at the time thought encircled the continents. From there, they would sail around Africa and reach the Pillars of Heracles, which flank the Strait of Gibraltar: this was to become a genuine world conquest. The Macedonians had already gone further than Dionysus and surpassed the achievements of Heracles. Turning back risked undoing this work since tribes left unconquered would incite those within the empire to revolt, causing a domino effect that would bring war back to Macedonia. Alexander could not stop now.

This speech encapsulates the way that Arrian characterizes Alexander. Later, he would describe Alexander as somebody who would not have been satisfied with conquering all of Europe as well as Asia, but who would have gone on and on, competing with himself when there were no other rivals left.[25] His men, however, had no interest in any of this, and the speech was met with stony silence. Eventually, the Macedonian nobleman Coenus spoke up on behalf of the army: the men had huge respect for Alexander's leadership and gratitude for his achievements, but they were exhausted. They had seen their compatriots die, not only on the battlefield but of disease too, or be left behind in garrisons; those who remained were wounded, dispirited and homesick, longing to see family, friends and their homeland again. Alexander deserved opportunities for further conquest, but this should be with new recruits while the veterans enjoyed the fruits of their victories. Alexander was furious and returned to his tent. He spent two days in solitude, a technique which had served him well after the death of Clitus and would work again at Opis a couple of years later. This time, however, his men were immutable. Recognizing this, Alexander let out the word: it was time to go home.

Those who subscribe to the 'great man' theory of history imagine that historical change is brought about primarily because of the actions of prominent individuals – Alexander so often stands out as a prime example of this. Critics of this school of thought sometimes point out the obvious: Alexander did not conquer the Persian Empire alone, he relied on his men, he inherited a successful army from his father, and so on. However, the shortcomings of 'great man' history run much deeper than this. This episode emphasizes that leadership requires consensus: once the Macedonian soldiers decided they would go no further into India, Alexander was forced to stop. This helps us appreciate that the campaign was a shared enterprise, and that Alexander was not the sole architect of events. Indeed, we have seen that it had its roots in Philip's reign and, though Alexander took crucial decisions that shaped how things played out, he did not have exclusive ownership of the endeavour. Thus far Alexander and his men had shared a vision, but we can see that, when this unity was fractured, he could be constrained by his subjects. At the Hyphasis, it was the collective opinion of the Macedonian army that changed the course of history.

Or was it? Historians have traditionally focused on the set-piece speeches and the image that emerges from them of the ambitious young king frustrated by his war-weary men, but the aftermath is equally telling. Rather than Alexander simply acknowledging that he had listened to his men, the event was carefully stage-managed. Religious rituals were a part of everyday life in antiquity, and Alexander supposedly performed the sacrifices that were expected before crossing a river.[26] It was only when the omens were unfavourable that he announced the army would turn around. By doing this, Alexander attempted to wrest control of the narrative: it was not his men who had thwarted his ambitions, but the gods. This image of a pious ruler was extended when Alexander ordered that twelve huge altars should be established on the banks of the river as an offering of thanks to the Olympian gods who had supported his endeavours.[27] Some sources report that the dimensions of these structures were deliberately exaggerated to impress future visitors to the spot. These altars were also a spatial marker, since setting up altars on the banks of the Hyphasis visibly demarcated the edge of Alexander's empire.[28] There are lots of earlier examples of this practice – Darius I, for instance, apparently put up two pillars to celebrate his crossing of the Bosporus.[29] This parallel shows how Alexander was inspired by Near-Eastern models of kingship, but the way that this was framed through a Greek religious lens perhaps gives a sense that an action like this could be presented to different audiences in varying ways.

The Malloi (326–325)

Like the events at the Hyphasis, the plans for the months that followed were laden with symbolic significance as Alexander announced his intentions to return to the Hydaspes and sail down it, into the Indus, and on to the Indian Ocean. Taking this route, rather than retracing his steps exactly, was another way to mark out the edge of his empire. The borders sketched out through this activity may have been influenced by the historical boundaries of the Achaemenid Empire, but we know so little about the actual experiences of the Achaemenids in India that this is hard to substantiate.

For modern readers, the period under discussion is most notable for a much darker story. The Malloi were an Indian tribe inhabiting territory around the confluence of the Hydaspes, Acesines and Hydraotes rivers.[30] As Alexander approached this region, Arrian explains that his policy – familiar to us from elsewhere – was to reach agreements with those communities that immediately surrendered and to subdue with force those which showed signs of resisting. There is little indication that either side attempted to establish a diplomatic relationship, but Alexander apparently learned that the Malloi had sent their women and children to the most secure cities and were preparing to fight. Quite how Alexander acquired this information is unclear but, given the way that Taxiles appears to have influenced the Macedonians' attitude to Porus, we might wonder what Alexander's Indian allies were telling him about their powerful neighbours.

What followed was a war of annihilation. Alexander split his army into three groups. Hephaestion would march five days ahead of the main force, which Alexander himself was to command. Any Indians who fled before Alexander would only run into Hephaestion's troops as they tried to escape. Meanwhile, Ptolemy would follow three days behind Alexander to catch anybody who slipped through the net. Advancing quickly and arriving unexpectedly at one Malloi city, Alexander caught the inhabitants by surprise in the fields. Despite being unarmed and offering no resistance, they were cut down. The city itself was stormed and some 2,000 people killed. Days later, he slaughtered another group of Malloi as they attempted to cross the Hydraotes. Some managed to escape to a city inhabited by the Brahmans; almost 5,000 are said to have been killed in the attack that followed, some burning to death in fires that they themselves had set to stop their homes falling into the hands of the invaders. Orders were now sent out to Macedonian forces across the country: any Indian who had escaped and did not give themselves up was to be killed.

Worse was to follow. The Malloi retreated to a stronghold across the Hydraotes, chased all the way by Alexander. His exhausted army was given a night to recover, and then Alexander launched a major attack. The city's walls were swiftly captured, and the defenders retreated to the citadel. Some Macedonians set about undermining its walls; others tried to bring up ladders to fight their way up. Alexander, however, was dissatisfied with the slow progress. He grabbed a ladder from a passing soldier and set it up against the wall himself. He climbed up, followed by Peucestas, Leonnatus and Abreas, an otherwise unknown Macedonian. But then, disaster: such was the crowd that tried to follow the four men that the ladder snapped under the added weight, sending soldiers tumbling and leaving Alexander isolated. He cut a conspicuous figure on the walls of the citadel, resplendent in his armour, and he was assailed from multiple sides – fired down upon by Indians in the towers, as those on the ground threw javelins up at him. He could stay where he was and be shot to pieces, or he could accept that the situation was hopeless and clamber down to his men.

But, no: Alexander, we are told, Alexandered. He jumped down, not back to safety but into the crowd of Indians. He then backed himself up against the inside of a wall so that he had some protection and started swinging. Of course he did. He was the descendant of Achilles, and it is moments like this that create legends. One Indian was dispatched, then another and another until no Indian dared come near him. Instead, they kept their distance and threw whatever they could find at him. Abreas, who had been given no choice but to follow Alexander's lead, was killed, leaving only Peucestas and Leonnatus to support the king. And then, inevitably, Alexander was hit. An arrow sneaked past his shield and buried itself deep in his breastplate. Blood spurted, and air could be heard escaping from the wound, a sure sign of a punctured lung. He fought on as best he could but weakened quickly as he lost blood. Dizziness came on, his legs gave way and he fell, slumped across his shield.

The Indians now crowded around Alexander, determined to strike the final blow. Peucestas, allegedly carrying the shield that Alexander had earlier taken from Troy, crouched over the king, offering what protection he could. Leonnatus too did his best to support Alexander, but both soon received wounds of their own. Things were looking hopeless, but now the Macedonians swarmed into the city. Some found ways up the walls, others broke through the gate with one last, huge effort. News of Alexander's injury had reached the Macedonian soldiers, and quickly rumours swirled through the city that the king was dead. Roused by a combination of fury and fear, the Macedonians ran amok. Men, women and children were slaughtered in their thousands, the invaders making no distinction between combatant and non-combatant. Eventually, the anger of the soldiers was exhausted, and the butchery subsided. Meanwhile, Alexander was carried away, his life hanging in the balance.

It is hard to know what to make of these events. We cannot judge Alexander and the Macedonians by the standards of today, and ancient rules of war essentially permitted victorious attackers to treat the inhabitants of a city that chose to offer a defence however they pleased. But, compared with the battles against the

Persians, and even the repression of resistance in Bactria and Sogdiana, something about the campaign against the Malloi sits uneasily. It is striking that ancient authors like Arrian and Curtius paint such a vivid picture of uncontrolled carnage. The latter, for instance, describes the Macedonians killing indiscriminately until they had worked off their rage at the apparent death of their king.[31] It is not just the modern reader who senses something extreme about the slaughter here.

Alexander had always been ruthless and had weaponized violence to terrorize his opponents from the earliest days of his reign, as the Thebans knew only too well. And yet somehow the treatment of the Malloi seems different. Partly, I wonder whether this is because we view reaching the Hyphasis as the climax of Alexander's campaign. We read descriptions of these events aware that Alexander would die only a few years later, having achieved little else of note, and knowing that his subsequent reputation rests on the conquests he had already completed. From that perspective, as when we hear reports of those killed after the armistice of November 1918, there seems something especially futile about the deaths that occurred at this stage of the campaign, not just on the Indian side, but among the Macedonians too. What was all of this for?

The fact that this takes place in India might also affect modern judgements, at least for English-speaking audiences. Is this all a little bit too familiar for those of us schooled on the excesses of the British in India, particularly when the precedent of Alexander was evoked by those who advocated on behalf of the British Empire? The image of Western troops slaughtering Indians indiscriminately, in their homes and as they tried to escape, calls to mind Delhi in 1857, Jallianwala Bagh in 1919 and so many other atrocities. So, perhaps the setting of these events strikes a chord with our own innate postcolonial guilt in a way that does not happen when we read descriptions of Alexander's behaviour elsewhere, making the narrative even more disquieting. That said, I do think that there is more to this than our own preconceptions. In particular, the way that Alexander divided his army to trap as many of the Indians as possible appears to be an ominous development. He was no longer content with capturing key strategic sites or destroying his enemy's ability to fight: killing for the sake of killing had become a feature of Alexander's warfare.

Alexander's wound was serious, and for several days it was unclear whether he would survive. Recognizing the impact that this uncertainty was having, as soon as he was well enough, Alexander had himself carried by ship down the Hydraotes to the main army camp. He waved at his men, then made a point of mounting a horse and showing himself to his soldiers; the response was euphoria – partly, one imagines, out of genuine affection for Alexander, but also, no doubt, out of relief.[32] The soldiers' fears about what would happen to them after Alexander's death, with no obvious successor in place and the army thousands of miles from home, surrounded by potentially hostile peoples, could be put aside – for now.

According to Arrian, Alexander's closest friends rebuked the king for risking his life and playing the part of a common soldier rather than a general.[33] He names as his source here Nearchus, who was purportedly one of Alexander's childhood friends and later commanded the fleet in the Indian Ocean; as part of the king's inner circle, he was well-placed to know the facts. Leading from the front was an integral part of Macedonian kingship: Philip II had lost an eye and walked with a limp because of his injuries, while Alexander himself had been wounded many times before this. But the requirements of kingship can change over time. Alexander had already proved his mettle, his authority was unquestioned within the army, and there was little to gain by exposing himself to further risks. Alexander, we are told, was furious at this recommendation, but recognized that his friends were right.

The Indus Valley and the Indian Ocean (325)

Unsurprisingly, the surviving Malloi sued for peace, but this was not the end of the fighting. As Alexander sailed down the Indus, while many tribes surrendered, he continued to encounter peoples prepared to show resistance. Two episodes are particularly revealing about how this developed. In the spring of 325, Alexander reached the territory of a ruler named Musicanus.[34] He had shown no signs of negotiating or surrendering, which Alexander took to be an indication of hostility. However, the speed of his arrival surprised Musicanus, who quickly offered his submission, apologized for hesitating and sweetened the deal with valuable gifts. Alexander then invaded the neighbouring kingdom, ruled by Sambus. Sambus, Arrian says, had fled when he heard that Alexander had allowed Musicanus to remain in control of his realm: the two, we are told, were old enemies. Sambus' family surrendered the capital city and went out to entreat with Alexander on behalf of their kinsman – Arrian does not record what happened to Sambus, but Diodorus suggests that he escaped.[35] If so, he was lucky, since some 80,000 of his people are reported to have been killed and thousands more enslaved.[36] Musicanus now rebelled for unknown reasons and was executed.

The most telling part of this episode is what Sambus' family allegedly told Alexander to justify his behaviour: Sambus had fled, they said, not because of hostility to Alexander but because Musicanus had been reinstated. This, I think, is the perfect microcosm of the Indian campaign. Like Taxiles and Porus, or Porus and his namesake, Musicanus and Sambus were so focused on one another that Alexander was essentially a secondary consideration. His arrival represented an opportunity to settle scores and reshape the regional balance of power, but they were affected more by the behaviour of their rival than anything that Alexander did. It is crucial to appreciate that Alexander did not engage with these

Indian communities – or, indeed, any of the peoples he encountered – in a vacuum. Had Alexander's first alliance been with somebody other than Taxiles, there is a good chance that we would be talking about a very different campaign and a very different set of characters. This is not an attempt to indulge in another game of *what if?*, but to stress that these pre-existing relationships affected every aspect of the expedition, including whom the Macedonians fought against.

Later that summer, as the Macedonians neared the coast, Alexander learned that the inhabitants of a city called Patala had abandoned the site and fled.[37] There is no sense that these Indians were planning to resist – in fact, the ruler of the region had apparently offered his submission only recently. If the response of some Indian communities to the Macedonians was affected by pre-existing relationships with their neighbours, perhaps we see here the psychological impact of the Macedonians' actions. Even people with ostensibly nothing to fear thought it best to abandon their homes and flee. This had an impact on not only the local people, but the Macedonians. Alexander wanted to sail down a branch of the Indus to the ocean, but the journey proved difficult because – and Arrian is explicit about this – the flight of the locals meant that there were no guides available. Several ships were wrecked in a storm and, later in the voyage, a similar disaster was averted only when some guides that Alexander had been able to find led the Macedonians to a sheltered canal.

While we often stress that Alexander was leading his men into the unknown, the practicalities of this can be overlooked. All ancient armies relied on local knowledge as they moved into unfamiliar terrain. Occasionally we hear reports of locals volunteering their assistance, but usually these people were coerced and perhaps even enslaved, either permanently or for the duration of a campaign. Guides are rarely mentioned by ancient authors so it is easy to ignore their vital contribution, but they played a pivotal role in shaping military expeditions.[38] After all, they helped choose the routes taken, which, among other things, meant deciding which communities the invader's army would pass through, with its potentially cataclysmic impact. We have seen how local rivalries affected high politics, and they likely played out here too. It is striking, however, that these guides were so taken for granted that their importance becomes clear only in their absence.

Finally, in the summer of 325, Alexander and the Macedonians reached the Indian Ocean. Arrian describes Alexander sailing out to an unidentified island where he sacrificed to the gods.[39] He then sailed further into the sea, pouring libations and making additional offerings. There is something of an explorer's zeal here – Arrian portrays Alexander as eager to reach the outer ocean and achieve the unthinkable. Efforts were also made to discern which branches of the Indus were navigable, and a major naval expedition along the coast of India and Persia was instigated.[40] But there is another side to Alexander's activity in the Indian Ocean. Earlier rulers of Mesopotamia had claimed to rule from the 'upper sea' (the Mediterranean) to the 'lower sea' (the Red Sea).[41] These were obvious territorial boundaries and using them to mark the limit of the realm was a way to suggest that the kingdom stretched to the limits of the earth. Over time, rulers like Sargon II and Ashurbanipal claimed to rule islands in the middle of the Mediterranean, and then Darius I crossed that sea to attack the Scythians in Europe. Consequently, traversing the seas became a way for kings to surpass their predecessors and establish themselves as rulers of a universal empire. Alexander was not only exploring the edges of the earth but laying claim to them. Meanwhile, the rivers of India ran red with blood. Alexander was king of the world, but at what cost?

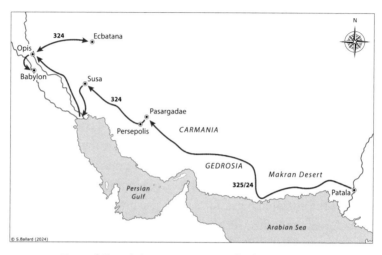

Route of Alexander's campaigns in Iran and Babylonia, 325–323.

6

Persia, 325–324

My formative years played out against a backdrop of war in the Middle East. I had more important things to do as a teenager than watch the news, but words like 'Mosul' and 'Helmand' percolated through. As I began to study Alexander in the late 2000s, the names of battlegrounds were familiar. It was sobering to discover that these places had been fought over then just as they are now, but they still felt very distant. Over the next decade or so, as I began an academic career, I found myself drawn increasingly to the margins of Alexander's life. I looked backwards into the Achaemenid period, exploring how far he engaged with Persian monarchical culture, and forwards into the Hellenistic era to understand what sort of impact he had on the world.

Meanwhile, the Middle East plunged further into chaos. The Western powers proved unable to rebuild Iraq and withdrew. What followed included a power vacuum, ISIS, civil war in Syria, a resurgent Taliban and a clear message: winning a war is just one part of the puzzle, and perhaps the easiest to solve. Closer to home, the multicultural world that I had embraced, but perhaps taken for granted, came under attack from extremism of all kinds. The notion that people from different backgrounds or with divergent beliefs could live side by side in harmony was challenged by bloodshed and angry rhetoric. It all felt radical, different, new; and yet somehow all too recognizable.

I am no expert on the modern Middle East. My interpretations come from cursory engagement with a handful of journalistic perspectives, and I do not really believe that we can learn from history in any strong sense or that history repeats itself in any meaningful way – life is too complicated for that. But it is only in the last few years that I have connected the dots between what was happening around me and the questions that I was asking about Alexander. For me, the most interesting and important part of Alexander's story actually begins only in 325, when he returned to Persia from India. Until then, his reign had been taken up by conquest. There had been few opportunities to think about the future and decisions had been taken with short-term military objectives in mind as this was the only way to win the war. But what now?

The headline moments from the next two years are easily established. Alexander returned to Persia in the winter of 325/4, where he began instigating changes to the personnel within the upper echelons of his administration. In the spring of 324, the Macedonians reached Susa, where Alexander married the daughters of Darius III and Artaxerxes III in a lavish ceremony. Later that year, the army took umbrage at Alexander's attempt to decommission the veteran soldiers and send them home. A mutiny was averted only with difficulty. Shortly afterwards, Hephaestion, the king's closest friend and possible lover, died at Ecbatana. A bereft Alexander stumbled on to Babylon, where he too fell ill and died in June 323.

Set against the high watermarks of Alexander's career, these two years can sometimes fade into insignificance, seemingly an ignominious footnote to a life otherwise filled with success and excitement. When the first decade or so of Alexander's reign is so packed full of drama and adventure – of stories worth telling, as Arrian would have put it – the temptation for a biographer is to rush through the final years of Alexander's life.[1] Instead, there is a self-conscious change of pace in the narrative here. With fewer noteworthy developments to explore, I have taken the opportunity to delve a little deeper. This reflects my belief that these events were not only important, but that, for a modern audience, they are perhaps the most relevant.

The key issue was what to do with the conquered peoples, particularly the Persian nobility. Other local elites could be integrated into the empire relatively straightforwardly. Provided they pledged their loyalty and then worked for Alexander by collecting taxes and the like, there was little reason to risk upsetting regional stability by introducing sweeping changes. Occasionally, one or two individuals who were thought to have been particularly close to the Persian administration might need to be replaced, but, in general, Macedonians could be placed into supervisory positions, with the imperial army ready to enforce discipline if required. This was essentially how things had worked in the Achaemenid Empire, and elite families had little to gain and much to lose by threatening the status quo. For them, one superpower had replaced another, and there was little reason to push back. The Persians were a different case, however. They would have to accept a new, subordinate status, so there was reason to think that Persia itself might prove tricky to govern in the future, while the Persian elite had connections across the empire that could prove troublesome. They also had lots to offer the Macedonians. After two centuries of running an empire, the Persians had knowledge and expertise that could prove valuable.

Sometimes, Alexander's critics argue that he was so fundamentally self-interested that he gave no thought to empire-building or to what would happen after his death. We will see in due course that his spectacular failure to develop a secure succession plan led to the implosion of his empire, but, once Alexander returned from India, we do see signs that he was beginning to think about the future. New marriages were contracted and there were administrative changes too. I will question how effective these measures were, but the mere fact that they were introduced is important. In the nineteenth and twentieth centuries, scholars often described this activity as being part of a policy of 'fusion'.² By this, they meant that Alexander sought to create a unified Macedonian–Persian ruling class, and perhaps encourage some cultural interchange too. Some saw this in positive terms, with Alexander cast as a dreamer who imagined all of his subjects living together harmoniously. Critics, however, saw an attempt to create a servile governing class, loyal only to the king, another sign of Alexander's increasing megalomania, or – much more problematically – as a betrayal of 'Western civilization'. The argument that Alexander pursued such a policy is less popular now, and I have no intention of resurrecting it. But in considering the way that Alexander envisaged the relationship between Macedonians and Persians, the notion of 'fusion' is reminiscent of another concept holding contemporary resonance: the idea of winning hearts and minds. Governing by force alone was impossible in an empire of Alexander's size. Self-interest and material rewards might be enough to win over some of the Persian elite, but would this be enough to control the Persian aristocracy in perpetuity? Alexander had left Persepolis in flames; as he returned, it appears that he was beginning to consider postwar reconstruction.

The Road to Persia (325)

The return to Persia proved perilous, and this was entirely Alexander's fault. Rather than take a safer, more roundabout route, he chose to lead the army westwards across the Makran desert in Baluchistan, which today extends across the southern border of Iran and Pakistan. Alexander allegedly knew that the journey would be difficult but had been told that both Cyrus the Great and Semiramis, a legendary Assyrian queen, had led expeditions across the desert alongside only a handful of companions and survived; as ever, Alexander was keen to surpass his predecessors. The desert did indeed prove arid and inhospitable, and the sources paint a bleak picture of the journey.³ Pack animals were slaughtered for food; wagons proved too tough to pull across the sands, meaning that the ill, injured and exhausted had to be abandoned. As in another war thousands of years later, knock-kneed men marched asleep, those who succumbed to tiredness dropping out of the columns and sleeping wherever they fell. Waking up hours later, abandoned, some managed to follow their comrades' footsteps and rejoin the army, but most were lost in the sandy sea. What little water there was proved a curse as parched soldiers frantically overdrank and died as a result.

On another occasion, the army camped next to a stream that was little more than a trickle; suddenly, rainwater gushed down the dried-up watercourse, sweeping most of the women and children away to their deaths. These people were camp followers, many of them having formed relationships with Macedonian soldiers during the campaign. As we will see, only six months or so later some 10,000 Macedonians apparently married Asian women, so plenty of people evidently survived the journey. This suggests that the reports are exaggerated, but they still give a sense of the hardships forced on the army by Alexander's reckless pursuit of his own legend. Even if we strip away the heroic talk and recognize that details in our sources are embellished, we must still acknowledge a rare strategic miscalculation by Alexander here. The desert was not impassable, but more reconnaissance and greater preparation were required for such an arduous journey to be completed successfully.⁴

Finally, the exhausted army limped into the capital of Gedrosia, the satrapy they had just crossed. Quick to pin the blame for the disaster on somebody else, Alexander removed Apollophanes from his position as satrap, claiming that his orders (presumably to gather appropriate supplies for the army) had been ignored.⁵ It soon transpired, however, that Apollophanes had died while fighting to ensure that the fleet exploring the southern coast was properly provisioned. This proves he was used as a scapegoat, and, as the army moved into Carmania, it became apparent that he would not be the last.

Two trends emerged. First, Craterus arrived, having led an army back from India by a different route. Along the way, he had subdued a revolt led by two Iranians, Ordanes and Zariaspes, who were brought to Carmania and executed.[6] Several other Iranians were arrested in this period for instigating rebellions.[7] It is difficult to judge how much of a threat these would-be usurpers posed. Anti-Macedonian agitation was obviously easier to perpetuate when the Macedonians were absent, and, since the sources doggedly follow in Alexander's footsteps, we get very few details about the activities of these rebels. In some instances, Alexander's own Iranian appointees subdued the revolts, which demonstrates that he did have some support among the Persian aristocracy, although it evidently was not universal. These challenges emphasize that Alexander's grip on his conquests was far from secure.

The second trend concerned the people Alexander had left governing the empire while he was in India. Cleander, Sitalces, Heracon and Agathon rejoined the main camp.[8] These were the men who had killed Parmenion, and they had remained in Media afterwards to run the satrapy. A litany of complaints emerged about their behaviour: they were accused of exploiting their subjects and enriching themselves by despoiling shrines and tombs. Cleander allegedly raped a noblewoman and handed her over to his own slave as a concubine. These charges may have been true – these men would not be the first imperial officials to act rapaciously – but they may also have been a pretext for removing another powerful faction.

Either way, Cleander and Sitalces were executed; Heracon was acquitted, but condemned on similar charges a few months later. This was just the beginning of a significant overhaul of the higher echelons of the administrative system. Ernst Badian calculated that by the time Alexander died in 323, only two satraps out of 22 appear to have avoided oppression entirely.[9] Eight are reported to have been removed from office, six of them executed, while the remainder may have come under some pressure through such measures as being summoned to court or being forced to send children to Alexander as potential hostages. For Badian, this amounted to a 'reign of terror' as Alexander, furious at the way his power had been challenged at the Hyphasis, took out his anger on those around him. However, there were perfectly good administrative reasons for a ruler to ask satraps to attend court from time to time so, as Badian himself admits, this picture has been exaggerated for effect.

The really interesting feature of this period is that new appointees appear to have been Macedonian or Greek, and to have been of lower status than those given roles in the years before the Indian expedition. Were Persians now unwilling to serve Alexander? Had Alexander lost trust in them? If so, a policy of governmental fusion was impossible. Badian thought lower-ranking Iranians may not have been considered appropriate for the most important administrative positions, whereas Greeks and Macedonians were. In this view, Alexander was appointing nobodies to high office; knowing that they were reliant on his patronage, their loyalty could be expected. However, there is another way to see this. This emerges from what I think is the most intriguing example of a Persian satrap being replaced by a Macedonian.

Persepolis (325/4)

In the winter of 325/4, Alexander returned to Persia and discovered that the man he had appointed as satrap there, Phrasaortes, had died. In his place, a Persian nobleman called Orxines was running things.[10] Arrian emphasizes that this was not Alexander's doing and that Orxines had simply decided that in the absence of another appointee he was the best man for the job. Alexander disagreed. When the court reached Persepolis, the Persians themselves are said to have complained that they had been mistreated by Orxines; Alexander sided with them, and Orxines was executed.

Curtius lays the blame for this outcome at the feet of a figure called Bagoas.[11] He was a eunuch, who had been one of Darius III's favourites and was inherited by Alexander; as we will see, the sources imply that their relationship was sexual. Curtius reports that on the way to Persepolis, Alexander stopped at Pasargadae, where he was met with a lavish display: horses, chariots, jewellery and vast sums of money, all gifts from Orxines. His friends were also honoured with gifts, but Bagoas was overlooked; when asked why, Orxines dismissed Bagoas as an effeminate whore, or words to that effect. Learning of this, Bagoas set out to ruin the man who had insulted him. The description of events at Pasargadae sounds similar to the ceremonial entrance seen earlier in Babylon and long a feature of Near-Eastern monarchy, so this may have been nothing out of the ordinary. Bagoas, though, spied an opportunity. When Alexander opened the tomb of Cyrus the Great, intent on paying his respects, he found none of the treasure that he imagined should be there. Bagoas was quick to whisper accusations that Orxines' largesse was made possible only by thievery. Alexander, unable to resist Bagoas' charms, was soon persuaded, and Orxines was executed.

Arrian also reports that Cyrus' tomb had been robbed and explains that Aristoboulos claimed to have been appointed by Alexander to restore the monument to its former glory.[12] This might reflect Alexander's personal admiration for Cyrus, one great conqueror acknowledging another, but, as Achaemenid kings were expected to venerate their predecessors, this was also a way of further establishing his credentials as a ruler in Persia. According to Arrian, nobody was ever convicted of robbing the tomb. Consequently, the way that Curtius connects this episode to Bagoas and Orxines is best understood as a demonstration of how he viewed imperial courts. As in lots of places, eunuchs had been prominent members of the Achaemenid royal court. Alexander had taken over

Darius III's material possessions, which will have included enslaved people, so it is perfectly plausible that Bagoas, or somebody like him, existed. The real problem with Curtius' tale is that Orxines seems ignorant of Bagoas' potential influence and deliberately slights him. Given his experience of Achaemenid politics, Orxines would surely have known better. Instead, he becomes a mouthpiece for Curtius to denounce the malignant impact of flatterers and favourites within a royal court. Without underplaying the very real influence that figures like Bagoas can exert on rulers, we should not place too much credence in Curtius' tale.

Set in the gardens of the city he built at Pasargadae, this structure has been identified as the Tomb of Cyrus. Aristoboulos claims he was commissioned by Alexander to restore the structure after it had been ransacked.

Modern historians tend to see the charges laid against Orxines as a smokescreen. Instead, they argue that Alexander was keen to punish somebody who had dared to assume power without his permission.[13] This is possible, but there was probably more to it than this. Though stating that Orxines had appointed himself satrap, Arrian does stress that he did so to preserve order in Persia for Alexander. Curtius also portrays Orxines as a loyal servant of Alexander, though this characterization is evidently affected by his desire to malign Bagoas. As the sources present things, this was not an arrogation of power or an attempt to undermine Alexander.

There is an interesting parallel here with an earlier event. During the siege of Mytilene in 333, the Rhodian commander Memnon fell ill and died. When he was on his deathbed, he apparently appointed his Persian nephew Pharnabazus as his replacement, but only until Darius could deal with the matter himself.[14] Might Phrasaortes, Orxines' predecessor, have done something similar? There are clear parallels between the two situations. Communication with Darius would have been difficult for the Persians besieging Mytilene, and things were even trickier when Alexander was in India. Communication lines were long and hazardous, and there will have been times when subordinates elsewhere simply did not know where Alexander was. No message could be guaranteed to reach the king quickly, and Persia could hardly remain without a governor for months. It is possible, therefore, that Orxines was simply following established Persian practice for dealing with the unexpected death of a satrap. If so, he may have been surprised to find his behaviour interpreted so negatively. This begins to suggest that Alexander may have had different expectations than the Persian elite about how satraps should operate.

A second clue is that Orxines' replacement was Peucestas, a leading Macedonian and one of the men who had saved Alexander's life in India.[15] As a reward for this, he had been made a member of Alexander's bodyguard, one of the most prestigious courtly roles.

Arrian suggests that Peucestas had embraced Persian culture and become the only Macedonian to learn the Persian language, leaving him well-placed to forge connections with the Persian elite. However, Arrian also claims that Alexander was already planning to make Peucestas the satrap of Persia when he had him enrolled in the royal bodyguard a few weeks earlier. This may involve some back-projection from Arrian, and one would certainly wonder how he could know what Alexander was planning at this point. If he is right, however, this is extremely significant: at this point Alexander was apparently unaware that Orxines was governing Persia, which would mean his replacement was predetermined and had nothing to do with Orxines' behaviour.

There are good reasons for thinking that Alexander might have struggled with managing the Persian satrapal system. He had taken over the Achaemenids' method of governing the empire primarily out of convenience, while individual satraps had been retained out of pragmatism and to fracture the Persian elite. Administrative arrangements will have evolved over two centuries of Achaemenid rule, but the overarching structure remained similar, and satraps always enjoyed significant power. For instance, there are several examples of satraps conducting negotiations with Greek powers on their own initiative, recruiting soldiers and even fighting with one another.[16] This was tolerated by the Achaemenids providing tribute was collected efficiently and the satraps accepted the king's overarching authority. This had proven effective, but it was also almost inevitable: the size of the empire meant that the kings had to cede significant authority to the governors on the ground.

Alexander will have appreciated this. At the same time, however, he grew up in a kingdom where rulers could be much more involved in decision-making at a local level. Of course, Philip still delegated, but it was easier for his representatives to refer decisions to the king. I wonder how this may have affected Alexander's own expectations about how his subordinates should behave. If he genuinely had not learned of Phrasaortes' death and Orxines' self-appointment, we must assume that Alexander had heard very little of substance from Persia while he was in India, and this may be true more generally. This would help to explain not only why there were so many new appointments in this period, but why the new satraps were all Macedonian or Greek. This was not so much about the status of these men or the reliance of the incoming satraps on Alexander's personal favour, but rather a reflection of a cultural clash about how to exercise power.

Susa (324)

From Persepolis, Alexander travelled to Susa, where further administrative changes were made. Aboulites, who had surrendered the city to Alexander after Gaugamela and retained his position as satrap, was charged with a litany of offences and executed along with his son.[17] As with Orxines, the accusations noted by Arrian are very generic and amount to corruption and misrule. Notably, this included mistreating the people they governed, so Alexander may have been posing as the defender of the common man in an effort to minimize the threat of popular revolt. Again, though, this might have been a smokescreen for another motive.

It was at Susa, in the spring of 324, that one of the most notable events in Alexander's reign occurred: he got married again, not once, but twice. Whereas his earlier marriage to Roxane had its origins in the need to bring the fighting in Bactria and Sogdiana to an end, this wedding appears to have been conceived with something grander in mind. The first clue to this is the identity of the brides: Stateira, the daughter of Darius III, and Parysatis, the daughter of Artaxerxes III.[18] Stateira had been captured after the Battle of Issus almost a decade earlier, so there had been ample opportunity for a marriage before 324. The decision to delay the marriage until now is instructive.[19] In an earlier marriage, Stateira would have been

a prize won in war, a symbol of the Persians' defeat. Alexander allegedly refused to accept a peace settlement that included Stateira's
hand, which reflects the inherent contradiction of marrying her
but continuing the war against her father.[20]

By 324, however, the political context was different. Darius
was long dead, and the Persians had been decisively defeated and
were facing serious questions about what role they would play in
Alexander's empire. The removal of men like Aboulites only added
to the uncertainty. In this environment, marrying into the Achaemenid line was a clear statement of its continued relevance and
meant acknowledging the value of Achaemenid blood as a means
of legitimizing rule in Asia. There was to be a place, and a prominent one at that, for Persians in the new order. Diodorus claims that
Stateira was left at Susa earlier in the campaign with instructions
to learn Greek, which might suggest that Alexander was always
planning to marry her at some stage.[21] She may already have been

Alexander and Stateira are the focal point of this 19th-century painting by
Andreas Müller (1811–1890). Other newlyweds can be seen around the royal couple.

in Susa, therefore, which might mean that the timing of the marriage was influenced by logistics, but she could have been sent east had Alexander wanted to wed her sooner. This suggests that returning to Iran prompted him to consider how to bring about reconciliation with the Persians.

That is the positive interpretation, but there is a more cynical possibility: marrying the daughters of the two previous Achaemenid kings stopped anybody else from doing so. This prevented any Persian nobleman from creating a marital link with the Achaemenid dynasty and using this to win support for a challenge to Alexander. Only a few months earlier, a Mede named Baryaxes had been executed for claiming to be king of the Persians and Medes.[22] He had been captured by Atropates, the satrap of Media, so some Iranians were prepared to back Alexander, but potential challengers evidently remained. Any such rivals would be made much more powerful with an Achaemenid wife and, in due course, an Achaemenid successor. From this longer-term perspective, these marriages also increased the security of the heirs that Alexander no doubt expected to father. A polygamous court meant increased competition to succeed to the throne, as Alexander himself knew only too well, but at least his heirs could avoid contesting the throne with an Achaemenid pretender.

Another crucial aspect of this event emphasizes that Alexander was thinking about the future: his was not the only marriage. Some eighty leading Companions were married to the most high-ranking Iranian women – Hephaestion to Stateira's sister Drypetis, Craterus to Darius' niece Amastrine. More than 10,000 common soldiers were also encouraged to make official their relationships with Asian women. This was an important part of the argument that Alexander pursued a policy of fusion because it was understood as an attempt to create a new Macedonian–Persian governing class for the empire. However, if Alexander's marriages to Stateira and Parysatis were partially defensive, then marrying other Achaemenid women to his closest supporters gave an added layer of insurance. Men like

Hephaestion could be trusted with an Achaemenid bride, and, even if some royal pretensions were to emerge in the future, the Macedonian nobility could hardly use an Achaemenid link to win support for a rebellion among their peers in the same way as Persian aristocrats. Furthermore, a genuine policy of 'fusion' surely requires some semblance of equality, but the weddings here only saw Macedonian and Greek men marry Asian women.[23] Of course, practical obstacles would have to be overcome if Persian men were to be matched with Macedonian brides since few, if any, noblewomen had travelled with the army, but these were hardly insurmountable. Either Alexander was not prepared to wait for women summoned from Macedonia to arrive, in which case his aims were less far reaching than some have thought, or the Susa weddings were deliberately one-sided.

This emphasizes that the marriages could have been seen by Persians as a symbol of Macedonian domination. Moreover, marrying some eighty Companions to the leading women of Asia meant that, at a stroke, the marriage prospects of an entire generation of young Persians were destroyed. Already scarred by war, the most eligible bachelors would be forced to settle for inferior matches. Fathers also lost the ability to select husbands for their daughters, which was an attack on their rights. Finally, can we be sure that all of the women involved were unmarried? Ptolemy and Eumenes were apparently married to two daughters of Artabazus, the nobleman who had retired due to old age in the days before the murder of Clitus in Bactria. Indeed, one of his granddaughters was apparently married to Nearchus in the same ceremony. Perhaps he did have daughters later in life who remained unmarried, or others who had been widowed during the war, but it is possible that some Persians may have lost their wives to Macedonians at Susa. This was fertile breeding ground for resentment.

Whatever their intention, the marriages do not appear to have been much of a success. After Alexander's death, Roxane apparently saw Stateira and Parysatis as a threat to her and her newborn son

Alexander IV, so had them killed.[24] The other women mentioned here disappear from the historical record after Alexander's death, so it is often – but problematically – assumed that the Macedonians repudiated these marriages as soon as they were able to do so without incurring Alexander's wrath.[25]

The one exception is Apama, the wife of Seleucus, a Macedonian army commander who would play a pivotal role in the events after Alexander's death. Her life offers a fascinating insight into the impact of Alexander's campaign on the people of Asia. She was the daughter of Spitamenes, whom we met earlier as one of the principal architects of the military resistance in Sogdiana. His precise relationship with the Achaemenid court is unclear, but he was among Bessus' entourage in 329 so evidently had important connections. In that sense, Apama was born into a position of privilege and was a part of the ruling elite, though perhaps more on the local than imperial level.

Alexander's arrival in the region shattered this and resulted in the death of her father. Curtius paints a bleak picture of how this happened.[26] Apama's mother, who is never named, apparently tired of the constant need to keep moving to escape capture. She urged Spitamenes to come to some agreement with Alexander, but succeeded only in angering her husband, who was prevented from killing her only with difficulty. The wife was briefly banished, but, when Spitamenes proposed a reconciliation, she pretended to agree. In a story reminiscent of the biblical tale of Judith and Holofernes, with Spitamenes passed out from drink, she crept into their bedchamber, removed a sword from beneath her clothes and cut off her husband's head. Sneaking out into the night, she went to the Macedonian camp and demanded an audience with Alexander, still wearing her blood-spattered clothes. Alexander, Curtius claims, was torn – grateful that his enemy had been killed but also outraged by the crime that the woman had committed. In the end, he had her cast out of the camp, and we hear no more about her fate.

We do not know how old Apama was at this point, though she gave birth to a son fathered by Seleucus within a year or so of their marriage, so she was probably born by the mid-330s at the latest. If Curtius' account is correct, we can only imagine the impact that her father's murder would have had on the young Apama. It gives a sense too of how Alexander's appearance could split families and communities, as individuals and peoples were forced to make choices about whether to fight or negotiate with the invader.

Arrian, however, claims that Spitamenes was killed by the Massagetae in an effort to keep Alexander out of their territory, and I am sceptical of Curtius' tale.[27] Nevertheless, we can still appreciate that the upheaval brought on by the conquest would have been traumatic for Apama. This is magnified when we acknowledge that we do not know where she was between 329, when this happened, and her appearance at Susa in 324, who she was with or how she was selected as one of the brides. How much warning did she have? Had she even been to Susa before? The Achaemenid princesses had apparently been taught Greek, but had Apama? Would she have been able to communicate with Seleucus from the off? Moreover, husband and wife will likely have met for the first time only shortly before their marriage, perhaps only at the ceremony itself. This must have been something of a whirlwind, and it is easy to cast Apama and the other women married at Susa as the passive victims of powerful men.

But there is a second, more remarkable act to Apama's dramatic story. Having given birth to a son, Antiochus, around the time of Alexander's death, Apama's marriage was not dissolved but endured into the 290s. Her fortunes changed significantly in this period as her husband built an empire that stretched from the borders of India to Asia Minor. In 305, with Alexander's own line extinguished, Seleucus declared himself king. Apama was now queen of the largest empire in the known world. Explanations for Seleucus' decision to maintain their relationship – and we must acknowledge that agency here probably did not lie with Apama – sometimes project backwards from these later events: Seleucus ended up controlling Apama's homeland, so he must always have thought the match might prove useful.[28]

However, it is hard to imagine that Seleucus was seriously dreaming of kingship in the period after Alexander's death when other Macedonians may have abandoned their Asian wives. At this juncture, he was among the second rank of Macedonian nobles, certainly important, but hardly on the cusp of carving out an empire. Moreover, one benefit of diplomatic marriage is access to kin networks, in this case ties to local elites in Sogdiana and Bactria. But how far did these survive Alexander's reign? Apama's inclusion in the weddings at Susa demonstrates that her status continued to be recognized, but we know very little about power structures in the region and nothing about what happened to her family after the death of her father. Was there anybody left in Sogdiana with a vested interest in supporting Apama's husband? Instead of seeing things only through a political lens, I wonder if there might be space here for genuine affection. In an otherwise dark tale, one would like to think so.

There is so much more I wish I could say about Apama: her public-facing role as Seleucus sought to establish a new dynasty, the potential effects of Seleucus' second marriage, her influence on Antiochus; but this is supposed to be Alexander's story. What I will say is that there is scope to envisage a remarkable woman. Somebody astute enough to play the politics of the early Hellenistic period and smart enough to act as a bridge between multiple cultures, a sounding board for Seleucus and Antiochus as they grappled with the challenges of ruling a multicultural realm, and a voice for the non-Greek communities within that empire.

That, though, is a romantic image created as much out of hope as it is born of the ancient sources, and we cannot know what she herself thought about her experience. Nevertheless, her life speaks to the limitations of seeing the effects of Alexander's campaign only in black or white. Born into one imperial apparatus, Apama's life was radically altered by the Macedonian conquest, but she then played an active role in establishing and perpetuating a new empire. This emphasizes that drawing a stark contrast between Macedonian 'conquerors' and Asian 'victims' is too simplistic. For all the undoubted trauma of her youth, Apama eventually reached a status likely inconceivable at her birth. Stories like this are usually overlooked in treatments of Alexander's reign; telling them brings his impact to life and gives a more rounded perspective on people who are often depicted as only two-dimensional and peripheral, but who were actually instrumental.

Returning to the occasion of Apama's marriage to Seleucus, the other important point to note about their wedding celebration is its setting. Susa was a major city and the site of a major royal palace built by Darius I. Rather than hold the ceremony there, however, Alexander preferred to use a lavish tent, which is described by Athenaeus and Aelian.[29] Both were writing at the end of the second and beginning of the third century CE, but the former names Chares as his source, and the similarities between their reports suggest that Aelian also used his account. As we have seen, Chares was involved in and perhaps even responsible for organizing major court events like the Susa weddings, so he is certainly a source to take seriously. We can always wonder how faithful later authors were to their source material, but the overlap between Athenaeus and Aelian is encouraging, so we seem to be dealing ultimately with eyewitness testimony here.

The accounts paint a vivid picture of the magnificence of the scene: extravagant draperies and linens decorated the walls, purple rugs with golden adornment covered the floor, while animals, weaved in gold, added sparkle to the curtains that surrounded the tent. All of these examples had clear Achaemenid antecedents. For instance, Aelian is explicit that the cloth that adorned the space was particularly prized by the Persians and guests had a parallel to the animal decorations close at hand in Darius' palace, where a frieze of lions proudly patrolled the perimeter of one of the court-yards.[30] Consequently, there are good reasons for thinking that the tent itself originally belonged to the Achaemenids and had been seized by Alexander.

One detail is particularly fascinating. Chares reports that the couches upon which the couples reclined had silver feet, but that Alexander's own had golden feet.[31] The materiality of these couches therefore marked Alexander out from the other grooms, highlight-ing his special status: he was worthy of gold, the others only of silver. This appears to have become a feature of Alexander's display after he returned from India. In Babylon the following year, Alexander apparently sat on a throne while his companions occupied silver-footed couches; again, this detail is said to have come from an eye-witness, Aristoboulos.[32] Like other aspects of the wedding tent at

The Persian palace at Susa, built during the reign of Darius I, was richly decorated. This frieze, which is made from glazed bricks, depicts a striding lion.

Susa, these items seem to have originated at the Achaemenid court. Aristoboulos, who supposedly restored the tomb of Cyrus the Great after it had been despoiled, allegedly found a golden-footed couch among the items there.[33] The best evidence, however, comes from Xenophon. He had served as a mercenary in the army of Cyrus the Younger, who sought to overthrow his brother, Artaxerxes II. After Cyrus was killed and the mercenary leaders annihilated, Xenophon was elected to command the survivors and successfully led them home. He records these events in the *Anabasis*, mentioning there that his men discovered silver-footed couches in the tent of the Persian general Tiribazus.[34] Since this description pre-dates Alexander's expedition and emerges from a different context, we do not need to worry about whether Alexander's practices have influenced Xenophon's writing, so we can be sure that these couches were used by the Persians.

Why does this matter? There are two reasons. First, there is no evidence that earlier Macedonian kings were distinguished visually from their Companions; in fact, everything suggests that this was not the case. Second, this example shows how features of Achaemenid royal display challenged the status quo at the Macedonian court, offering an alternative template of what monarchy might look like. Alexander is often presented as having deliberately adopted aspects of Persian monarchical culture, and perhaps to have begun to model himself on the Achaemenid kings he had defeated.[35] We have seen examples which show that there is something to that argument, but this case reveals that this interpretation does not tell the whole story. We do not know when Alexander encountered these couches for the first time, but, when he did, he would have sat on the golden-footed couch. It is unlikely that his motivation was to change radically the way he presented his relationship with the leading members of the Macedonian nobility; instead, he will have sat there simply because that was where the king was supposed to sit. He did not need Persian courtiers or Darius' attendants to tell him this – though they might well have done so – because it was visually obvious; the setting made it clear that this was the king's chair.

More than that, Alexander could hardly countenance allowing somebody else to sit in the golden-footed couch while he himself reclined in another seat. Perhaps he could have shunned the golden-footed couch entirely and had everybody use the silver-footed couches, but what about when Persians were present, as they evidently were not just on this occasion – when we might imagine that the families of the brides were among the guests – but more generally by this stage of the campaign? After two hundred years of Achaemenid rule, they had expectations of what a ruler looked like and how he behaved: failure to live up to this standard would undermine Alexander's authority. Persian royal spaces were designed to make visitors think about the Achaemenid kings in particular ways, and they remained imbued with those qualities and ideals even after the demise of their creators. Simply by using them, the Macedonians became exposed to these ideas. We tend to think of agency only on a human level, but the spaces and material culture of the Persian world exerted their own force on Alexander and the Macedonians, prompting and nagging away, always saying: there is another way to be king.

There was one other important part of events at Susa in 324 that pointed towards the future.[36] Some 30,000 Iranian teenagers arrived, equipped in Macedonian armour. They had been recruited some years earlier – now, their training in Macedonian military fashion was complete and they were joining the main army. Their given name, apparently, was the *epigonoi* – the 'offspring', or, perhaps, the 'successors'. At first glance, these youths look like the embodiment of a policy of fusion: they were ethnic Iranians, who had taken on Macedonian military and cultural markers, and they were being offered a clear role in Alexander's empire. But would young Iranians necessarily have embraced this? After all, they were being forced to abandon their own cultural traditions in favour of alien habits and to leave their homes to serve in a foreigner's army. Perhaps this last point was Alexander's motivation: young men were one of the most likely sources of trouble within the empire, so removing them from peripheral territories and keeping them close at hand was a way of increasing security in their native satrapies. In the long term, integrating them into the imperial hierarchy through military service was a means of breaking their ties to their homeland. For Alexander, it promised an added advantage: a generation that owed no loyalty to any one place or community, only to him. Again, we have a choice between identifying idealistic, pragmatic or cynical motives. One's interpretation of this episode says much about one's view of Alexander – I tend towards the pragmatic. Either way, the arrival of an Iranian military unit with a name implying their future prominence represented a challenge to the status of the Macedonians within the army.

7

Iran and Babylonia, 324–323

If Alexander was indeed beginning to look to the future, a fundamental question to pose is: what role would Macedonians play
in his empire? The Macedonians themselves were keenly aware
of this, and incidents like the *proskynesis* affair and the murder of
Clitus demonstrate that this had long been a source of tension.
However, events at Susa appear to have exacerbated this and things
came to a head shortly afterwards.

The Mutiny at Opis (324)

At Opis (near modern Baghdad), Alexander assembled the whole
army and announced that older soldiers and those unfit for active
service would be discharged and sent home.[1] This had been their
central demand at the Hyphasis, but the troops did not react well.
Feeling slighted and underappreciated, they insisted that they should
all go home. The assembly swiftly turned ugly and took on a mutinous tone, with soldiers shouting their criticisms of Alexander and
mockingly suggesting that he carry on campaigning alone, with his
so-called father, Ammon, for company. Alexander's response was
brutal: he jumped into the crowd, pointed out thirteen principal
agitators and ordered their immediate execution. Reporting this,
Arrian explains that Alexander was increasingly short-tempered and
less indulgent of the Macedonians because he had become accustomed to being feted like a barbarian king. As with his treatment

of the murder of Clitus and the Pages' Conspiracy, Arrian presents Persian monarchical culture as a corrupting influence. This is an important reminder that the perspectives of the Roman-period authors permeate our sources.

This display of force succeeded in quieting the crowd, and Alexander addressed his men again.[2] The speech that Arrian has Alexander make is full of techniques to manipulate the emotions of his audience. He opens by describing the transformative effect of Philip's reign, exaggerating to make the point. Philip is said to have found the Macedonians a poor, mountain-dwelling people unable to protect themselves from their neighbours. He is portrayed as playing a civilizing role, giving the Macedonians proper clothes and establishing cities and laws before leading them to glory in Greece. However, Alexander's own achievements dwarf those of his father. Alexander stresses that he has not sat idly by while his men risked life and limb to win victory but has shared in the dangers and been injured several times: 'you show me your wounds, and I'll show you mine', or words to that effect, he declares with bravado. He also emphasizes the honours bestowed on those killed in the fighting and practical matters like the tax breaks afforded to their relatives. The speech reaches an emotional climax as Alexander says his men should go home and tell people that they have abandoned their king – the man who had conquered the known world – and left him dependent on barbarians for his safety. It ends with a single word, a daring challenge to his men to do the unthinkable: 'Go!'

This speech has been hailed as a masterpiece – recently it was listed among a collection of 'speeches that changed the world' – but the rhetoric here is almost certainly Arrian's own doing.[3] Thucydides, the great historian of the Peloponnesian War, famously explained that he had been unable to remember exactly what had been said on key occasions and so had made his speakers say what he thought seemed appropriate.[4] He was stating the obvious, but this set the tone for how ancient historians approached their speeches, and students have long been taught to be especially sceptical about this feature of ancient historical writing. To take Alexander's speech at Opis seriously, we would have to believe that Arrian had found a verbatim account in one of his sources and copied it directly. This seems unlikely, not least because Alexander had apparently spoken off the cuff, so there was no original written version for a well-placed source like Ptolemy to reproduce.

More than this, speeches were an opportunity for ancient historians to demonstrate their own literary skills and were integral to how they characterized their subjects. This emerges clearly in the subtly contrasting tone of Alexander's speech in Curtius' account, which is harsher towards the Macedonians – at one point Alexander is dismissive of their military abilities – and perhaps angrier too, though Arrian's Alexander is certainly self-indulgent, defensive and frustrated. The key twist is in the ending. Whereas Arrian claims that the thirteen most vocal critics were condemned to death before the speech, Curtius' Alexander works himself into a lather before jumping into the crowd. By making this the denouement, Curtius has Alexander leave the Macedonians cowed into silence by his threats, which, in keeping with his overall portrayal of Alexander, heightens the impression of a tyrannical ruler.

That said, there are some similarities between the speeches. For instance, both Curtius and Arrian have Alexander stress the impact of Philip on the Macedonian way of living, and they give the same figures for the debts he inherited. This might suggest that some kernels of truth underpin the surviving accounts, but it may simply be that such details had become canonical by the time that Curtius and Arrian were writing. It is also evident that words akin to those reported could be considered appropriate in these circumstances. A ruler facing a crowd of critics may well seek to hammer home their achievements, just as a general confronting a mutinous army might present himself as one of the boys who, like them, laughs in the face of danger. So, elements of the speeches are plausible, but this does not necessarily mean we should have all that much faith in them as accurate accounts of what Alexander said to his men at this pivotal juncture. Instead, they tell us much more about the attitudes of the men who composed them.

The sources broadly agree on what came next.[5] Alexander retreated into his quarters and refused to admit any of his men for several days. This strategy had proven successful after Clitus' death, but this time there was an extra layer of political posturing. Arrian reports that Alexander summoned the leading Persians, appointed them as the new commanders of his army, and called them his 'kinsmen', a title which came with the privilege of being allowed to kiss the king. New, Asian, military units were also created, their names echoing their Macedonian counterparts. Alexander cannot seriously have expected to survive had he abandoned his Macedonian power base entirely, unless one subscribes to the view that he was so caught up in his own self-aggrandizement that he was entirely delusional, but these moves were enough to break the resolve of the Macedonians: they came unarmed to Alexander's door and begged for forgiveness. Their spokesman, Callines, allegedly explained that they were especially upset that Persians were acknowledged as Alexander's kinsmen when no Macedonians held this title. Alexander immediately shared this honour with them and allowed everybody to kiss him.

Given the underlying grievances that had prompted the Macedonians' insubordination, it seems strange that this would be all that was said, or that the Macedonians would fixate on a courtly title rather than the redistribution of military commands, so Arrian or his source likely recorded events selectively. However, this focus is telling. Xenophon describes the closest courtiers of Cyrus the Great as his 'kinsmen', so this might be a Greek rendering of an honorific title used at the Persian court.[6] Macedonians not just accepting, but actively advocating for, a Persian or Persian-inspired title would represent a significant step in the Persianization of the royal court. Furthermore, the ritual of exchanging kisses brings us back to the issue of *proskynesis*. As we have seen, in Chares' version of this controversy, courtiers performed the gesture, kissed Alexander and sat back down.[7] There is no mention of *proskynesis* at Opis, and surely there would be if it was mooted, which reinforces my earlier point that it might be something of a red herring, only a part of broader changes to protocol in 328/7 that were designed to re-imagine the balance of power at court. By 324, Macedonians were apparently prepared to embrace courtly practices they had rejected a few years earlier. It is unlikely that the Persians retained the military commands they were given at Opis when they had replaced Macedonians, but there is no indication that the title they were awarded was rescinded. Macedonians and Persians were now all Alexander's kinsmen and therefore in some sense on an equal footing to one another when it came to interacting with the king.

The Banquet of Reconciliation, Opis (324)

This set the scene for one of the most important showpieces of Alexander's reign. Arrian reports that Alexander performed a sacrifice and then invited Macedonians, Persians and other notable people from across his empire to a banquet – some 9,000 apparently attended.[8] Guests shared in the same libations, following the lead of Greek and Persian priests, and Alexander then delivered a public prayer which requested concord and partnership in empire for Macedonians and Persians. The aim was evidently to draw a line under events at Opis, but this moment lies at the heart of one of the most significant twentieth-century debates about Alexander.

In the 1930s and '40s, William Woodthorpe Tarn suggested that Alexander sought to bring about the 'unity of mankind', a shorthand for a cosmopolitan world with national differences elided and people from different cultures treating one another as equals.[9] The banquet at Opis was the most important evidence used to support this argument. Tarn described people from all over the empire sitting alongside Alexander, sharing wine from the same mixing bowl. 'No witness', Tarn writes, 'could ever have forgotten the sight of that great krater on Alexander's table and people of every nationality drawing wine from it for their common libation.'[10] Alexander's prayer, Tarn suggests, went even further. The usual translation of the key sentence in Arrian's text presents Alexander as praying for Macedonians and Persians to share concord and partnership in empire. Tarn, though, saw 'concord' as something 'substantive' in its own right. In reading the text like this, he made this desire for concord – unity – a generalizing statement. This was not merely about bringing Macedonians and Persians together and resolving the tension that had prompted chaos within the camp just a few days earlier, but about uniting all of humanity, even peoples beyond Alexander's rule. Seen like this, the prayer becomes a wish for global unity and universal peace.

That wishful interpretation represents the high watermark of the romantic traditions around Alexander, but it is based on a misinterpretation. This was demonstrated in 1958 in a famous article by Ernst Badian, who argued that Tarn's conclusions were tenable only with 'violent distortion of the Greek'.[11] His own view of Alexander was much more cynical, as was made clear in a lecture delivered a few years later. Entitled 'Alexander the Great and the Loneliness of Power', Badian presents Alexander's life in tragic terms:

on the personal level, the story of Alexander the Great appears to us as an almost embarrassingly perfect illustration of the man who conquered the world, only to lose his soul. After fighting, scheming and murdering in pursuit of the secure tenure of absolute power, he found himself at last on a lonely pinnacle over an abyss, with no use for his power and security unattainable . . . Alexander illustrates with startling clarity the ultimate loneliness of supreme power.[12]

Badian and Tarn had two very different conceptions of Alexander, and they strike at the heart of what it means to examine the past. In his influential book *What Is History?*, published in 1961, E. H. Carr famously advises readers to 'study the historian before you begin to study the facts', noting that 'by and large, the historian will get the kind of facts he wants.'[13] We find exactly that here.

Born in 1869 and educated at Eton and Cambridge, Tarn was in many respects the archetypal Victorian gentleman.[14] Initially a lawyer, he retired due to ill health in 1905, moved to Scotland and established himself as an independent scholar. He worked in intelligence during the First World War, before returning to academic pursuits. In Tarn's work we see a view, shared by some contemporaries, of how empire and imperial power can be a force for good. His interpretation of Alexander grew out of the social and intellectual environment into which he was born, but he was also part of a generation repulsed by the slaughter seen on the battlefields of France. Promised that this would never occur again, they witnessed further horrors only two decades later.

The first volume of Tarn's biography of Alexander, published in 1948 but grounded in his inter-war thinking, closes with a vivid illustration of this. He paints a picture of Alexander as a visionary dreamer, who believed in a world where national differences were transcended and who inspired an ideal that ran through Zeno, the Stoic philosopher, into Christian thinking and was eventually realized with the French Revolution. Tarn writes that the idea might 'only smoulder' in his own day, but 'it never has been, and never can be, quite put out.' He ends with a despondent footnote: 'I have left the latter part of this paragraph substantially as written in 1926. Since then we have seen new and monstrous births, and are still moving in a world not realised; and I do not know how to rewrite it.'[15]

If Tarn could not come to terms with the Second World War, Badian could not escape its shadow. Born in 1925 in Vienna, Badian, who was Jewish, saw his father attacked on Kristallnacht and then briefly interned in Dachau, before the family escaped to New Zealand in 1939.[16] From there, he studied and taught in the UK, and then moved to the USA, spending most of his career at Harvard. The events of his youth clearly affected Badian's later scholarship. Discussing Coenus, who had spoken up on behalf of the army in India and advocated for a return home but died shortly afterwards, Badian writes: 'We cannot be certain as to the circumstances surrounding the death of this sinister man. But those who remember the fate of Rommel are entitled to be cynical.'[17] There is little in the sources to support this. Arrian simply reports Coenus' death, while Curtius suggests Alexander made some barbed comment that suggested his intervention at the Hyphasis had brought Coenus little gain. There is nothing to justify the characterization of Coenus as 'sinister'.[18]

Even as late as the turn of the millennium, Badian continued to draw on the 1940s to understand Alexander. In an article discussing conspiracies, he explains that the absence of hard evidence means that interpretations of Alexander must rest on inferences about his character.[19] Rulers who engage in conspiracies themselves are likely to imagine conspiracies against them, Badian argues, which explains why Alexander's reign is apparently so full of them. He also suggests that allegations of conspiracies can be a useful tool for autocratic regimes to tighten their grip on power. I would not dispute this. However, as part of the justification of his approach, Badian notes: 'those of us who have lived through the age of Stalin and Hitler will find plenty of examples of this.'[20] This might be because Stalin and Hitler were uniquely given to conspiratorial thinking, but it might also be because Badian's generation were conditioned to see things in a particular way by their own experiences. So, while Badian was right to reject Tarn's interpretation of the banquet at Opis, and especially correct to criticize his handling of the ancient sources, we see here how the tyrants who so profoundly shattered and shaped the world during his formative years loom large in his own treatment of

Alexander: Tarn's vision of a dreamer was incompatible with Badian's world view. Again, we see how Alexander's story is as much the story of his interpreters as it is a historical tale. We all have our own Alexander.

It should be no surprise, therefore, that my own interests in this event emerge from the intellectual currents of the last thirty years or so. For me, what matters most are the spatial arrangements made for the banquet of reconciliation.[21] Something of this has appeared already in my discussion of the setting of the Susa weddings, and this focus reflects the effect of the so-called 'spatial turn' on the humanities. The basic idea behind this is that the spaces we occupy – both natural and man-made – affect the way we behave. Examples from our own day-to-day lives make this obvious: we know that places like churches or mosques have particular codes of conduct, so we adjust our behaviour accordingly as we enter. Sometimes this knowledge comes from our understanding of societal norms, which we pick up over time by observing the world around us, but often we are reminded of the rules by what we see as we enter a space. These 'cues' encourage us to think and behave in particular ways.[22]

Consequently, it is not just what Alexander said during the banquet that matters, but also how the room was laid out. Tarn imagined people from all over the empire sharing Alexander's own table in a powerful display of cosmopolitanism, but this is not what Arrian's text says. Instead, he states that Alexander sat down, the Macedonians sat 'around him', the Persians sat 'next to them', and then came the elites from elsewhere. The way that this is phrased, particularly the notion that the Macedonians sat 'around' Alexander, implies a series of concentric circles, with Alexander in the middle. Proximity to the king is one way to accord status to individuals and groups, so what this seems to suggest is that Alexander envisaged an empire in which he reigned supreme, his compatriots represented his most significant supporters, the Persians the next most important group, and then everybody else. Nationality was apparently elided in this

Sultan Muhammad Nur, 'Alexander at a Banquet', folio 321b from a Khamsa (Quintet) of Nizami of Ganja. In one of the five poems in his Khamsa, produced in the late 13th century, Nizami wrote Alexander into Persian traditions as the half-brother of Darab, the king whom he conquers. This 16th-century illustration of the poem depicts Alexander at a banquet, wearing clothing emblematic of the Safavid period.

outermost circle, but it was integral to the overall display. Alexander may have prayed for partnership in empire between Macedonians and Persians, but the spatial setting as he was saying these words implied that this would not be a relationship between equals.

The real difficulty lies in understanding how much importance we should attach to this event because the context makes it difficult to know whether this was supposed to be a permanent model for the empire. The banquet was a response to unrest among the Macedonian soldiery, who were especially concerned that they were to be replaced by Alexander's new Asian subjects. There was an urgent need to reassure them that they remained vital and to stress their continued superiority. Yet Alexander could hardly neglect the Persians. A few days earlier, he had awarded them special privileges and promoted them to important positions; backing away from that dispensation so quickly would reveal that it had been nothing more than a stunt to manipulate the Macedonians. This risked damaging their future relationship, so Alexander had good reason to ensure that the Persians did not feel slighted. The spatial arrangement was thus a delicate solution to this immediate problem, since the Macedonians were given special status, but the Persians were marked out from everybody else. This was something the Persian elite had become accustomed to after two centuries of Achaemenid rule.[23] These pressures suggest that we should not necessarily imagine that the hierarchical model of empire on display during the banquet at Opis was intended to endure indefinitely.

Whether or not the banquet was designed with the long-term future of the empire in mind, it appears to have had a short-term impact. The veterans of the army now willingly departed for home under the command of Craterus, one of Alexander's leading generals, with a healthy bonus to boot.[24] Alexander ordered them to leave behind any children they had fathered with Asian women in case taking them to Macedonia destabilized society – if Alexander really did believe in the unity of mankind, he evidently recognized that he was alone in this vision. He promised to raise these children in the Macedonian military tradition and return to Macedonia with them when they were adults. A cynic might put this alongside the recruiting of the Iranian *epigonoi* and see it as an attempt to create an army devoid of regional and personal ties, whose only loyalty was to the king. However, this is also an important insight into the challenges of managing such a long military campaign. Thousands of Macedonians had apparently recorded marriages to Asian women at Susa.[25] Without underplaying the sexual violence that inevitably accompanied the sacking of cities, this indicates that Macedonian soldiers had formed long-lasting relationships with Asian women and implies a huge camp following. What happened to these women after their husbands left, Arrian does not say. One wonders too about the world these soldiers were returning to and how any pre-existing relationships had been affected by their prolonged absence.

As a general rule, I have sought to avoid too many judgements on Alexander's character because the source problem means we are so often at arm's length from the historical figure. At Opis, however, one gets a sense of his political acumen. The stick is deftly counterbalanced by carrot, while a clear understanding of factionalism enables him to tug on the heartstrings of the Macedonians to force their requital. Just as Alexander used the common soldiery to break the power of the Macedonian nobility during the trial of Philotas, the influence of those very same soldiers was undermined by the promotion of the Persians. What we should make of this is another question. Is this to be admired? Is it good leadership to force through an unpopular policy against the will of those whom it most affects? And yet, if we describe this behaviour with words like 'Machiavellian', we introduce negative connotations of a conniving king who will stop at nothing to get his own way. Is this any better? How do we square the reports of Alexander's anger with what ultimately appears a cool-headed way of managing the situation? Is a hot temper incompatible with rational thinking or was this anger staged, part of Alexander's arsenal of persuasion? Should we be sceptical and connect Alexander's fury here to his murder of Clitus in order to identify – and critique – a debilitating character trait? That said, Alexander was apparently offering his men something they had previously demanded. Some frustration at their reaction is understandable, so is it fair to compare this moment with others?

This emphasizes the problems that emerge when we try to understand Alexander's life through a study of his personality or attempt to connect together all of the glimpses of Alexander that come down to us into something more cohesive than the vignettes which appear in the ancient sources. In the end, perhaps all we can say is that Alexander appears to have achieved his own aims, but that trust between the king and the Macedonian soldiery was eroding.

The Death of Hephaestion (324)

If his relationship with his Macedonian soldiers had deteriorated to breaking point at Opis, there had always been one person Alexander believed he could trust – Hephaestion. However, at Ecbatana in the autumn of 324, disaster struck: Alexander's closest confidant fell ill and died.[26] Alexander's grief at Hephaestion's death was already legendary by the time our sources were writing. They report a host of despairing actions, from the plausible, like cutting his hair as a sign of mourning, to the far-fetched – executing the doctor who failed to save Hephaestion, and even burning down a temple of Asklepios, the Greek god of medicine, who had stood idly by as Hephaestion died. A memorial appears to have been commissioned, but the sources cannot decide whether this was built in Babylon or Ecbatana. The latter, where Hephaestion died, seems more likely and some have identified a stone lion found there as a possible monument.[27]

This sort of confusion is hardly unusual, but disagreement and exaggeration are particularly pronounced here because of Hephaestion's perceived importance to Alexander. He is usually presented as one of Alexander's oldest friends, their companionship said to date back to childhood. This tradition may be correct, but the evidence supporting it is surprisingly thin, essentially amounting to one throwaway remark by Curtius.[28] In reality, surprisingly little is known about Hephaestion's background, though some have speculated that his father, Amyntor, had Athenian connections which were perhaps shared by Hephaestion himself.[29] Hephaestion's first major role came after the death of Philotas, when he was one of two men appointed to share the command of the Companion Cavalry. Given this context and his apparent lack of ties to the wider Macedonian elite, Hephaestion's emergence is best explained as the result of a personal connection with Alexander. Other friends were promoted in this period, and it makes sense that the person who

The Stone Lion of Hamadan. It has been suggested that this Hellenistic sculpture in Hamadan, ancient Ecbatana, was set up on Alexander's orders to commemorate the death of Hephaestion.

rose fastest and furthest was the man to whom Alexander felt closest. This comes through most clearly during the Susa weddings, when Hephaestion married Drypetis, the sister of one of Alexander's own brides.[30] Arrian claims Alexander wanted his children to be related to Hephaestion's. This is guesswork, but, as I explained earlier, it was important that Achaemenid women were married only to people whom Alexander trusted, and a royal marriage was a clear symbol of Hephaestion's status.

Hephaestion does appear earlier in the campaign but often in stories that seem unlikely to be true. We saw, for instance, how Sisygambis supposedly performed *proskynesis* to him, thinking he was Alexander. In another tale, when Alexander had visited Troy, the king had supposedly laid a wreath on the tomb of Achilles, while Hephaestion had done the same at the tomb of Patroclus.[31] These stories cast Hephaestion as the 'other' Alexander, his mirror or alter ego. This closeness, and particularly the parallel with Achilles and Patroclus, perhaps the most famous pair of male lovers in antiquity, hints at a sexual relationship between Alexander and Hephaestion. Picking up this thread, Justin claims that his beauty was one reason why Alexander was so fond of Hephaestion, while Curtius compares him unfavourably to Euxenippus, whom he euphemistically says rivalled Hephaestion for Alexander's favour because of his youth and good looks.[32] According to Arrian, the Stoic philosopher Epictetus, the former's teacher, claimed Alexander had the temple of Asclepius burned when his *eromenos* ('beloved') died.[33] Arrian reports that the temple was set alight after Hephaestion's death, but he does not describe Hephaestion as Alexander's lover. Rather than coming from contemporary accounts by authors like Ptolemy, who was best placed among our sources to know about any sexual relationship, this might suggest that the terminology adopted by Epictetus reflects later gossip. Arrian, though, was certainly keen to present the relationship between the two men in a particular light – he included a description of events at Troy despite admitting that these were not found in Ptolemy or Aristoboulos, his preferred sources, and he only ever mentions Achilles in connection with Patroclus and Hephaestion.[34]

It is hardly surprising that the evidence for a sexual relationship between Alexander and Hephaestion is elusive, since, for the most part, these matters largely remained a private concern. However, this question opens up an important discussion about Alexander's sex life and its connection with sexuality in the Greek world more broadly.[35] Since we know that some people had sex with men and women, it is tempting to describe ancient Greeks as bisexual. Modern labels like this are essentially about who we want to have sex with, but the hierarchical nature of ancient societies makes it hard to apply these terms to antiquity. I am sure that some ancient Greeks will have preferred same-sex partners, but it was only adult, citizen men who had much opportunity to explore their desires. Female sexuality was tightly controlled and, with enslaved people seen as possessions of their masters, sexual violence and exploitation was endemic. In these contexts, for men like Alexander, the choice of sexual partner was perhaps as much about exerting status as anything else.

Furthermore, our public discourse about relationships between men in ancient Greece remains dominated by a conception that emerges from Athens. This famous model juxtaposes an older man, known as the *erastes* ('the lover'), with an adolescent *eromenos* ('the beloved').[36] The *erastes* plays the active role in pursuing his beloved, and the affair is broken off once the *eromenos* reaches maturity. Whether the relationship included penetrative sex or was confined to non-penetrative activity is debated. Against this backdrop, a long-term relationship between Alexander and Hephaestion, which endured into adulthood, seems unusual. But examining other Greek communities reveal alternative models of male–male sexual activity. Perhaps the best example comes from Thebes, where the so-called 'Sacred Band', an elite military unity, was purportedly made up of

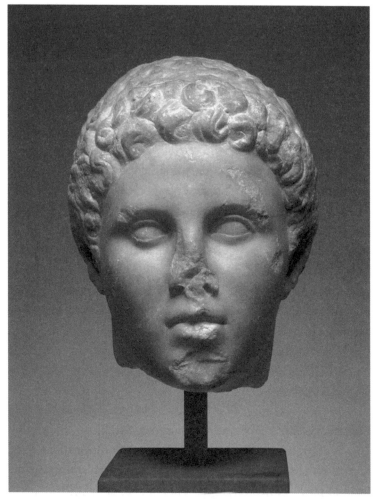

Images of Alexander and his contemporaries are few and far between. This head, *c.* 320 BCE, has been identified as a representation of Hephaestion.

150 pairs of lovers.[37] These were evidently adult free men, who publicly celebrated their relationships.

There are clear indications of sexual activity between men in Macedonia too. We have already seen how Philip was murdered by Pausanias; Archelaus, an earlier king, also apparently died at the hands of a former lover.[38] Aristotle is the main source for the latter example. He may have been writing more than half a century after these events, but he was close to the Macedonian court and had experienced the patterns of behaviour there. Consequently, there are good reasons for thinking that Alexander's predecessors, and most notably his own father, had engaged in sexual relationships with men. The Pages who conspired to kill Alexander provide another example.

What we know of Alexander's sexual relationships reflects these contemporary patterns. In addition to his marriages to Roxane, Stateira and Parysatis, Alexander is said to have had a long-lasting relationship with a woman called Barsine.[39] She was the daughter of the Persian nobleman Artabazus and had previously been married to Memnon of Rhodes, who had played a pivotal role on the Persian side in the opening years of the invasion. Barsine allegedly bore Alexander a son named Heracles, who briefly emerged as a pawn in the struggle to succeed Alexander. Plutarch claims she was Alexander's only female sexual partner before his marriage to Roxane, but he makes this remark while discussing the capture of Darius' family, so it is designed to emphasize Alexander's magnanimous treatment of the Persian royal women. We should not necessarily take this comment too seriously, therefore, and Plutarch was probably thinking only about free women here. However, this stresses that Alexander's sexual conduct became a way of representing his character and thus another area in which representation was divorced from reality. In that spirit, there are a host of other stories concerning Alexander's sexual exploits with women, including a supposed tryst with an Amazonian queen, but none of these are particularly convincing.[40]

On the male side, the firmest evidence concerns Bagoas. As discussed above, he was a Persian eunuch whom Alexander inherited from Darius and who allegedly played a role in the downfall of Orxines; Curtius is clear that their relationship was sexual.[41] We might worry that he was using the stock figure of the Persian eunuch as a means to highlight the corrupting influence of Eastern luxuries on Alexander's character. If that reflects Roman preoccupations, an alternative reading might stress that Bagoas was essentially a sex slave and see him struggling to find a way to survive and exert influence. His perspective, we might say, like so many others, is irrecoverably lost, hidden behind the sneers of the privileged. Plutarch and Athenaeus also describe Alexander publicly kissing Bagoas in a theatre to vociferous approval from the Macedonians present.[42] Athenaeus attributes this story to Dicaearchus, who was writing within a few years of Alexander's death. This does not mean that the tale is true, but it at least suggests that contemporaries considered it plausible that Alexander would kiss another man – and why wouldn't they when many of them would have had same-sex partners of their own?[43]

None of this proves that Alexander had sex with Hephaestion, but this wider context clearly demonstrates that a sexual relationship with a free, Macedonian man would not have been out of place. In fact, given contemporary practices, only having sex with women would have been more unusual. So, while labels like 'gay' or 'bisexual' are anachronistic, Alexander probably did have sex with men. Hephaestion may have been among those partners, but that is less clear-cut.

Return to Babylon (324–323)

Alexander wallowed for a period after Hephaestion's death, but eventually pulled himself together the only way he knew how – with a cathartic expedition against a warlike tribe, this time the Cossaeans, who inhabited the mountains near Ecbatana.[44] He then returned to Babylon, where the court was largely based over the next six months. Alexander's thoughts were apparently turning to the future. A scientific expedition was sent to explore the Caspian Sea, and a major new naval campaign was planned for the coast of

Arabia, which was to be the next military target. The army was also reorganized. Peucestas had arrived in Babylon with some 20,000 Persian troops and these were integrated into Macedonian units. The Macedonians were to be paid more, but this was a significant new step and perhaps suggests that the disgruntled troops at Opis had been right to fear for the future.

During this period, Alexander received scores of Greek envoys, largely as a response to his own diplomatic initiatives. During the Olympic Games of 324, his envoy Nicanor had made a major announcement.[45] Known as the Exiles Decree, Alexander declared that almost all of the Greeks who had been banished from their cities would be allowed to return home. Diodorus suggests that he was motivated partly by a desire for fame and partly by security considerations: the exiles would be indebted to Alexander and could be expected to champion his interests upon their return. The latter seems especially plausible – after the threat of Agis' war in 331/30 and with Graeco-Macedonian relations marred by mutual suspicion for over a century, this was perhaps seen as a way to ensure the compliance of Greek communities. The decree had significant practical implications. For instance, exile was usually accompanied with forfeiture of property, so disputes could be expected as men returned home and demanded either the restoration of their land and possessions or financial compensation. Consequently, the decree was likely to have a destabilizing effect on Greek cities. Furthermore, as a major intervention in the internal affairs of the Greek cities, it also constituted a breach of the oath of the League of Corinth, which was nominally an alliance of independent Greek city-states. From that perspective, this was a tyrannical act, so it is little wonder that Greeks might want to push back against this imposition. But this is the other crucial point about the Exiles Decree: exceptions could be discussed only with Alexander himself, which reinforced his position as the supreme powerbroker in the Greek world.

But what could the Greeks offer the man who had everything? Arrian reports that some ambassadors arrived in Babylon wearing golden crowns and crowned Alexander too, as though honouring a god. This statement is loaded with irony because he contrasts this information with his own remark that Alexander was close to death. Juxtaposing these divine-like honours with Alexander's mortality was an effective way to undercut those claims, so this may be as much literary technique as it is a historical detail. That said, Greek communities were discussing Alexander's potential divinity in the final year of his life. The best indication of this comes from Athens in the years after his death, when a faction traditionally opposed to Macedonian power sought revenge on a rival political bloc that had advocated on Alexander's behalf. This led to a series of trials featuring prominent politicians, and, though the evidence is fragmentary, one of the contentious topics seems to concern behaviour during debates about whether to bestow divine honours on Alexander.[46] It is unlikely that people who saw themselves as supporters of Alexander would be proposing honours like this unless they thought they would be well received by the king, but this demonstrates that Alexander's association with the divine was not driven exclusively by the king himself. It also emphasizes just how far Alexander's campaign had transformed the balance of power in Greece. The honours traditionally bestowed upon benefactors by Greek communities – prime seats at the theatre, a free dinner – were no longer appropriate for a king with the resources of Asia at his disposal. This was one of Alexander's most important long-term legacies, and it paved the way for the emergence of ruler cults in the Hellenistic world.

8

Babylon and Beyond, 323–Present

As Alexander returned to Babylon, he supposedly received a stream of grim omens which warned that his death was imminent. Given that the ancient authors were writing retrospectively, it is difficult to know how much store to set by these stories. According to one, a gust of wind blew the diadem off Alexander's head while he was sailing.[1] A quick-thinking sailor swam after it; not wanting to get it wet as he returned to the ship, he put the diadem on his own head. This was interpreted as an ominous sign, and Alexander apparently had the sailor beheaded or, according to the apologetic account of Aristoboulos, whipped. In one version, however, the diadem was retrieved not by an anonymous sailor but by Seleucus, who would go on to become king of the Asian part of Alexander's empire. Here, the tale predicts Seleucus' own succession and is certainly a later invention.

In another story, Alexander briefly wandered away from the throne during a council meeting and returned to find that it had been occupied by a random person, perhaps a prisoner.[2] The man was tortured in case this was a plot, but he denied this, saying his behaviour was impulsive. Arrian attributes this to Aristoboulos, meaning it must at least have had a contemporary resonance. For Arrian, this was a worrying sign of what was to come, but we might see here a Greek interpretation of the old Babylonian 'substitute-king' ritual.[3] This was a means of counteracting ominous portents that involved the king temporarily being replaced by somebody else, who would enjoy the trappings of royalty but no real power. Eventually the stand-in would be removed, perhaps killed, to fulfil the prophecy.

If this ritual was performed, it did not work.[4] In late May 323, Alexander developed a serious fever. He attempted to continue with regular business, but his condition gradually worsened. As news filtered through the camp, and it began to become clear that he would not recover, his men forced their way into the palace, demanding to see him one last time. A sombre procession filed silently past the king, who could no longer speak but struggled to acknowledge individuals as best he could with subtle movements of his eyes and head. Alexander's illness apparently began after a heavy night of drinking at a symposium organized by his friend Medius. The ancient accounts report that conspiracy theories were quick to emerge, and the origins of the illness naturally led to suspicion that he had been poisoned. In antiquity, fingers for this were pointed at Antipater. He had recently been summoned to Babylon and, perhaps fearing that he was to be replaced or would suffer the same fate as Parmenion, allegedly acted out of anticipatory self-defence. In one version, Aristotle – who now feared Alexander after his treatment of Callisthenes – created a poison for Antipater, who had his son Cassander carry it to Babylon, where it was handed over to Iolas, another of Antipater's sons, who just so happened to be responsible for pouring the drinks at Alexander's court. This all sounds a bit far-fetched.

There may have been some motivation for Antipater to act, but the notion that Alexander was poisoned is entirely conjectural. More sober accounts of a fever that progressively worsened seem more convincing. Indeed, it may have been purely coincidental that Alexander's final illness began after attending Medius' symposium, or doing so may merely have left him susceptible to another disease. Modern medical theories have suggested a whole host of possibilities, including malaria, typhoid, West Nile fever and

Guillain-Barré Syndrome.[5] However, these are just as unconvincing as the poisoning theory because they rely on the ancient accounts, and we cannot be sure that the reported symptoms are exhaustive or accurate. Ultimately, all we can know for sure comes from our only contemporary source. In one of the Babylonian astronomical diaries, buried among remarks about the position of the planets and data about the price of the goods in the marketplace, there is a simple statement: 'the king died.'[6] It was 11 June 323.

Contested Legacies: The Wars of the Successors and Hellenistic Macedonia (323–146)

As rumours of Alexander's death swirled through Babylon, there was uncertainty about what would happen. Roxane was pregnant, but not due to give birth for months and there was obviously no guarantee that Alexander's only legitimate child would be male. He may have had a son with Barsine, but this is disputed, and a bastard could hardly be expected to succeed. After the bloodletting at the start of his reign, when Alexander had purged Macedonia of potential challengers, his only surviving male relative was his half-brother Arrhidaeus, the son of Philip II and Philinna. On bloodline alone, Arrhidaeus was the obvious successor, but he apparently suffered from some form of mental disorder, which meant he would require a regent.

Some sources claim that Alexander was asked on his deathbed to whom he was leaving his empire. 'To the strongest' or 'the best', he is said to have replied, foreseeing the fighting that would soon break out; some suggested that he meant 'to Craterus' because the Greek words are similar. In other accounts, he handed his signet ring, a key symbol of his authority, to Perdiccas, perhaps indicating his chosen successor. Determining the right version is impossible, and I think it is doubtful that any arrangements at all were made at this late stage. In any case, any last-minute solution was unlikely to hold much credence in the long term. Without clear promulgation by Alexander himself, the claims made by the people who were with him when he died would have had little credibility.

Faced with uncertainty, the leading generals gathered in the room around Alexander's corpse, arguing about what to do.[7] Perdiccas, apparently, proposed waiting to see whether Roxane's child was a boy; Nearchus argued for Heracles, Barsine's son; Ptolemy suggested that the leading generals rule as a war council; Aristonous recommended that Perdiccas be made king. Whether there is any truth in these reports is debatable – later authors may simply be outlining the various possibilities to their readers and ascribing each option to different characters makes this easier to digest. When Alexander's closest friends could not find a solution, an even greater dispute broke out between the cavalry and the infantry. The infantry, led by Meleager, argued that the only legitimate candidate for the throne was Arrhidaeus and acclaimed him as king under the throne name Philip III.

Things deteriorated to such an extent that the cavalry, led by Perdiccas, exited Babylon and essentially besieged the infantry, who remained holed up in the city. Eventually an agreement was reached: Arrhidaeus would remain king as Philip, but power would be shared between Perdiccas, Meleager and Craterus, who was leading the veterans dismissed from the army at Opis back to Macedonia when Alexander died. To heal the rift, a purification ritual was organized. It involved the army marching between the two halves of a mutilated dog and was meant to reunite the infantry and cavalry. It was a ruse. At Perdiccas' insistence, Philip demanded the punishment of the infantrymen who had caused the breach. Three hundred men were seized and, in full view of the whole army, trampled to death by the elephants. These, of course, were Meleager's principal allies and Meleager himself was killed shortly afterwards.

The remaining leaders agreed that Perdiccas would take up the regency, while they took control of key provinces across the empire. Most notably, Ptolemy was made the satrap of Egypt while Antipater and Craterus, neither of whom were in Babylon but who were so powerful that they had to be accounted for, were to share Europe between them. As this was being finalized, Roxane gave birth to a son; he was named after his father and immediately proclaimed as joint-king, Alexander IV. The promotion of co-kings created the potential for factional divisions in the future.

The uneasy truce between the Macedonians just about held for two years but there were always divisions, which made conflict likely. The spark that eventually ignited civil war involved Alexander's corpse. Perdiccas had ordered the construction of an elaborate funerary carriage that would carry Alexander home. This took time to build, so it was not until 321 that the hearse began its journey to Macedonia. When it reached Damascus in Syria, it was intercepted by Ptolemy's soldiers, who diverted it to Egypt, where Alexander's body was buried, first in Memphis and then in Alexandria. Perdiccas could hardly ignore this challenge to his authority and invaded Egypt. After his prestige was diminished by a disastrous attempt to cross the Nile, he was murdered by some of his own officers.

Ptolemy declined the opportunity to take over the regency, leaving Antipater to take up the position. A new power-sharing agreement replaced Perdiccas' supporters with those loyal to Antipater and his allies. Meanwhile in Greece, Athens and her allies attempted to reassert their independence in a conflict known as the Lamian War. The Greeks were defeated in 322 by Antipater and Craterus, who imposed harsh terms on them. Most significantly, the Athenian political system was reconfigured, effectively ending democracy, at least for the time being.

Antipater, now in his eighties, died in 319, leaving Alexander's contemporaries to shape the next forty years. The main players were Antigonus the One-Eyed, Alexander's satrap of Phrygia, who had already built up a significant power base in Asia Minor; Ptolemy, Alexander's close friend, now the satrap of Egypt; Seleucus, Perdiccas' second-in-command, who was given the plum satrapy of Babylonia, likely as a reward for facilitating his superior's death; Lysimachus, another veteran of the campaign, who controlled Thrace; and Cassander, Antipater's son. There were a host of secondary characters too – like Eumenes, Alexander's Greek secretary – who shone brightly but briefly, and, almost without exception, came to grisly ends. This was also an era of remarkable women: Olympias, Alexander's mother who now championed her grandson's interests; Cynane, Alexander's half-sister, who forced through the marriage of her daughter to Philip III; Adea-Eurydice, Cynane's daughter, who sought to use her status as the wife of Philip to influence policy; Thessalonike, another of Alexander's half-sisters, who eventually married Cassander.

I cannot do justice here to the complexities of this period, but the headlines are straightforward. Driven by their own ambitions, Alexander's generals fought viciously with one another and, in doing so, dismembered his empire. Antigonus is traditionally seen as the prime mover in the period from 321 to 301, his efforts at expansion often characterized as an attempt to seize control of Alexander's whole empire. His activity drove the other major figures into a grand alliance, which eventually triumphed in 301 at the Battle of Ipsus in Phrygia. Antigonus, by now perhaps an octogenarian, was killed in the fighting, which says everything about the character of the people involved in this struggle. His son, Demetrius, escaped to carry the Antigonid name forward.

Alexander's family were the inevitable casualties of these wars. By 317, Philip III and Alexander IV were controlled by opposing factions. Alexander's chief advocate was Olympias. She had attached herself to Polyperchon, to whom Antipater had entrusted control of Europe when he died. However, Cassander, furious at having been sidelined by his father, allied with Adea-Eurydice and Philip.

The motif of Alexander on horseback is a popular one. This statue overlooks the sea at Thessaloniki, a city in northern Greece founded by Cassander and named after Alexander's half-sister.

In one of the most exceptional moments in antiquity, Olympias and Adea-Eurydice are said to have led troops personally onto the battle-field, but Adea-Eurydice's men refused to fight against Alexander the Great's mother. Adea-Eurydice and her husband were captured and killed, and Olympias instigated a bloody purge of Cassander's supporters in Macedonia. Cassander, however, was undeterred and soon captured Olympias; she too was executed. This gave Cassander control of Alexander IV, to whom the generals theoretically owed allegiance even as they fought with one another. This situation was clearly untenable, and, in the late 310s or early 300s, Cassander had Alexander IV and Roxane killed. Alexander's generals now declared themselves kings – Antigonus was first, in 306/5, followed swiftly by the others. The era of the 'Successor' kingdoms had arrived.

Alexander IV was the last male Argead, but his death was not the end of the dynasty. Alexander's sister Cleopatra was still alive, so too his half-sister Thessalonike. Their family connections made them especially attractive brides for the Successors, and Cleopatra was apparently killed by Antigonus after agreeing to marry Ptolemy. Thessalonike married Cassander in the mid-310s, which gave him a strong claim to Macedonia because, when their children came to the throne, Macedonia would again be ruled by descendants of Philip II. Cassander reigned until 297, when he died of illness. His eldest son, Philip, succeeded him, but he was perhaps already suffering from the same disease and died shortly afterwards.

A struggle broke out between Cassander's two remaining sons. Thessalonike apparently backed the youngest, Alexander, to the fury of the middle child, Antipater, who orchestrated the murder of his mother. Alexander sought external help, inviting Demetrius, the son of Antigonus the One-Eyed, and Pyrrhus, ruler of neighbouring Epirus, to help him regain the throne. This was a disastrous move. Pyrrhus occupied the western part of Macedonia, so Demetrius arrived to be told that his help was no longer required. This went down as well as can be expected, and Demetrius had Alexander murdered. Antipater fled to Lysimachus in Thrace, hoping for assistance. Instead, Lysimachus killed him and recognized Demetrius as the ruler of Macedonia. He did not fare much better. After a six-year reign characterized by thwarted ambitions, Pyrrhus invaded Macedonia and Demetrius' own soldiers abandoned him. Demetrius fled abroad, reached an ill-thought-out alliance with Seleucus, and then drank himself to death in luxurious captivity.

Meanwhile, things were also going wrong for Lysimachus in Asia. Taking a new wife sparked dynastic competition at court, which led to the execution of his heir. Recognizing these splits, Seleucus spied an opportunity and invaded. Lysimachus was killed in battle, and his kingdom fell to Seleucus, who now crossed the Hellespont, striking out for Macedonia intent on reaching his homeland and reuniting the two halves of Alexander's empire. But he too was killed. His assassin was Ptolemy Ceraunus (the 'thunderbolt'), the eldest son of Ptolemy I. After being sidelined by a younger brother in Egypt, he had fled to Lysimachus' court and now sensed a chance to seize a kingdom of his own. However, within a year or so, he died in battle against an invading army of Gauls. A series of short-lived kings followed until eventually a general called Sosthenes ruled – but not, apparently, as king. This period of chaos is one of the low points in Macedonian history. Then, in 277, Antigonus II, the son of Demetrius, won a significant victory over the Gauls in Thrace. The prestige from this allowed him to return to Macedonia and lay claim to the throne his father had abandoned: his Antigonid dynasty would rule for more than a century.

After the breathlessness of the forty years after Alexander's death, the establishment of Antigonid control of Macedonia in the 270s, after successful transfers of power in both the Ptolemaic and Seleucid realms in the late 280s, saw the political picture stabilize somewhat. These empires still fought with one another, but the basic shape of the eastern Mediterranean was fixed: the Antigonids controlled Macedonia and dominated Greece, the Ptolemies held Egypt and the Seleucids ruled in Asia. In some sense, this was the defining geopolitical legacy of Alexander's campaign – a unipolar world dominated by a single superpower became multipolar, with several kingdoms competing with one another, much as had been the case before the conquests of Cyrus the Great. This was exacerbated further as new powers emerged, such as Pergamon in Asia Minor and Parthia in Central Asia. However, the biggest impact, at least on Macedonia, came from the west. By the end of the third century, diplomatic relations between the Antigonids and Rome were strained as expansion brought the Romans to Illyria, Macedonia's western neighbour. Hostility was ensured when Philip V agreed an alliance with Hannibal, during the Carthaginian's famous invasion of Italy. The Romans would remember this and, in the first half of the second century, they won a series of wars against the Macedonians. This culminated in 146 with the creation of the Roman province of Macedonia. Macedonia's centuries of independence were over.

Contested Legacies: Alexander's Tomb

The underlying dynamics meant that war between Alexander's generals was always likely, but it is striking that conflict was sparked by Ptolemy's seizure of Alexander's corpse. This highlights the importance of being seen to control Alexander's legacy and the extent to which Alexander remained a legitimizing force in the years after his death. The Ptolemies made much of their possession of Alexander's body, constructing an elaborate mausoleum for it and connecting their own tombs to Alexander's. Despite vigorous debate over the last two centuries, this building remains lost and there are scores of competing theories about its location. I do not pretend to have a solution to this, but there is an important point to make about where Alexander should have been buried.

In 1977 Manolis Andronikos made a spectacular discovery at the village of Vergina. Hidden beneath a large tumulus were three royal tombs, Tombs I, II, and III. Andronikos named Philip II as the occupant of Tomb II, which was the grandest of the tombs and where the most significant grave goods were discovered. Others, however, assigned Philip II to Tomb I and argued that Tomb II belonged to his son, Philip III. Hanging over this disagreement is a cynical question with little relation to ancient history: is Tomb II less important if it belongs to Philip III rather than his father? The debate has several facets, covering matters like the architecture and decoration of the structures, and the material culture found within them.[8] This can get very technical, but two pieces of evidence are especially worth mentioning.

The first concerns the human remains that were discovered in the tombs. Analysis of the cremated remains indicate that the occupant of Tomb III was an adolescent; it is widely accepted that this must be Alexander IV, who died in his early teens. Tomb I contained the bones of a middle-aged man, a younger woman likely around the age of twenty and a newborn. Likewise, Tomb II held the cremated remains of a woman reaching the end of her teens and an older man. Andronikos, based on one forensic analysis, argued that the skull of the male occupant of Tomb II showed damage to the eye socket, which would correspond with reports that Philip II lost an eye during a siege. However, newer technology has challenged this.[9] The literary sources also suggest that Philip walked with a limp, the result of another battlefield injury.[10] The remains in Tomb II shows no sign of damage to the legs, but the bones of the male figure in Tomb I indicate significant damage to the knee, likely the result of a major wound.[11] Of course, other Macedonian kings may have suffered a similar injury, but this would seem to indicate that Philip II was buried in Tomb I along with his final wife, Cleopatra, and their child; Philip III Arrhidaeus was laid to rest in Tomb II, together with his wife, Adea-Eurydice; and Alexander IV was placed in Tomb III.

As we have seen, Cleopatra and her child were killed after Philip's death. Advertising this ruthless act by burying them with Philip might seem counterintuitive, but there was real value in making sure the world knew that they were dead. If this was accepted, no pretender could rise up claiming to be the infant, nor could hostile factions seize control of Philip's youngest child and use this as leverage against Alexander. Similar considerations surround the burial of Philip III and Adea-Eurydice, who may have been reinterred a year or so after their deaths by their former ally Cassander.[12] For him, this was a chance to cement relationships with the faction that had supported Philip III, and to stress his loyalty to the Argead family in the wake of his own killing of Olympias.

The second important point is that Tomb II was built in two phases.[13] Andronikos reports that the main chamber was constructed first and the antechamber second, noting that the plastering in the main chamber was done hurriedly and never finished.

Why? There is, I think, an answer to this question, one which resolves many of the problems relating to the identities of the people buried at Aegae: Tomb II was not intended for Philip III, but for Alexander. Perdiccas had made significant preparations for the funeral cortege that would transport Alexander back to his final resting place in Macedonia, and he would hardly have taken the body home to nothing. His intention presumably was to enter Macedonia and bury Alexander with the two co-kings by his side. This would have been a powerful statement. It would have firmly established his regency, and perhaps set the ground for something more. For this to work, a tomb must have been constructed.

This would have been a significant monument, and it would have been natural to situate it close to Philip's burial place as a means of emphasizing that this was a dynastic centre. But then, as work on the tomb progressed, came the news that Ptolemy had hijacked Alexander's corpse. Tools were downed in the confusion, and the structure was never finished – there was little point doing so without a body to bury. A few years later, Philip III died. Quickly completing Alexander's tomb and burying Philip and Eurydice in it was a neat solution to the problems of what to do with them and with the unfinished tomb. This argument is naturally a little speculative, but it fits with the archaeological evidence, and responds to an important logical proposition: we know that Alexander's body was sent back to Macedonia, and there must have been a tomb to house it. His eventual resting place remains a mystery, but perhaps we can point to Alexander's 'tomb' after all.

Contested Legacies: Macedonia after Alexander

The way that Alexander's empire fell apart so quickly after his death poses a significant challenge to his short-term legacy. Alexander blitzed across the Persian Empire and established a new world order, but the fact that this new empire effectively died with him seems to make all of this a little bit pointless. Even more damagingly, after ruling Macedonia for generations, the Argead line was extinguished without his heirs ever establishing themselves on the throne. Alexander may represent the high watermark of the Argead family, but he was also essentially its end-point. If a king's first duty is dynastic, Alexander spectacularly failed on that score. The question, however, is how much responsibility for this should be laid at his door.

The obvious criticism is that Alexander failed to father a legitimate son during his lifetime and did not make alternative arrangements for the succession. Although Roxane was pregnant when Alexander died and a boy was eventually born, he was hardly set up for success – examples of infants who were born into kingship and reached maturity to exercise their office are few and far between in the ancient world. This situation emerged because Alexander did not marry until he met Roxane in 327: why did he delay for so long? If we were looking to defend Alexander, we might point to his youth – he was only around twenty when his father died in an era when men probably wed around the age of thirty. Once the campaign had begun, we might say that the focus needed to remain on the immediate military objectives. As ever, Philip is a useful contrast. He cannot have been much older than Alexander when he came to the throne, and yet within a couple of years he had contracted multiple marriages and produced children, all while leading military expeditions.

One potential problem for Alexander when he first came to power was whom to marry. The obvious candidates were the daughters of leading Macedonian noblemen like Parmenion and Antipater. These men had been instrumental in securing the succession for Alexander and their support was vital in the early years of his reign. But marrying into one of their families would have meant promoting one Macedonian faction over another, which risked jeopardizing the balance of power within the kingdom.[14]

With hindsight, Alexander's best option may have been to mimic Philip's strategy and marry at the conclusion of the campaign against his northern and western neighbours in 335. Arrian reports that during this expedition, Langarus, the king of the Agrianians, offered to tackle the rebellious Autariatae on Alexander's behalf.[15] Langarus supposedly had a strong relationship with Philip, so this represents a renewal of that alliance. To strengthen these ties, Alexander promised to marry his half-sister Cynane to Langarus, but Langarus died before this could happen. This suggests that Alexander was thinking about marriage as a diplomatic tool in the first year of his reign. The most prudent course of action may have been to find himself an appropriate match at this juncture – putting this off was evidently a deliberate decision.

Throughout the campaign, there were plenty of moments which should have reminded Alexander of the need to secure the succession. What would have happened to Macedonia if Clitus had reacted just a fraction of a second slower to Spithridates' attack on Alexander at the Granicus, for instance? In the aftermath of that battle, Alexander reached an agreement with Ada, a Hecatomnid ruler.[16] The Hecatomnids were a local dynasty who ruled Caria as sub-satraps for the Achaemenids. They are most well-known for the Mausoleum of Halicarnassus, one of the seven wonders of the ancient world. Ada surrendered the city of Alinda to Alexander and adopted him as her son; in return, she was restored as the ruler of Caria. This fictive kinship worked for both parties: it helped Ada return to power, but the arrangements presumably meant that Alexander would inherit her position upon her death. Ada herself was probably too old to be a viable wife for Alexander or to give birth to his heirs, but this shows that he was thinking about how to benefit from new family ties.

This happened towards the end of 334 at the same time as Alexander supposedly sent his newly married troops back to Macedonia to spend winter with their wives.[17] This was not done out of compassion, but so that these men could do their duty to the state by fathering children. For them, fighting against the Persians was not incompatible with planning for the future, and the same should have been true for Alexander. I am not saying that he could or should have married into the Hecatomnid family, or that any particular marriage alliance was an especially attractive proposition, but it is legitimate to ask whether there was really nobody for Alexander to marry before Roxane, when he had reigned for almost a decade.

Alexander is sometimes accused of being more interested in new conquests than building an empire, and of caring too little about what would happen after his death. I tend to think that these criticisms are overegged, but on the question of his failure to produce an heir I do have more sympathy with those who judge Alexander harshly. That said, it is only fair to point out that Alexander could have married in 335 and still been childless in 323: bad luck, difficulty conceiving and miscarriage were all possibilities, while infant mortality rates were very high. Indeed, the *Metz Epitome* reports that Roxane gave birth to a son who died in infancy in India, though none of the main sources confirm this and there is no obvious motivation for them to suppress this information.[18] But this only emphasizes how important it was to maximize the window for fathering an heir by marrying early, and perhaps often. By the conventional standards of the time, failing to produce an heir was a major black mark against Alexander.

However, even if Alexander had married in 335 and had a son soon afterwards, his successor would still only have been a boy in 323. Any child could have prospered only with the cooperation of others, which emphasizes that Alexander cannot bear sole responsibility for the disintegration of his empire. The period after his death is characterized by the personal ambitions of the leading actors. Antigonus is usually held up as the prime example of somebody whose pursuit of his own objectives destabilized the empire, but others were just as aggressive. Seleucus, for instance, may have played a longer game than his great rival, but was still pursuing his own aspirations in the late 280s. Similarly, while Thessalonike's motivations are obscure, her machinations after the death of Cassander apparently led to the implosion of her family, and it was miscalculations by her sons that actually extinguished the Argead line.

In a sense, we should hardly be surprised that Alexander's generals behaved as they did. They had proven their abilities during Alexander's campaign, and negotiating the court politics of his reign attests to their ruthlessness and political savvy. At the same time, the way that people like Ptolemy – men who Alexander counted among his closest friends – turned against his heirs so quickly represents a striking departure from Macedonian history, in which the Argead dynasty seems to have enjoyed the loyalty of the Macedonian nobility, even if individual kings did not. Their behaviour reflects the way that Alexander's conquests had changed the dynamics of Macedonian society and raised the stakes.

After a decade of continuous service, ordinary soldiers had become more professional and more prepared to make their voices heard, while those who had risen through the ranks and reached the very top had done so through a mix of talent, ambition and nepotism. Ironically, their personal allegiance to Alexander may have meant a weakening of the ties that bound them to one another, to the Argead dynasty and even to Macedonia itself. After Alexander's death, it transpired that their only loyalty was to themselves: the empire fell apart because too few people were prepared to make the compromises necessary to keep it together. Alexander, however, was the architect of this situation and must carry the can for the fact that his greatest political achievement, the creation of a new Macedonian Empire, was so short-lived.

The question about Alexander's culpability for the end of the Argeads plays into a wider discussion about the impact of his reign on Macedonia itself. After all, though he would take up new roles, he was first and foremost a Macedonian king and his primary duty was to the people of Macedonia. Clearly, Alexander's victories catapulted the Macedonians to greater prominence in the ancient world, but it is questionable how far Macedonia itself benefitted from his reign. Cyrus had founded Pasargadae with the proceeds of his campaigns, while Darius I had built Persepolis. For centuries, the Persians had exploited the people that they had conquered, extracting resources as best they could in the form of manpower and material wealth. This was the archetype of imperialism: goods flowed to the Persian homeland from across the empire. But how far did the emptying of the Persian treasuries enrich Macedonia? There is little sense that the wealth of Asia made it back to Macedonia. Indeed, as we have seen, by the 280s Macedonian politics had descended so far that the rule of kings was interrupted. Alexander may not have been solely responsible for events after his death, but it is apparent that Macedonia did not become a new global centre in the way that Persia had under the Achaemenids or that Rome would by the end of the millennium.

One reason for this may have been the impact of Alexander's wars on the Macedonian soldiery. Brian Bosworth suggested that Alexander's need for troops essentially emptied Macedonia of military-age men, which, among other effects, significantly lowered the birth rate. In the medium term, this reduced the Macedonian population, limiting the kingdom's ability to churn out replacements for the soldiers killed or settled overseas. Alexander, he argued, was responsible for creating a 'dead generation' and so also for the decline of Macedonia.[19] A lack of precise information about the Macedonian population, or reliable statistics for the Macedonian army, means that substantiating some of these claims is impossible, but the general notion that Alexander's campaign saw a large proportion of military-age men leave Macedonia is clear. The impact of this is hard to quantify, and male fertility is not necessarily the

Alexander captured the imagination of later writers and artists, and his legend evolved
far beyond his historical exploits. Here, in an illustration of the Iranian epic poem the
Shahnameh, Alexander is shown marching on Andalusia in southern Spain. The poem
was written by Ferdowsi from the late 10th to the early 11th century, but this copy dates
to the Safavid era (1501–1736).

dominant factor in societal birth rates, but Bosworth obviously has a point: removing thousands of elite soldiers inevitably leaves a kingdom less able to defend itself.

However, I am not sure that we should see this as resulting in the decline of Macedonia, which is ultimately a question of perspective. Macedonia was obviously a less significant political force under the Antigonids than it had been in 323 when Alexander controlled much of the known world. But was it weaker than in 359, when Philip came to power with the Illyrians threatening to run riot across the kingdom, or 336, when Macedonia controlled the Greek peninsula but had only a limited wider influence? The Antigonids dominated Greek affairs throughout the third century, and it was only with the rise of Rome that Macedonian power eventually dwindled. We might see Macedonian history in the century or so after Alexander's death as regression to the mean: Macedonia was a regional power, but not a world empire. In a sense, this magnifies the achievements of Alexander and Philip, who led their kingdom to new and, as it turned out, unsustainable heights.

At the same time, though, this might tarnish their legacy. Was there anything about Persia, Rome or any other imperial entity in terms of underlying manpower or resource base that meant they were better suited to exercising long-term hegemonic power than Macedonia? Or did the founders of these empires do a better job than Alexander of establishing an imperial system that could endure? We should remember that the descendants of the Successors continued to consider themselves part of a Macedonian dynasty, even if they had rarely, if ever, visited the land they regarded as home. So, if we speak of a Macedonia in decline after Alexander's death, we must be clear that we mean the territory in which he was born. Beyond that, Macedonians continued to reign supreme until new powers emerged.

Contested Legacies: Alexander Today

I had planned to close this book by sketching a rough outline of the way that Alexander's legacies developed in the millennia after his death. From the dual traditions in medieval Iran that we have seen something of, to the present day, with his symbolic role as the face of a debate between Greece and North Macedonia about whether the latter is entitled to include Alexander's homeland in its name (the core of the ancient kingdom lies within modern-day Greece, but at various points its boundaries extended across contemporary borders). In the end, there is not enough space to do justice to these topics, but Alexander evidently remains just as much of a touchstone for contemporary debate as he was for Roman-era writers like Arrian and Curtius.

One example gives a good illustration of this. In January 2024, Netflix released a new drama-documentary, *Alexander: The Making of a God*. Reviews were mixed, but coverage – and criticism – focused almost exclusively on depictions of the relationship between Alexander and Hephaestion.[20] I was struck by the disconnect between much of the public commentary and the views expressed by experts. This made me think about the role of history and historians in today's world. Like most drama-documentaries, *Alexander* is didactic and definitive. Historians appear as talking heads to add some context and blur the picture a little, but the series is presented as a conclusive account of Alexander's reign: this, the audience is told, is what happened. But imagine an alternative, where viewers are put in control with the experts as their guide. Scenes could be played through multiple times, with historical figures characterized in different ways. How do things look and feel if Clitus really was needling Alexander in the run-up to his death? What happens if your Alexander does become increasingly paranoid? How does that compare with a drunk or a daydreamer? A choose-your-own Alexander on the model of the old children's adventure series.

Rather than facts, obtuse and contested as they are, debate could take centre stage.

For this to work, historians must become more comfortable in making clear the difference between what we know and what we think. It also means stepping back a little from the lectern, democratizing discourse and giving audiences more scope to reach their own, well-informed, conclusions. I have tried to do something of that here, though inevitably this approach has its limits. If historians are to be upfront about the challenges we face when studying the past, what should we do when, as with Alexander, everything is problematic? Almost every detail that I have presented as a fact could be, and often has been, challenged. But dissecting every single issue is impossible in a book like this, and, inevitably, I have had to prioritize what I think matters most.

This statue overlooks the central square in Skopje, the capital of North Macedonia. Its presence reflects ongoing debates about who can claim Alexander as part of their history.

'Alexander Is Lowered into the Sea', folio from a Khamsa (Quintet) of Amir Khusrau Dihalvi, 1597–8. As Amir Khusrau told it, Alexander's campaign stretched as far as China and Russia. In this 16th-century illustration, Alexander is lowered into the sea in a diving bell. In the poem, an angel forewarns him of his death, but this imagery also plays on the image of Alexander as not only a conqueror, but an explorer.

For instance, I could have said more about Stateira, Darius' wife, but I chose instead to use Sisygambis as a means of thinking about how the Achaemenid royal family may have experienced their captivity. Some of my favourite figures did not make the final cut. How I wish I could have discussed Harpalus, a childhood friend of Alexander. Excused military service due to a disability, he was eventually made the treasurer in Babylon, only to abscond in 324 with a sizeable fortune and then die in mysterious circumstances after a failed attempt to rouse up Athens against Alexander. Occasionally, I have been able to point out and even justify omissions like these, but often I have not. More than that, historians must eventually do more than weigh up the sources or we would all end up saying the same thing: at some point, we must take a position on the issues that matter.

In that spirit, it seems worth closing by summarizing my own view of Alexander. Essentially, he was everything that people have said he was. He could be cruel and yet simultaneously magnanimous, visionary and delusional in equal measure. He was good and bad, a killer as well as a dreamer. But trying to discover the real Alexander is a waste of time. Beyond the obvious source problems, prioritizing character fundamentally misrepresents what makes history happen. Focusing on Alexander alone perpetuates the notion that individuals are the sole drivers of real historical change and risks justifying narratives of individual exceptionalism in the modern world as well as the ancient. If 'great men' are supposed to transcend their situation, the story that I have told shows that this is impossible in practice.

In my reading of events, Alexander could not extricate himself from his context. Parmenion, Antipater and the expectations foisted upon him as the heir of Philip pushed him to invade the Persian Empire, just as much as any desire for fame and glory on his own part. Once the campaign was underway, only total military victory could bring peace. Maybe Alexander genuinely did get his kicks from the thrill of a cavalry charge, but long-term security meant that the sort of limited war that historians sometimes imagine was envisaged by Philip – as much as a means of juxtaposing his supposedly more pragmatic character against Alexander's ambition – was inherently risky. Peace with Darius, perhaps after the Battle of Issus in 333, may have brought territory and a marriage alliance, but there was always the danger that the Persians would view this merely as breathing space while they prepared for war, and subsequent Achaemenids would always see any land surrendered to the Macedonians as part of their birthright. Capturing Iran meant it was perhaps always likely that Alexander would be drawn into Bactria, but it was Bessus' attempts to establish himself as the successor to Darius that made this inevitable. Taxiles and Porus then dragged him further east, and we have seen how influential preexisting relationships were on the shape of events in India. Then, when Alexander's own ambitions finally diverged from the aims of his men at the Hyphasis, he was stopped. In all of this, Alexander was reactive just as much as he was proactive.

There was brilliance – of course there was brilliance – and recklessness and folly too. The nature of his reign meant that Alexander faced challenges that only a few leaders in history have shared. He found resolutions to some, though not to others, but time and again these problems were posed, and their solutions proposed, by others. If Alexander ever had a master plan, it was never truly his alone. When we really think about the big historical picture, these factors matter much more than whether Alexander was a bit short-tempered after a few drinks. Do I think Alexander was great? Yes, I suppose I do – but only insofar as any one person can be great, and, really, that is not very great at all.

In the end, Alexander matters most because of what he came to represent. Describing the assault on the Malloi city in India, I used his name as a verb, and that is how his life has ultimately been remembered: Alexander Alexandering. Careering around Asia, choosing the heroic option when it was available, manufacturing it when it was not. Whether this is seen positively or negatively, the whole point of Alexander is that he Alexandered. But this is an illusion and a distraction, an image that tells us more about the people who have commentated on Alexander and their time than the man himself.

That's my Alexander – what's yours?

REFERENCES

Abbreviations

Greek literature and Latin literature are referenced in a different way to modern texts. They include book, chapter and, where appropriate, section numbers. This means that the relevant information can easily be found regardless of the edition/translation. The abbreviations used throughout these notes are listed below.

Ancient Authors

Ael. *VH.*	Aelian, *Varia Historia*
App. *Syr.*	Appian, *Syrian Wars*
Arist. *Pol.*	Aristotle, *Politics*
Arr. *Anab.*	Arrian, *Anabasis*
Arr. *Epict. diss.*	Arrian, *Epicteti dissertationes*
Arr. *Ind.*	Arrian, *Indica*
Ath.	Athenaeus, *Learned Banqueteers*
Curt.	Curtius, *The History of Alexander*
Diod.	Diodorus Siculus, *Library of History*
Hdt.	Herodotus, *Histories*
Just.	Justin, *Epitome of the Philippic History of Pompeius Trogus*
Plut. *Alex.*	Plutarch, *Life of Alexander*
Plut. *Artax.*	Plutarch, *Life of Artaxerxes*
Plut. *Demetr.*	Plutarch, *Life of Demetrius*
Plut. *Eum.*	Plutarch, *Life of Eumenes*
Plut. *Lys.*	Plutarch, *Life of Lysander*
Plut. *Mor.*	Plutarch, *Moralia*
Plut. *Pel.*	Plutarch, *Life of Pelopidas*
Strabo	Strabo, *Geography*
Thuc.	Thucydides, *History of the Peloponnesian War*
Xen. *An.*	Xenophon, *Anabasis*
Xen. *Cyr.*	Xenophon, *Cyropaedia*
Xen. *Symp.*	Xenophon, *Symposium*

Other Abbreviations

AD	A. Sachs and H. Hunger, *Astronomical Diaries and Related Texts from Babylonia*, 7 vols (Vienna, 1988–2022)
BM	British Museum
FGrH	F. Jacoby, *Fragmente der griechischen Historiker* (1923–)

Introduction

1 This sketch of characterizations of Alexander is drawn from a huge range of scholarly treatments. See particularly the works of the following, listed in the Bibliography: Ernst Badian, Albert (Brian) Bosworth, Pierre Briant, Elizabeth Carney, Paul Cartledge, Hans-Joachim Gehrke, Peter Green, Nicholas Hammond, Robin Lane Fox, Sabine Müller, John O'Brien, Fritz Schachermeyr, William Woodthorpe Tarn and Ian Worthington. The wealth of material on Alexander means that citations are potentially limitless. Consequently, I have used notes rather sparingly and generally cited only works written in English and which readers are likely to find accessible.

1 Macedonia and Greece, 356–334

1 Plut. *Alex.* 3.3–5.

2 Ibid. 6.

3 Plut. *Demetr.* 1.5–8.

4 Plut. *Alex.* 1.1–3.

5 Diodorus, Books 15 and 16 contain most of the key historical details for Philip's reign, but other sources provide supplementary details; most important are speeches by Philip's Athenian contemporaries, like Demosthenes and Aeschines. On Philip's reign, see, for example, Edward Anson, *Philip II, the Father of Alexander the Great: Themes and Issues* (London, 2020), and Ian Worthington, *Philip II of Macedonia* (New Haven, CT, 2008).

6 Thuc. 2.49.1–3.

7 Diod. 16.2.4–5.

8 Ibid. 16.4.7.

9 Mary Beard, 'Alexander: How Great?', *New York Review of Books*, LVIII/16 (27 October 2011).

10 Diod. 16.86.1–4.

11 Accessible discussions of the Persian Empire include Lloyd Llewellyn-Jones, *Persians: The Age of the Great Kings* (London, 2022), and Matt Waters, *Ancient Persia: A Concise History of the Achaemenid Empire, 550–330 BCE* (New York, 2014). The most important scholarly synthesis remains Pierre Briant, *From Cyrus to Alexander: A History of the Persian Empire* (Winona Lake, IN, 2002).

12 The most important Achaemenid inscriptions, and much other related evidence, are collected in Amélie Kuhrt, *The Persian Empire: A Corpus of Sources from the Achaemenid Period* (London and New York, 2007). Achaemenid inscriptions are referenced using the following convention. The first letter refers to the king in whose name the inscription was written (D = Darius I, X = Xerxes I, etc.); the second letter indicates where the

inscription was put up (P = Persepolis, S = Susa, etc.); and the final letter
to the specific inscription. Any numbers that follow refer to particular
paragraphs of the inscription.

13 Herodotus is the key source for the information that follows.
14 Aeschylus' *Persians* is perhaps the archetypal demonstration of this. See
   Edith Hall, *Inventing the Barbarian: Greek Self-Definition through Tragedy*
   (Oxford, 1989).
15 Hdt. 5.21.
16 Ibid. 8.136, 140–44.
17 Ibid. 9.44–5.
18 Ibid. 5.17–21.
19 Edward Said, *Orientalism* (Harmondsworth, 1978). For a succinct sense of
   the Achaemenid Workshop's central thesis, see the introduction by Heleen
   Sancisi-Weerdenburg and Amélie Kuhrt to their edited volume, *The Greek
   Sources: Proceedings of the Groningen 1984 Achaemenid History Workshop*
   (Leiden, 1987), esp. pp. ix–x.
20 Peter Rhodes and Robin Osborne, *Greek Historical Inscriptions, 404–323 BC*
   (Oxford, 2003), no. 76.
21 Diod. 16.89.
22 Ibid. 16.91.2.
23 The events are described by Diodorus (Diod. 16.91.4–95).
24 Plut. *Alex.* 10.4. Ernst Badian is perhaps the strongest modern proponent
   of this view: see 'The Death of Philip II', *Phoenix*, XVII (1963), pp. 244–50,
   and 'Conspiracies', in *Alexander the Great in Fact and Fiction,* ed. Albert
   Bosworth and Elizabeth Baynham (Oxford, 2000), pp. 50–95 (p. 54).
25 Plut. *Alex.* 9.4–5.
26 Ibid. 9.1–2.
27 The evidence for the aftermath of Philip's assassination is piecemeal and
   includes Arr. *Anab.* 1.25.1–2; Diod. 17.1–5.2; Plut. *Alex.* 10; Curt. 7.1.3–6;
   Just. 11.1–2, 5.1–2.
28 Pausanias, *Descriptions of Greece* 8.7.7.
29 The narrative here is based on Arr. *Anab.* 1.1.4–1.6.11.
30 Ibid. 1.7.1–1.9.10.
31 Ibid. Pref. 3.
32 Ibid. 1.12.1–5.
33 Ibid. Pref. 1–2.
34 Brian Bosworth's work was key to the re-evaluation of Arrian, especially
   A Historical Commentary on Arrian's History of Alexander, 2 vols (Oxford,
   1980–95), and *From Arrian to Alexander: Studies in Historical Interpretation*
   (Oxford, 1988).
35 Diod. 17.8–14. Just. 11.3–4 gives another slightly different version.
36 See Luisa Prandi, 'New Evidence for the Dating of Cleitarchus (*Poxy* LXXXI.
   4808)?', *Histos*, VI (2012), pp. 15–26.

2 Asia Minor, the Levant and Egypt, 334–331

1 Diod. 17.17.2; Just. 11.5.10.
2 Arr. *Anab.* 1.11.7–12.1; Just. 11.5.12.
3 Arr. *Anab.* 1.13.2.

4 Diod. 17.19.1–3.

5 To be fully transparent: I put some key points (based on Arrian's account) into ChatGPT and asked for a 'lively' paragraph. I rendered a few versions and mixed between them to produce the final text: so, this is not entirely AI-generated, but none of the words are my own.

6 Joseph Pietrykowski, *Great Battles of the Hellenistic World* (Barnsley, 2009), pp. 54–5.

7 Arr. *Anab.* 1.17.1–2.3.4.

8 Ibid. 2.3.7–8; Just. 11.7.4–16.

9 Pierre Briant, *From Cyrus to Alexander: A History of the Persian Empire* (Winona Lake, IN, 2002), pp. 769–80, on Darius III's rise to power. For a detailed treatment of Darius, see Pierre Briant, *Darius in the Shadow of Alexander* (Cambridge, MA, 2015).

10 Arr. *Anab.* 3.22.6; Diod. 17.5.3–6.3.

11 BM 40623, Albert Grayson, *Babylonian Historical-Literary Texts* (Toronto, 1975), no. 3 iii. 4–8.

12 Diod. 17.6.1–2; Just. 10.3.3–6.

13 Description of troop movements after Arr. *Anab.* 2.4.1–2.8.4.

14 Ibid. 2.4.7–11; Plut. *Alex.* 19.2–5; Curt. 3.6.1; Just. 11.8.3–9.

15 The main sources for the battle are Arr. *Anab.* 2.8–11; Plut. *Alex.* 20; Curt. 3.9–11; Diod. 17.33–5; Just. 11.9.

16 Arr. *Anab.* 2.11.8–9.

17 See Briant, *Darius*, esp. pp. 425–48.

18 For example, Herodotus (8.90) describes Xerxes watching the Battle of Salamis from a nearby hill. Xenophon (*An.* 1.8.22–3) suggests Persian kings habitually occupied the centre as it was considered the safest place and best for communicating with troops.

19 The sources for what follows are Arr. *Anab.* 2.11.9–2.12.8; Curt. 3.12; Diod. 17.37.3–38.6; Plut. *Alex.* 21; Just. 11.9.11–16.

20 Plut. *Alex.* 30.1; Just. 11.12.6. Curtius (4.10.18–34) claims Alexander had seen her only on the day she was captured and that she died from exhaustion.

21 On 'everyday resistance', see especially James C. Scott, *Weapons of the Weak: Everyday Forms of Peasant Resistance* (New Haven, CT, 1985); 'Everyday Forms of Resistance', *Copenhagen Papers*, IV (1989), pp. 33–62; and *Domination and the Arts of Resistance: Hidden Transcripts* (New Haven, CT, 1990).

22 Arr. *Anab.* 3.17.6.

23 Ibid. 2.14.1–9; Curt. 4.1.7–14; Just. 11.12.1–5.

24 The following narrative is based on Arr. *Anab.* 2.16–24; Curt. 4.2–4; Diod. 17.40–46; Just. 11.10.10–14.

25 Arr. *Anab.* 2.16.7.

26 The details differ from source to source. Arrian does not mention the crucifixion of prisoners, which might lead us to suspect that the more brutal details have been suppressed, but it is he who suggests 30,000 people were enslaved, whereas Diodorus gives 13,000.

27 Arr. *Anab.* 2.25.1–3; Curt. 4.5.1–9 – he places Alexander's rebuke of Parmenion later at 4.11.

28 Arr. *Anab.* 2.27.1–7.

29 Curt. 4.6.26–9.

30 Arr. *Anab.* 3.1.1–2.2.
31 Diod. 17.49.2–51.
32 Curt. 4.7.
33 Just. 11.11.6.
34 Plut. *Alex.* 27.5.
35 Arr. *Anab.* 3.3.1–4.5.
36 Ian Worthington, *Alexander the Great: Man and God* (Harlow, 2004), p. 279.
37 Strabo 17.1.43.
38 Strabo does refer to Aristoboulos (e.g., 11.7.3, 11.11.5, 14.5.9, 15.1.45, 15.1.61–2, 15.3.7) but mainly for episodes and places situated in the second half of Alexander's reign. This suggests that his description of Siwah is based exclusively on Callisthenes, and that Aristoboulos drew on this too.
39 Thuc. 5.11.1.
40 Plut. *Lys.* 18.3–4 = Duris of Samos, *FGrH* 76 F71.

3 Mesopotamia and Iran, 331–330

1 Arr. *Anab.* 3.6.1–3.8; Plut. *Alex.* 31–4.
2 My account of the battle follows Arr. *Anab.* 3.8.7–3.15.7, cross-referenced against Diod. 17.56–61; Curt. 4.12–16; Plut. *Alex.* 31–3; Just. 11.13–14.7.
3 Plut. *Alex.* 33.1–2.
4 Arr. *Anab.* 3.16.3–5; Curt. 5.1.17–23.
5 AD-204 C rev. l.10; AD–381 A obv. l.7.
6 AD-330 obv. l.15.
7 AD-330 rev. ll.3–14.
8 For a useful summary of Mazaeus' career, see Ernst Badian, 'Mazaeus', *Encyclopaedia Iranica*, https://iranicaonline.org, 21 April 2015.
9 Arr. *Anab.* 3.16.4–5.
10 Ibid. 3.16.6–9.
11 Ibid. 3.18.2–9.
12 Diod. 17.68.5–7; Curt. 5.4.3–34.
13 Diod. 17.69.1–2; Curt. 5.5.2–3.
14 Diod. 17.70–71; Curt. 5.6.
15 Curt. 5.7; Diod. 17.72.
16 Arr. *Anab.* 3.18.10–12.
17 Ibid. 5.7.1–5.
18 Cleitarchus *FGrH* 137 F11 = Ath. 13.576d-e; Plut. *Alex.* 38.1; *SIG* I 314.
19 Arr. *Anab.* 6.30.1; Curt. 5.7.11.
20 Albert Bosworth, *Conquest and Empire: The Reign of Alexander the Great* (Cambridge, 1988), p. 92, after Erich Schmidt, *Persepolis I: Structures, Reliefs, Inscriptions* (Chicago, IL, 1953), p. 179; Eugene Borza, 'Alexander at Persepolis', in *The Landmark Arrian: The Campaigns of Alexander*, ed. J. Romm (New York, 2010), pp. 367–70 (pp. 367–8).
21 Overall consensus, Pierre Briant, *From Cyrus to Alexander: A History of the Persian Empire* (Winona Lake, IN, 2002), p. 851. On the significance of the removal of the treasure for Alexander's intentions, Eugene Borza, 'Fire from Heaven: Alexander at Persepolis', *Classical Philology*, LXVII/4 (1972), pp. 233–45 (p. 243); Bosworth, *Conquest and Empire*, p. 93. For

scholars accepting the Vulgate's story, see for example, Edmund Bloedow and Heather Loube, 'Alexander the Great "Under Fire" at Persepolis', *Klio*, LXXIX/2 (1997), pp. 341–53 (p. 352); Bosworth, *Conquest and Empire*, p. 93; Robin Lane Fox, *Alexander the Great*, revd edn (London, 2004), pp. 261–4; John O'Brien, *Alexander the Great: The Invisible Enemy* (London and New York, 1992), p. 105; Hans-Joachim Gehrke, *Alexander der Grosse* (Munich, 1996), p. 60. See also Julian Degen, *Alexander III. zwischen Ost und West. Indigene Traditionen und Herrschaftsinszenierung im makedonischen Weltimperium* (Stuttgart, 2022), pp. 178–201. The Greek audience is foregrounded by Ernst Badian, 'Agis III', *Hermes*, XXIII (1967), pp. 170–92 (pp. 186–90), and 'Alexander in Iran', in *Cambridge History of Iran*, vol. II: *The Median and Achaemenian Periods*, ed. I. Gershevitch (Cambridge, 1985), pp. 420–501. The Persian audience is stressed by Heleen Sancisi-Weerdenburg, 'Alexander and Persepolis', in *Alexander the Great: Reality and Myth*, ed. J. Carlsen et al. (Rome, 1993), pp. 177–88; Borza, 'Fire from Heaven'; Briant, *Cyrus to Alexander*, p. 852; and Pierre Briant, *Alexander the Great and His Empire: A Short Introduction* (Princeton, NJ, 2010), p. 110.

22 Diod. 17.62–3. See also Curt. 6.1. on the Battle of Megalopolis.

23 Sancisi-Weerdenburg, 'Alexander and Persepolis', pp. 181–2.

24 This is true throughout Alexander's campaign, as Degen stresses: see *Alexander III*, pp. 156, 190, 324, for example.

25 See Stephen Harrison, *Kingship and Empire under the Achaemenids, Alexander the Great and the Early Seleucids* (Edinburgh, forthcoming), ch. 1.

26 XPa §4, trans. Amélie Kuhrt, *The Persian Empire: A Corpus of Sources from the Achaemenid Period* (London and New York, 2007), p. 581. Other examples include A1Pa, A2Ha.

27 DPd §3, trans. ibid., p. 487.

28 *Ardā Wirāz Nāmag*, 1.1–9; see Fereydun Vahman, ed., *Ardā Wirāz Nāmag: The Iranian 'Divina Commedia'* (London, 1986), pp. 76–9 (text), p. 191 (translation).

29 *Bundahišn* 33.19; see Domenico Agostini and Samuel Thrope, *The Bundahišn: The Zoroastrian Book of Creation* (New York, 2020), p. 173. For critical Iranian portraits of Alexander, see Josef Wiesehöfer, 'The "Accursed" and the "Adventurer": Alexander the Great in Iranian Tradition', in *A Companion to Alexander Literature in the Middle Ages*, ed. Z. David Zuwiyya (Leiden, 2011), pp. 113–32 (pp. 124–8); Pierre Briant, *Darius in the Shadow of Alexander* (Cambridge, MA, 2015), pp. 366–70. More generally, see Haila Manteghi, *Alexander the Great in the Persian Tradition: History, Myth and Legend in Medieval Iran* (London, 2018).

30 O'Brien, *Invisible Enemy*, p. 105; Briant, *Alexander*, p. 108 n. 20 warns against exaggerations like O'Brien's.

31 Examples of defectors include Bisthanes (Arr. *Anab.* 3.19.4, 3.20.2), Bagistanes and Antibelos (Arr. *Anab.* 3.21.1, but see Curt. 5.13.1).

32 The following narrative is based on Arr. *Anab.* 3.19–3.22.

33 Just. 11.15.5–15.

34 *Alexander Romance* (Greek), 2.20. For an accessible translation, see Richard Stoneman, *The Greek Alexander Romance* (London, 1991).

35 Arr. *Anab.* 3.22.1.

36 Plut. *Alex.* 45.1 dates this specifically to Alexander's arrival in Parthia in early autumn 330.

37 The most detailed descriptions of Alexander's clothing are found in Diodorus (17.77.5) and Plutarch (*Alex.* 45.1–2). Arrian (*Anab.* 4.7.4) claims that Alexander did wear the tiara, but this is part of a description of Alexander's moral decline where the tiara has a symbolic effect, so this is likely Arrian's own insertion. Ephippus (*FGrH* 126 F5 = Ath. 537e–f) discusses Alexander's later clothing; his account is hostile, but there are useful details here.

38 Xen. *Cyr.* 8.3.13 for the claim that only the king wore this garment.

39 Greeks used a variety of terms for this headgear (tiara, *kurbasia*, *kidaris*) and their various meanings are contested; see, for example, Christopher Tuplin, 'Treacherous Hearts and Upright Tiaras: The Achaemenid King's Head-Dress', in *Persian Responses: Political and Cultural Interaction with(in) the Achaemenid Empire*, ed. Christopher Tuplin (Swansea, 2007), pp. 67–98; Nicholas Sekunda, 'Changes in Achaemenid Royal Dress', in *The World of Achaemenid Persia: History, Art and Society in Iran and the Ancient Near East*, ed. John Curtis and St. John Simpson (London, 2010), pp. 255–72 (p. 256); Lloyd Llewellyn-Jones, *King and Court in Ancient Persia 559 to 331 BCE* (Edinburgh, 2013), p. 61. What really matters is that this item was either unique to the king or worn in a way that was distinctive.

40 For instance, Albert Bosworth, 'Alexander and the Iranians', *Journal of Hellenic Studies*, C (1980), pp. 1–21 (pp. 4–10), sees a 'limited experiment' (p. 7) that gradually became more permanent. Historians also emphasize that Alexander's dress was a compromise, which still had potential to upset Macedonians: Paul Cartledge, *Alexander the Great: The Hunt for a New Past* (London, 2004), pp. 201–2; Peter Green, *Alexander of Macedon: A Historical Biography*, 2nd edn (Harmondsworth, 1974), pp. 333–5; Sabine Müller, *Alexander der Grosse: Eroberung, Politik, Rezeption* (Stuttgart, 2019), pp. 165–7; and Ian Worthington, *Alexander the Great: Man and God* (Harlow, 2004), pp. 160, 251.

41 I outline the arguments on this point more fully in Harrison, *Kingship and Empire*, Chapter One.

42 Xen. *Cyr.* 8.3.13.

43 Curt. 6.6.4 suggests this possibility for Alexander's diadem.

44 Curt. 6.7–7.2; Diod. 17.79–80; Plut. *Alex.* 48–49 calls the initial conspirator Limnus; Arr. *Anab.* 3.26–3.27.

45 Ernst Badian, 'The Death of Parmenio', *Transactions and Proceedings of the American Philological Association*, XCI (1960), pp. 324–38; 'Conspiracies', in *Alexander the Great in Fact and Fiction*, ed. Albert Bosworth and Elizabeth Baynham (Oxford, 2000), pp. 50–95 (pp. 64–9).

46 This has been stressed especially by, among others, Waldemar Heckel. See his 'The Conspiracy Against Philotas', *Phoenix*, XXXI/1 (1977), pp. 9–21; *The Marshals of Alexander's Empire*, 2nd edn (London, 2016) pp. 58–9; 'King and "Companions": Observations on the Nature of Power in the Reign of Alexander', in *Brill's Companion to Alexander the Great*, ed. Joseph Roisman (Leiden, 2003), pp. 197–226 (pp. 216–19).

References

4 Bactria and Sogdiana, 330–327

1 Arr. *Anab.* 3.29.6–30.5.
2 Ibid. 4.7.3.
3 DB §32–33.
4 See Joseph Naveh and Shaul Shaked, *Aramaic Documents from Ancient Bactria from the Khalili Collections* (London, 2012), with discussion of the archive's collection, provenance and publication in the introduction, esp. pp. 15–18.
5 Ibid. C1 (Khalili IA 21), with dating discussed pp. 19, 259.
6 Ibid. C4 (Khalili IA 17).
7 Arr. *Anab.* 4.1.1–3, 4.15.1–5.
8 Ibid. 4.3.6–4.5.1, 4.15.1–5.
9 Ibid. 4.18.4–4.19.4; Curt. 7.11.
10 Arr. *Anab.* 4.5.6–4.6.2.
11 Ibid. 4.17.3; Curt. 8.1.19.
12 Arr. *Anab.* 4.8.1–4.9.7; Curt. 8.1.19–8.2.13; Plut. *Alex.* 50–52; Just. 12.6.
13 Arr. *Anab.* 4.8.9.
14 Ibid. 4.8.5, 4.9.1.
15 Curt. 8.1.49–52.
16 Arr. *Anab.* 4.9.2–8; Curt. 8.2.1–12.
17 Arr. *Anab.* 4.17.3–7.
18 The following events are described by Arr. *Anab.* 4.18.4–4.20.4; Curt. 8.4.21–30; Strabo 11.11.4.
19 Arr. *Anab.* 4.19.5–6; Plut. *Alex.* 47.4; Plut. *Mor.* 332f.
20 For instance, Albert Bosworth, *Conquest and Empire: The Reign of Alexander the Great* (Cambridge, 1988), p. 117; Hans-Joachim Gehrke, *Alexander der Grosse* (Munich, 1996), p. 71; Elizabeth Carney, 'Women in Alexander's Court', in *Brill's Companion to Alexander the Great*, ed. Joseph Roisman (Leiden, 2003), pp. 227–52 (p. 245); Waldemar Heckel, *Who's Who in the Age of Alexander the Great: Prosopography of Alexander's Empire* (Oxford, 2006), p. 242; Pierre Briant, *Darius in the Shadow of Alexander* (Cambridge, MA, 2015), p. 343; Sabine Müller, *Alexander der Grosse: Eroberung, Politik, Rezeption* (Stuttgart, 2019), pp. 175–6; Waldemar Heckel, *In the Path of Conquest: Resistance to Alexander the Great* (New York, 2020), pp. 193, 199–200; Julian Degen, *Alexander III. zwischen Ost und West. Indigene Traditionen und Herrschaftsinszenierung im makedonischen Weltimperium* (Stuttgart, 2022), pp. 317, 403–4.
21 Elizabeth Baynham, 'Alexander and the Amazons', *Classical Quarterly*, LI/1 (2001), pp. 115–26 (p. 125); Elizabeth Carney, 'Alexander and Persian Women', *American Journal of Philology*, CXVII/4 (1996), pp. 563–83 (p. 576); Paul Cartledge, *Alexander the Great: The Hunt for a New Past* (London, 2004), pp. 125, 283–4.
22 Arr. *Anab.* 4.21, 6.15.3; Curt. 8.2.19–35. Curtius (8.8.9) suggests Oxyartes was accused of mismanaging his satrapy and acquitted only after a trial; it seems unlikely that other sources would ignore something like this involving Alexander's father-in-law.
23 Diod. 19.48.2.
24 Arr. *Anab.* 4.15.1–4; Curt. 8.1.9.

25 Arr. *Anab.* 2.25.1; Curt. 4.5.1, 4.11.5; Diod. 17.54.2; Just. 11.12.10; Plut. *Alex.* 29.7.
26 *Metz. Epit.* 28–31.
27 Albert Bosworth, *A Historical Commentary on Arrian's History of Alexander*, vol. II: *Commentary on Books IV–V* (Oxford, 1995), p. 135; Heckel, *In the Path of Conquest*, pp. 198–9.
28 On these source problems, see Bosworth, *Commentary*, vol. II, pp. 124–34.
29 Ancient accounts: Arr. *Anab.* 4.9.9–4.12.6; Curt. 8.5.5–22.
30 Hdt. 1.134.1.
31 Examples include Xen. *An.* 1.8.21; Plut. *Artax.* 13.2; Hdt. 3.86.
32 Plut. *Artax.* 22.4; Ael. *VH.* 1.21.
33 Hdt. 7.136.
34 Sophocles, *Electra* 1374. Other examples include: Aeschylus, *Prometheus Vinctus* 936; Sophocles, *Philoctetes* 657, *Oedipus Coloneus* 1654; Aristophanes, *Plutus* 771.
35 Xen. *An.* 3.2.9.
36 Hugh Bowden, 'On Kissing and Making Up: Court Protocol and Historiography in Alexander the Great's "Experiment with Proskynesis"', *Bulletin of the Institute of Classical Studies*, LVI/2 (2013), pp. 55–78 (p. 59); Chiara Matarese, 'Proskynēsis and the Gesture of the Kiss at Alexander's Court: The Creation of a New Élite', *Palamedes*, VIII (2013), pp. 75–85; Chiara Matarese, 'Sending a Kiss to the King: The Achaemenid *Proskynēsis* between Explanations and Misunderstandings', *The Ancient World*, LXV/2 (2014), pp. 122–33; Christopher Tuplin, 'The Great King, His God(s) and Intimations of Divinity: The Achaemenid Hinterland of Ruler Cult?', *Ancient History Bulletin*, XXXI (2017), pp. 92–111.
37 Arr. *Anab.* 4.9.9–4.12.2; Curt. 8.5.5–24.
38 Curt. 8.5.22–24, though he names Polyperchon as the Macedonian involved.
39 Arr. *Anab.* 7.29.3.
40 Important voices on this include Bosworth, *Conquest and Empire*, p. 287; Albert Bosworth, *Alexander and the East: The Tragedy of Triumph* (Oxford, 1996), pp. 109–12; Ernst Fredricksmeyer, 'Alexander's Religion and Divinity', in *Brill's Companion to Alexander the Great*, ed. Roisman, pp. 253–78 (p. 275); Ian Worthington, *Alexander the Great: Man and God* (Harlow, 2004), p. 280.
41 For example, Worthington, *Alexander the Great*, p. 280.
42 Arr. *Anab.* 4.12.3–5; Plut. *Alex.* 54.3.
43 Bowden, 'On Kissing'.
44 Lara O'Sullivan, 'Reinventing *Proskynesis*: Callisthenes and the Peripatetic School', *Historia*, LXIX/3 (2020), pp. 260–82.
45 For example, John Balsdon, 'The "Divinity" of Alexander', *Historia*, I/3 (1950), pp. 363–88 (pp. 371–82); J. R. Hamilton, *Plutarch Alexander: A Commentary* (Oxford, 1969), pp. 150–52; Anthony Spawforth, 'The Court of Alexander the Great between Europe and Asia', in *The Court and Court Society in Ancient Monarchies*, ed. Spawforth (Cambridge, 2007), pp. 82–120 (p. 104); Matarese, 'The Kiss at Alexander's Court', esp. pp. 81–3; Frances Pownall, 'Callisthenes in Africa: The Historian's Role at Siwah and in the *Proskynesis* Controversy', in *Alexander in Africa*, ed. Philip Bosman (Pretoria, 2014), pp. 56–71 (pp. 55–6, 67–8).
46 The following account is based on Arr. *Anab.* 4.13.1–4.14.4; Curt. 8.6–8.

47 Curt. 8.6.8–10.

48 Arr. *Anab.* 4.14.3–4.

49 Plut. *Alex.* 55.5; Just. 15.3.3–9. Curtius (8.8.21) also claims Callisthenes died during torture.

50 See Cartledge, *Alexander the Great*, pp. 287–9.

51 Ath. 1.18a. For the importance of situating this episode within these cultural traditions, see Pierre Briant, 'Sources gréco-hellenistiques, institutions perses et institutions macédoniens: continuités, changements et bricolages', in *Achaemenid History VIII: Continuity and Change*, ed. Heleen Sancisi-Weerdenburg, Amélie Kuhrt and Margaret Root (Leiden, 1994), pp. 283–310 (pp. 305–7); Elias Koulakiotis, 'Domination et resistance à la cour d'Alexandre: Le cas des basilikoi paides', in *Esclavage Antique et Discriminations Socio-Culturelles*, ed. Vasilis Anastasiadis and Panagiotis Doukellis (Bern, 2005), pp. 167–82 (p. 176).

52 Ctesias *FGrH* 688 F14 = Photius, p. 40a5–41b37 §43. On the parallel between these two incidents, see Pierre Briant, 'Chasses royales macédoniennes et chasses royales perses: le theme de la chasse au lion sur la chasse de Vergina', *Dialogues d'histoire ancienne*, XVII (1991), pp. 211–55 (pp. 217–18); Briant, 'Sources gréco-hellenistiques', pp. 303–4; Elizabeth Carney, 'Hunting and the Macedonian Elite: Sharing the Rivalry of the Chase (Arrian 4.13.1)', in *The Hellenistic World: New Perspectives*, ed. Daniel Ogden (Swansea, 2002), pp. 59–80 (pp. 63–4); Eran Almagor, 'Hunting and Leisure Activities', in *A Companion to the Achaemenid Empire*, ed. Bruno Jacobs and Robert Rollinger, 2 vols (Hoboken, NJ, 2021), pp. 1107–20 (pp. 1114–15). Sabine Müller is sceptical: 'In the Shadow of His Father: Alexander, Hermolaus, and the Legend of Philip', in *Philip II and Alexander the Great: Father and Son, Lives and Afterlives*, ed. Elizabeth Carney and Daniel Ogden (Oxford 2010), pp. 25–32 (p. 28).

53 Carney, 'Hunting', p. 64. See further Stephen Harrison, *Kingship and Empire under the Achaemenids, Alexander the Great and the Early Seleucids* (Edinburgh, forthcoming), ch. 5.

5 India, 327–325

1 Hdt. 3.98–105.

2 Arr. *Anab.* 5.1.1–5.3.4; Just. 12.7.6–8.

3 See Julian Degen, *Alexander III. zwischen Ost und West. Indigene Traditionen und Herrschaftsinszenierung im makedonischen Weltimperium* (Stuttgart, 2022), pp. 382–402.

4 Arr. *Anab.* 7.1.5–3.4; Plut. *Alex.* 64–5.

5 The work of Brian Bosworth was key to this, especially *Alexander and the East: The Tragedy of Triumph* (Oxford, 1996).

6 Diod. 17.86.4.

7 Arr. *Anab.* 4.22.8. For more detailed discussion of Alexander in India, see Stephen Harrison, 'Alexander in Bactria and India, and the Spanish in America: Agency and Interaction on the Fringes of Empire', in *Theorising Comparative History for the Ancient Mediterranean: Asking New Questions of Old Evidence*, ed. Dylan James and Stephen Harrison (Liverpool, forthcoming).

8 Arr. *Anab.* 5.8.4–5.
9 Description of the pre-battle movements after Arr. Anab. 5.9–14; Curt. 8.13.
10 See Arr. *Anab.* 5.9.3.
11 Ibid. 5.14.3–6.
12 Ibid. 5.15.4. The battle narrative is based on Arr. *Anab.* 5.13.3–5.19.3; Curt. 8.14; Diod. 17.87–9.
13 Arrian (*Anab.* 3.8.6) suggests that Darius had elephants at Gaugamela, but they do not appear to have played a part in the fighting and their presence may be an error.
14 Arrian says Coenus was sent 'to the right' (5.16.23) but does not specify whether that means to Alexander's or Porus' right, so the precise movements have been debated.
15 Arr. *Anab.* 5.18.2.
16 Curt. 8.14.31–3.
17 Pierre Briant, *Darius in the Shadow of Alexander* (Cambridge, MA, 2015).
18 Arr. *Anab.* 5.18.4–5.
19 The narrative here follows Arr. *Anab.* 5.18.6–5.19.3; Curt. 8.14.35–46; Plut. *Alex.* 60.6–8.
20 Curt. 8.14.35–37 has Alexander send Taxiles' brother, but the effect is the same.
21 Arr. *Anab.* 5.19.1–3, Plut. *Alex.* 60.8.
22 Arr. *Anab.* 5.21.1–3.
23 Ibid. 5.22–5.24.
24 Ibid. 5.25.3–5.26.8.
25 Ibid. 7.1.4.
26 Ibid. 5.28.4
27 Ibid. 5.29.1–2; Curt. 9.3.19.
28 Degen, *Alexander III*, pp. 332–74.
29 Hdt. 4.87.
30 Discussion of the campaign against the Malloi after Arr. *Anab.* 6.4.3–6.11.8; Curt. 9.4.15–9.5.30; Diod. 17.98–9.
31 Curt. 9.5.20.
32 Arr. *Anab.* 6.13.1–3; Curt. 9.6.1–2.
33 Arr. *Anab.* 6.13.4.
34 Ibid. 6.15.5–6.17.3.
35 Diod. 17.102.6.
36 Curt. 9.8.15; Diod. 17.102.6.
37 Arr. *Anab.* 6.17.2–18.5.
38 See Dylan James, 'Nearchus, Guides, and Place Names on Alexander's Expedition', *Mnemosyne*, LXXIII/4 (2020), pp. 553–76.
39 Arr. *Anab.* 6.19.4–5, Arr. *Ind.* 20.10 where Nearchus is named as the source.
40 This voyage is described at length in Arrian's *Indica*, based on Nearchus' own account.
41 For discussions of the ideology described here, see Mario Liverani, *Prestige and Interest: International Relations in the Near East, ca. 1600–1100 BC* (Padua, 1990), pp. 48–50, and Robert Rollinger and Julian Degen, 'Alexander the Great, the Indian Ocean, and the Borders of the World', in *Achemenet. Vingt ans après: Études offertes à Pierre Briant à l'occasion des vingt ans du Programme Achemenet*, ed. Damien Agut-Labordère et al. (Leuven, Paris

and Bristol, CT, 2021), pp. 321–42. My own ideas are described in Stephen Harrison, *Kingship and Empire under the Achaemenids, Alexander the Great and the Early Seleucids* (Edinburgh, forthcoming), ch. 3.

6 Persia, 325–324

1 Arr. *Anab*. Pref. 3.
2 I cannot give a detailed history of the concept of 'fusion' here, but for a useful summary see Albert Bosworth, 'Alexander and the Iranians', *Journal of Hellenic Studies*, C (1980), pp. 1–2.
3 Arr. *Anab*. 6.24.1–6.26.5; Plut. *Alex*. 66.
4 Albert Bosworth, *Conquest and Empire: The Reign of Alexander the Great* (Cambridge, 1988), pp. 143–6.
5 Arr. *Anab*. 6.27.1, *Ind*. 23.5–8.
6 Arr. *Anab*. 6.27.3, Curt. 9.10.19, 10.1.9. Curtius names Ozines and Zariaspes, Arrian only Ordanes. These might be three separate people, or Curtius and Arrian may have confused the identity of Ozines/Ordanes; either way, the general point is clear.
7 For a list, see Ernst Badian, 'Conspiracies', in *Alexander the Great in Fact and Fiction*, ed. Albert Bosworth and Elizabeth Baynham (Oxford, 2000), pp. 50–95 (pp. 89–95).
8 Arr. *Anab*. 6.27.3–6; Curt. 10.1.1–8.
9 Ernst Badian, 'Harpalus', *Journal of Hellenic Studies*, LXXXI (1961), pp. 16–43, esp. pp. 16–25.
10 Arr. *Anab*. 6.29.1–2.
11 Curt. 10.1.22–38. He calls the satrap Orsines, but it is evidently the same person.
12 Arr. *Anab*. 6.29.3–11.
13 Bosworth, *Conquest and Empire*, p. 240; Maria Brosius, 'Alexander and the Persians', in *Brill's Companion to Alexander the Great*, ed. Joseph Roisman (Leiden, 2003), pp. 169–96 (p. 189); Badian, 'Conspiracies', p. 93.
14 Arr. *Anab*. 2.1.3.
15 Ibid. 6.28.3–4, 6.30.2–3.
16 For a detailed study of Achaemenid satraps, see Hilmar Klinkott, *Der Satrap: ein achaimenidischer Amtsträger und seine Handlungsspielräume* (Frankfurt, 2005). For the effects of satrapal competition, see Michael Weiskopf, *The So-Called 'Great Satraps' Revolt', 366–360 BC: Concerning Local Instability in the Achaemenid Far West* (Stuttgart, 1989).
17 Arr. *Anab*. 7.1.1–3.
18 Arrian calls Darius' daughter Barsine, but the other sources give her name as Stateira, which is usually preferred. Arr. *Anab*. 7.4.4; Diod. 17.107.6; Plut. *Alex*. 70.2. Curtius (10.3.11–12) does not describe the wedding but alludes to it.
19 See Elizabeth Carney, *Women and Monarchy in Ancient Macedonia* (Norman, OK, 2000), p. 112.
20 Curt. 4.5.1, 4.11.5, 4.11.20; Arr. *Anab*. 2.25.1–3.
21 Diod. 17.67.1. See Carney, *Women and Monarchy*, p. 109.
22 Arr. *Anab*. 6.29.3.
23 This point is stressed by Bosworth, 'Alexander and the Iranians', pp. 11–12; *Conquest and Empire*, pp. 156–7.

24 Plut. *Alex.* 77.4.

25 For the problems of assuming that the Susa marriages were abandoned, see David Engels and Kyle Erickson, 'Apama and Stratonike – Marriage and Legitimacy', in *Seleukid Royal Women: Creation, Representation and Distortion of Hellenistic Queenship in the Seleukid Empire*, ed. Altay Coşkun and Alex McAuley (Stuttgart, 2016), pp. 67–86 (p. 41).

26 Curt. 8.3.1–15.

27 Arr. *Anab.* 4.17.7. See Albert Bosworth, *A Historical Commentary on Arrian's History of Alexander*, vol. II: *Commentary on Books IV–V* (Oxford, 1995), p. 121.

28 For a balanced discussion of different interpretations of Seleucus' actions, see Engels and Erickson, 'Apama and Stratonike', pp. 41–5, and Ann-Catrin Harders, 'The Making of a Queen – Seleukos Nikator and His Wives', in *Seleukid Royal Women*, ed. Coşkun and McAuley, pp. 25–38 (pp. 31–3).

29 On Alexander's tents and their possible Persian origins, the evidence is usefully collected by Anthony Spawforth, 'The Court of Alexander the Great between Europe and Asia', in *The Court and Court Society in Ancient Monarchies*, ed. Spawforth (Cambridge, 2007), pp. 82–120 (pp. 112–18). Athen. 538b–539a = Chares FGrH 125 F4; Ael. VH. 8.7.

30 Jean Perrot, 'Restoration, Reconstruction', in *The Palace of Darius I at Susa: The Great Royal Residence of Achaemenid Persia*, ed. Jean Perrot (London, 2013), pp. 209–39 (p. 220).

31 For more detailed discussion, see Stephen Harrison, 'Changing Spaces, Changing Behaviours: Achaemenid Spatial Features at the Court of Alexander the Great', *Journal of Ancient History*, VI/2 (2018), pp. 185–214, esp. pp. 202–6.

32 Arr. *Anab.* 7.24.2. Athenaeus reports something similar but without specifying the location, Athen. 537d = Ephippus FGrH 126 F4.

33 Arr. *Anab.* 6.29.5.

34 Xen. *An.* 4.4.21.

35 For example, Ernst Fredricksmeyer, 'Alexander the Great and the Kingship of Asia', in *Alexander the Great in Fact and Fiction*, ed. Bosworth and Baynham, pp. 136–66 (pp. 165–6); Spawforth, 'Court of Alexander', pp. 99, 102, 109.

36 Arr. *Anab.* 7.6.1–2; Diod. 17.108.1–3; Curt. 8.5.1; Plut. *Alex.* 47.3, 71.1.

7 Iran and Babylonia, 324–323

1 Events are described by Arr. *Anab.* 7.8.1–3; Curt. 10.2.8–14; Diod. 17.108.3, 109.1–3; Just. 12.11.1–12.12.10.

2 For the speeches discussed here, Arr. *Anab.* 7.9.1–10.7; Curt. 10.2.15–29.

3 Simon Sebag Montefiore, *Voices of History: Speeches that Changed the World* (London, 2019), pp. 248–52.

4 Thuc. 1.22.1.

5 Arr. *Anab.* 7.11.4–7; Diod. 17.109.3. Curt. 10.3.1–14 includes a speech Alexander purportedly delivered to his Persian soldiers, but the text breaks off midway through and there is a large gap in what survives.

6 Xen. *Cyr.* 8.3.13. For discussion, see Pierre Briant, *From Cyrus to Alexander: A History of the Persian Empire* (Winona Lake, IN, 2002), pp. 309–10.

7 Plut. *Alex.* 54.3; Arr. *Anab.* 4.12.3–5.
8 Arr. *Anab.* 7.11.8–9.
9 William Woodthorpe Tarn, *Alexander the Great and the Unity of Mankind*
   (London, 1933); *Alexander the Great*, 2 vols (Cambridge, 1948), vol. II,
   pp. 399–451, esp. pp. 434–51.
10 Tarn, *Alexander*, vol. II, p. 442.
11 Ernst Badian, 'Alexander the Great and the Unity of Mankind', *Historia*, VII/4
   (1958), pp. 425–44 (p. 431).
12 Ernst Badian, 'Alexander the Great and the Loneliness of Power', *Journal
   of the Australasian Universities Language and Literature Association*, XVII/1
   (1962), pp. 80–91 (pp. 90–91).
13 Edward Carr, *What Is History?* (Harmondsworth, 1961), p. 23.
14 Biographical details after Frank Adcock, rev. K. Reynolds, 'Tarn, Sir
   William Woodthorpe', *Oxford Dictionary of National Biography* (2004,
   revd 2016). For a detailed discussion of how Tarn's background shaped his
   interpretations of Alexander and his historiographical practices, see Albert
   Bosworth, 'The Impossible Dream: W. W. Tarn's *Alexander* in Retrospect',
   Karanos, II (2019), pp. 77–95, first published in *Ancient Society: Resources for
   Teachers*, XIII (1983).
15 Tarn, *Alexander the Great*, vol. I, p. 148 n. 1.
16 Biographical details after William Harris, 'Badian, Ernst, 1925–2011',
   Biographical Memoirs of Fellows of the British Academy XVI,
   www.thebritishacademy.ac.uk, 25 April 2017.
17 Badian, 'Loneliness', p. 87. See also, his 'Harpalus', *Journal of Hellenic Studies*,
   LXXXI (1961), pp. 16–43 (p. 20).
18 Arr. *Anab.* 6.2.1; Curt. 9.3.20. Indeed, Badian later rowed back on this
   somewhat, suggesting that Alexander was merely fortunate that Coenus
   died of disease so quickly after opposing the king; see Ernst Badian,
   'Conspiracies', in *Alexander the Great in Fact and Fiction,* ed. Albert
   Bosworth and Elizabeth Baynham (Oxford, 2000), pp. 50–95 (p. 74).
19 Badian, 'Conspiracies', p. 52.
20 Ibid., p. 51, reiterated p. 52.
21 For more detailed discussion, see Stephen Harrison, *Kingship and Empire
   under the Achaemenids, Alexander the Great and the Early Seleucids*
   (Edinburgh, forthcoming), chs 4 and 5.
22 Amos Rapoport, *The Meaning of the Built Environment: A Nonverbal
   Communication Approach* [1982] (Tucson, AZ, 1990), and 'Systems of
   Activities and Systems of Settings', in *Domestic Architecture and the Use of
   Space*, ed. Susan Kent (Cambridge), pp. 9–20.
23 The Achaemenids often presented the Persians as distinct from, and superior
   to, the other peoples in their empire. See Harrison, *Kingship and Empire*,
   chs 3 and 4.
24 Arr. *Anab.* 7.12.1–4.
25 Ibid. 7.4.8.
26 Ibid. 7.14; Plut. *Alex.* 72.3; Diod. 17.110.7–8, 17.114–115; Just. 12.12.11–12.
27 Heinz Luschey, 'Der Löwe von Ekbatana', *Archäologische Mitteilungen
   aus Iran*, I (1968), pp. 115–29; Robin Lane Fox, *Alexander the Great* [1973]
   (London, 2004), pp. 434–5; Paul McKechnie, 'Diodorus Siculus and
   Hephaestion's Pyre', *Classical Quarterly*, XLV (1995), pp. 418–32 (p. 430).

28 Curt. 3.12.16. This point has been stressed particularly by Sabine Müller, who has written extensively about Hephaestion's background and his relationship with Alexander, for example, *Alexander der Grosse: Eroberung, Politik, Rezeption* (Stuttgart, 2019), pp. 231–6; 'Hephaistion: A Re-Assessment of His Career', in *Ancient Macedonians in Greek and Roman Sources: From History to Historiography*, ed. Timothy Howe and Frances Pownall (Swansea, 2018), pp. 77–102 (pp. 91–2).

29 Müller, *Alexander*, pp. 231–2; 'Hephaistion', p. 78.

30 Arr. *Anab.* 7.4.5.

31 Ibid. 1.12.1–2.

32 Just. 12.12.11; Curt. 7.9.19.

33 Arr. *Epict. diss.* 2.22.17–18.

34 Arr. *Anab.* 1.12, 7.14.4–5, 7.16.8.

35 For treatments that set the relationship within its broader Graeco-Macedonian context, see Jeanne Reames, 'An Atypical Affair? Alexander the Great, Hephaistion Amyntoros and the Nature of Their Relationship', *Ancient History Bulletin*, XIII (1999), pp. 81–96; Daniel Ogden, 'Alexander's Sex Life', in *Alexander the Great: A New History*, ed. Waldemar Heckel and Lawrence Tritle (Oxford, 2009), pp. 203–17, esp. pp. 210–17; Borja Antela Bernárdez, 'El Alejandro homoerótico: homosexualidad en la Corte Macedonia', *Klio*, XCII (2010), pp. 331–43.

36 See Kenneth Dover, *Greek Homosexuality* (London, 1978).

37 Plut. *Pel.* 18; Plut. *Mor.* 618d, 761b; Xen. *Symp.* 8.32–5.

38 Diod. 14.37.6; Arist. *Pol.* 1311b. See also Pseudo-Plato, *Alcibiades II* 141c–141e; Ael. *VH* 8.9.

39 Plut. *Alex.* 21.4–5; Plut. *Eum.* 1.3; Just. 11.10.2–3.

40 Diod. 17.77.1.–3, Curt. 6.5.24–32. Detailed discussion by Elizabeth Baynham, 'Alexander and the Amazons', *Classical Quarterly*, LI/1 (2001), pp. 115–26.

41 Curt. 6.5.23, 10.1.29.

42 Plut. *Alex.* 46.3–4; Ath. 13.603a–c.

43 For Bagoas' historicity, see Ernst Badian, 'The Eunuch Bagoas', *Classical Quarterly*, VIII/3–4 (1958), pp. 144–57.

44 Details here after Arr. *Anab.* 7.15.1–7.23.4.

45 Diod. 18.8.3–5.

46 For example, Hyperides, *Against Demosthenes* 31.

8 Babylon and Beyond, 323–Present

1 Arr. *Anab.* 7.22.2–5; App. *Syr.* 56.

2 Arr. *Anab.* 7.24.1–3; Plut. *Alex.* 73.3–4.1.

3 Klaas Smelik, 'The "Omina Mortis" in the Histories of Alexander the Great', *Talenta*, X–XI (1978–9), pp. 92–111 (pp. 100–107).

4 The information here is based on Arr. *Anab.* 7.24.4–7.27.3; Diod. 17.117–18; Plut. *Alex.* 75–77.3; Just. 12.13.7–16.1.

5 Medical discussions include David Oldach et al., 'A Mysterious Death', *New England Journal of Medicine*, CCCXXXVIII/24 (1998), pp. 1764–9; Louise Cilliers and François Retief, 'The Death of Alexander the Great', *Acta Academica*, XXXI/1 (1999), pp. 63–76; John Marr and Charles Calisher, 'Alexander the Great and West Nile Virus Encephalitis', *Historical Review*,

IX/12 (2003), pp. 1599–603; Katherine Hall, 'Did Alexander the Great Die from Guillain-Barré Syndrome?', *Ancient History Bulletin*, XXXII (2018), pp. 106–28.

6 AD-322, B 'obv', 8.

7 The main evidence is Curt. 10.6–10.10; Diod. 18.1–2; Just. 13.1–4. Arrian's *Events after Alexander* survives only in an excerpt from Photius but describes events in Babylon and the initial stages of the Wars of the Successors. Books 18 to 20 of Diodorus give the most details of that conflict, with supplementary information in Plutarch's accounts of figures like Eumenes and Demetrius, and Books 13 to 15 of Justin. For readable modern accounts of this period, see James Romm, *Ghost on the Throne: The Death of Alexander the Great and the Bloody Fight for His Empire* (New York, 2012); Robin Waterfield, *Dividing the Spoils: The War for Alexander the Great's Empire* (Oxford, 2013).

8 Discussions include Manolis Andronikos, *Vergina: The Royal Tombs* (Athens, 1984), and 'Reflections on the Macedonian Tombs', *Annual of the British School at Athens*, LXXXII (1987), pp. 1–16; Nicholas Hammond, 'Philip's Tomb in Historical Context', *Greek, Roman and Byzantine Studies*, XIX/4 (1978), pp. 331–50, 'The Evidence for the Identity of the Royal Tombs at Vergia', in *Philip II, Alexander the Great, and the Macedonian Heritage*, ed. Winthrop Adams and Eugene Borza (Washington, DC, 1982), pp. 111–27, 'The Royal Tombs at Vergina: Evolution and Identities', *Annual of the British School at Athens*, LXXXVI (1991), pp. 69–82; Eugene Borza, 'The Royal Macedonian Tombs and the Paraphernalia of Alexander the Great', *Phoenix*, XLI/2 (1987), pp. 105–21; Antonis Bartsiokas, 'The Eye Injury of King Philip II and the Skeletal Evidence from the Royal Tomb II at Vergina', *Science*, CCLXXXVIII/5465 (2000), pp. 511–14; Eugene Borza and Olga Palagia, 'The Chronology of the Macedonian Royal Tombs at Vergina', *Jahrbuch des deutschen archäologischen Instituts*, CXXII (2007), pp. 81–125; Antonis Bartsiokas et al., 'The Lameness of King Philip II and Royal Tomb I at Vergina, Macedonia', *Proceedings of the National Academy of Sciences of the United States of America*, CXII/32 (2015), pp. 9844–8; Antonis Bartsiokas, Juan Luis Arsuaga and Nicholas Brandmeir, 'The Identification of the Royal Tombs in the Great Tumulus at Vergina, Macedonia, Greece: A Comprehensive Review', *Journal of Archaeological Science: Reports*, LII (2023), no. 104279. Discussion of the human remains follows the analyses by Bartsiokas. Antonis Bartsiokas has recently re-examined material found in Tomb II, arguing that it is the remains of a cotton garment comprising a purple layer between two white layers; this is reminiscent of the Persian robe adopted by Alexander so would potentially be conclusive proof that Tomb II postdates Alexander. See Antonis Bartsiokas, 'The Identification of the Sacred "Chiton" (*Sarapis*) or Pharaoh Alexander the Great in Tomb II at Vergina, Macedonia, Greece', *Journal of Field Archaeology* (2024), https://doi.org/10.1080/00934690.2024.2409503.

9 Bartsiokas, 'Eye Injury'. He also argues that the bones of the occupant of Tomb II were cremated quite a while after the person died, which likely fits Philip III more than Philip II, see Borza and Palagia, 'Chronology', p. 107.

10 For example, Demosthenes 11.22, 18.67.

11 Bartsiokas et al., 'Lameness', p. 9845; Bartsiokas et al., 'Identification', pp. 5–6.

12 See Borza and Palagia, 'Chronology', p. 107.
13 Andronikos, *Vergina*, p. 228.
14 Elizabeth Baynham, 'Why Didn't Alexander Marry Before Leaving Macedonia? Observations on Factional Politics at Alexander's Court in 336–334 BC', *Rheinisches Museum für Philologie*, CXLI/2 (1998), pp. 141–52.
15 Arr. *Anab.* 1.5.1–5.
16 Ibid. 1.23.5–7.
17 Ibid. 1.24.1–2.
18 *Metz Epitome* 70.
19 Albert Bosworth, 'Alexander the Great and the Decline of Macedon', *Journal of Hellenic Studies*, CVI (1986), pp. 1–12 (p. 9). After methodological criticisms, he rowed back on some of his remarks: Albert Bosworth, *The Legacy of Alexander: Politics, Warfare, and Propaganda* (Oxford, 2002), pp. 64–97.
20 Sian Cain, 'Alexander the Great Netflix Show Labelled "Extremely Poor-Quality Fiction" by Greek Minister', *The Guardian*, www.theguardian.com, 20 February 2024; Reuters Fact Check, 'Fact Check: "Gay" Storyline in Alexander the Great Netflix Series Based on Historical Context', *Reuters*, www.reuters.com, 16 February 2024; Matthew Cox, 'Netflix Show Is Being Review Bombed for Being too WOKE as Fans Slam New Drama', *Daily Mail*, www.dailymail.co.uk, 11 February 2024.

BIBLIOGRAPHY

Adcock, Frank, rev. K. D. Reynolds, 'Tarn, Sir William Woodthorpe', *Oxford Dictionary of National Biography* (2004, revd 2016)

Agostini, Domenico, and Samuel Thrope, *The Bundahišn: The Zoroastrian Book of Creation* (New York, 2020)

Almagor, Eran, 'Hunting and Leisure Activities', in *A Companion to the Achaemenid Empire*, ed. Bruno Jacobs and Robert Rollinger, 2 vols (Hoboken, NJ, 2021), pp. 1107–20

Andronikos, Manolis, 'Reflections on the Macedonian Tombs', *Annual of the British School at Athens*, LXXXII (1987), pp. 1–16

——, *Vergina: The Royal Tombs* (Athens, 1984)

Anson, Edward, *Philip II, the Father of Alexander the Great: Themes and Issues* (London, 2020)

Antela Bernárdez, Borja, 'El Alejandro homoerótico: homosexualidad en la Corte Macedonia', *Klio*, XCII/2 (2010), pp. 331–43

Badian, Ernst, 'Agis III', *Hermes*, XXIII (1967), pp. 170–92

——, 'Alexander in Iran', in *The Cambridge History of Iran*, vol. II: *The Median and Achaemenian Periods*, ed. I. Gershevitch (Cambridge, 1985), pp. 420–501

——, 'Alexander the Great and the Loneliness of Power', *Journal of the Australasian Universities Language and Literature Association*, XVII/1 (1962), pp. 80–91

——, 'Alexander the Great and the Unity of Mankind', *Historia*, VII/4 (1958), pp. 425–44

——, *Collected Papers on Alexander the Great* (London and New York, 2012)

——, 'Conspiracies', in *Alexander the Great in Fact and Fiction*, ed. Albert Bosworth and Elizabeth Baynham (Oxford, 2000), pp. 50–95

——, 'The Death of Parmenio', *Transactions and Proceedings of the American Philological Association*, XCI (1960), pp. 324–38

——, 'The Death of Philip II', *Phoenix*, XVII/4 (1963), pp. 244–50

——, 'The Eunuch Bagoas', *Classical Quarterly*, VIII/3–4 (1958), pp. 144–57

——, 'Harpalus', *Journal of Hellenic Studies*, LXXXI (1961), pp. 16–43

——, 'Mazaeus', *Encyclopaedia Iranica*, https://iranicaonline.org, 21 April 2015

Balsdon, John P.V.D., 'The "Divinity" of Alexander', *Historia*, I (1950), pp. 363–88

Bartsiokas, Antonis, 'The Eye Injury of King Philip II and the Skeletal Evidence from the Royal Tomb II at Vergina', *Science*, CCLXXXVIII/5465 (2000), pp. 511–14

——, et al., 'The Lameness of King Philip II and Royal Tomb I at Vergina, Macedonia', *Proceedings of the National Academy of Sciences of the United States of America*, CXII/32 (2015), pp. 9844–8

——, Juan Luis Arsuaga and Nicholas Brandmeir, 'The Identification of the Royal Tombs in the Great Tumulus at Vergina, Macedonia, Greece: A Comprehensive Review', *Journal of Archaeological Science: Reports*, LII (2023), no. 104279

Baynham, Elizabeth, 'Alexander and the Amazons', *Classical Quarterly*, LI/1 (2001), pp. 115–26

——, 'Why Didn't Alexander Marry Before Leaving Macedonia? Observations on Factional Politics at Alexander's Court in 336–334 BC', *Rheinisches Museum für Philologie*, CXLI/2 (1998), pp. 141–52

Beard, Mary, 'Alexander: How Great?', *New York Review of Books*, LVIII/16 (27 October 2011)

Bloedow, Edmund, and Heather Loube, 'Alexander the Great "Under Fire" at Persepolis', *Klio*, LXXIX/2 (1997), pp. 341–53

Borza, Eugene, 'Alexander at Persepolis', in *The Landmark Arrian: The Campaigns of Alexander*, ed. J. Romm (New York, 2010), pp. 367–70

——, 'Fire from Heaven: Alexander at Persepolis', *Classical Philology*, LXVII/4 (1972), pp. 233–45

——, 'The Royal Macedonian Tombs and the Paraphernalia of Alexander the Great', *Phoenix*, XLI/2 (1987), pp. 105–21

——, and Olga Palagia, 'The Chronology of the Macedonian Royal Tombs at Vergina', *Jahrbuch des deutschen archäologischen Instituts*, CXXII (2007), pp. 81–125

Bosworth, Albert B., *Alexander and the East: The Tragedy of Triumph* (Oxford, 1996)

——, 'Alexander and the Iranians', *Journal of Hellenic Studies*, C (1980), pp. 1–21

——, 'Alexander the Great and the Decline of Macedon', *Journal of Hellenic Studies*, CVI (1986), pp. 1–12

——, *Conquest and Empire: The Reign of Alexander the Great* (Cambridge, 1988)

——, *From Arrian to Alexander: Studies in Historical Interpretation* (Oxford, 1988)

——, *A Historical Commentary on Arrian's History of Alexander*, vol. I: *Commentary on Books I–III* (Oxford, 1980)

——, *A Historical Commentary on Arrian's History of Alexander*, vol. II: *Commentary on Books IV–V* (Oxford, 1995)

——, 'The Impossible Dream: W. W. Tarn's *Alexander* in Retrospect', *Karanos*, II (2019), pp. 77–95, first published in *Ancient Society: Resources for Teachers*, XIII (1983)

——, *The Legacy of Alexander: Politics, Warfare, and Propaganda* (Oxford, 2002)

Bowden, Hugh, 'On Kissing and Making Up: Court Protocol and Historiography in Alexander the Great's "Experiment" with *Proskynesis*', *Bulletin of the Institute of Classical Studies*, LVI/2 (2013), pp. 55–77

Briant, Pierre, *Alexander the Great and His Empire: A Short Introduction* (Princeton, NJ, 2010)

——, 'Chasses royales macédoniennes et chasses royales perses: le theme de la chasse au lion sur la chasse de Vergina', *Dialogues d'histoire ancienne*, XVII/1 (1991), pp. 211–55

——, *Darius in the Shadow of Alexander* (Cambridge, MA, 2015)

——, *From Cyrus to Alexander: A History of the Persian Empire* (Winona Lake, IN, 2002)

——, 'Sources gréco-hellenistiques, institutions perses et institutions macédoniens: continuités, changements et bricolages', in *Achaemenid History*, vol. VIII: *Continuity and Change*, ed. Heleen Sancisi-Weerdenburg, Amélie Kuhrt and Margaret Root (Leiden, 1994), pp. 283–310

Brosius, Maria, 'Alexander and the Persians', in *Brill's Companion to Alexander the Great*, ed. Joseph Roisman (Leiden, 2003), pp. 169–96

Carney, Elizabeth, 'Alexander and Persian Women', *American Journal of Philology*, CXVII/4 (1996), pp. 563–83

——, 'Hunting and the Macedonian Elite: Sharing the Rivalry of the Chase (Arrian 4.13.1)', in *The Hellenistic World: New Perspectives*, ed. Daniel Ogden (Swansea, 2002), pp. 59–80

——, *Women and Monarchy in Ancient Macedonia* (Norman, OK, 2000)

——, 'Women in Alexander's Court', in *Brill's Companion to Alexander the Great*, ed. Joseph Roisman (Leiden, 2003), pp. 227–52

Carr, Edward H., *What Is History?* (Harmondsworth, 1961)

Cartledge, Paul, *Alexander the Great: The Hunt for a New Past* (London, 2004)

Cilliers, Louise, and François Retief, 'The Death of Alexander the Great', *Acta Academica*, XXXI (1999), pp. 63–76

Degen, Julian, *Alexander III. zwischen Ost und West. Indigene Traditionen und Herrschaftsinszenierung im makedonischen Weltimperium* (Stuttgart, 2022)

Dover, Kenneth J., *Greek Homosexuality* (London, 1978)

Engels, David, and Kyle Erickson, 'Apama and Stratonike – Marriage and Legitimacy', in *Seleukid Royal Women: Creation, Representation and Distortion of Hellenistic Queenship in the Seleukid Empire*, ed. Altay Coşkun and Alex McAuley (Stuttgart, 2016), pp. 67–86

Fredricksmeyer, Ernst, 'Alexander the Great and the Kingship of Asia', in *Alexander the Great in Fact and Fiction*, ed. Albert Bosworth and Elizabeth Baynham (Oxford, 2000), pp. 136–66

——, 'Alexander's Religion and Divinity', in *Brill's Companion to Alexander the Great*, ed. Joseph Roisman (Leiden, 2003), pp. 253–78

Gehrke, Hans-Joachim, *Alexander der Grosse* (Munich, 1996)

Grayson, Albert K., *Babylonian Historical-Literary Texts* (Toronto, 1975)

Green, Peter, *Alexander of Macedon: A Historical Biography*, 2nd edn (Harmondsworth, 1974)

Hall, Edith, *Inventing the Barbarian: Greek Self-Definition through Tragedy* (Oxford, 1989)

Hall, Katherine, 'Did Alexander the Great Die from Guillain-Barré Syndrome?', *Ancient History Bulletin*, XXXII (2018), pp. 106–28

Hamilton, J. R., *Plutarch Alexander: A Commentary* (Oxford, 1969)

Hammond, Nicholas G. L., *Alexander the Great: King, Commander and Statesman*, 3rd edn (London, 1994)

——, 'The Evidence for the Identity of the Royal Tombs at Vergia', in *Philip II, Alexander the Great, and the Macedonian Heritage*, ed. Winthrop L. Adams and Eugene N. Borza (Washington, DC, 1982), pp. 111–27

——, *The Genius of Alexander the Great* (London, 1997)

——, Philip's Tomb in Historical Context', *Greek, Roman and Byzantine Studies*, XIX/4 (1978), pp. 331–50

——, 'The Royal Tombs at Vergina: Evolution and Identities', *Annual of the British School at Athens*, LXXXVI (1991), pp. 69–82

Harders, Ann-Catrin, 'The Making of a Queen – Seleukos Nikator and His Wives', in *Seleukid Royal Women: Creation, Representation and Distortion of Hellenistic Queenship in the Seleukid Empire*, ed. Altay Coşkun and Alex McAuley (Stuttgart, 2016), pp. 25–38

Harris, William, 'Badian, Ernst, 1925–2011', *Biographical Memoirs of Fellows of the British Academy* XVI, www.thebritishacademy.ac.uk, 25 April 2017

Harrison, Stephen, *Kingship and Empire under the Achaemenids, Alexander the Great and the Early Seleucids* (Edinburgh, forthcoming)

——, 'Alexander in Bactria and India, and the Spanish in America: Agency and Interaction on the Fringes of Empire', in *Theorising Comparative History for the Ancient Mediterranean: Asking New Questions of Old Evidence*, ed. Dylan James and Stephen Harrison (Liverpool, forthcoming)

——, 'Changing spaces, Changing Behaviours: Achaemenid Spatial Features at the Court of Alexander the Great', *Journal of Ancient History*, VI/2 (2018), pp. 185–214

Harrison, Thomas, *The Emptiness of Asia: Aeschylus' 'Persians' and the History of the Fifth Century* (London, 2000)

Heckel, Waldemar, 'The Conspiracy Against Philotas', *Phoenix*, XXXI/1 (1977), pp. 9–21

——, *In the Path of Conquest: Resistance to Alexander the Great* (New York, 2020)

——, 'King and "Companions:" Observations on the Nature of Power in the Reign of Alexander', in *Brill's Companion to Alexander the Great*, ed. Joseph Roisman (Leiden, 2003), pp. 197–226

——, *The Marshals of Alexander's Empire*, 2nd edn (London, 2016)

——, *Who's Who in the Age of Alexander the Great: Prosopography of Alexander's Empire* (Oxford, 2006)

James, Dylan, 'Nearchus, Guides, and Place Names on Alexander's Expedition', *Mnemosyne*, LXXIII/4 (2020), pp. 553–76

Klinkott, Hilmar, *Der Satrap: ein achaimenidischer Amtsträger und seine Handlungsspielräume* (Frankfurt, 2005)

Koulakiotis, Elias, 'Domination et resistance à la cour d'Alexandre: Le cas des basilikoi paides', in *Esclavage Antique et Discriminations Socio-Culturelles*, ed. Vasilis I. Anastasiadis and Panagiotis N. Doukellis (Bern, 2005), pp. 167–82

Kuhrt, Amélie, *The Persian Empire: A Corpus of Sources from the Achaemenid Period* (London and New York, 2007)

Lane Fox, Robin, *Alexander the Great* [1973] (London, 2004)

Liotsakis, Vasileios, *Alexander the Great in Arrian's 'Anabasis'* (Berlin and Boston, MA, 2019)

Liverani, Mario, *Prestige and Interest: International Relations in the Near East, ca. 1600–1100 BC* (Padua, 1990)

Llewellyn-Jones, Lloyd, *King and Court in Ancient Persia 559 to 331 BCE* (Edinburgh, 2013)

——, *Persians: The Age of the Great Kings* (London, 2022)

Luschey, Heinz, 'Der Löwe von Ekbatana', *Archäologische Mitteilungen aus Iran*, I (1968), pp. 115–29

McKechnie, Paul, 'Diodorus Siculus and Hephaestion's Pyre', *Classical Quarterly*, XLV/2 (1995), pp. 418–32

Manteghi, Haila, *Alexander the Great in the Persian Tradition: History, Myth and Legend in Medieval Iran* (London, 2018)

Marr, John S., and Charles H. Calisher, 'Alexander the Great and West Nile Virus Encephalitis', *Historical Review*, IX/12 (2003), pp. 1599–603

Matarese, Chiara, 'Proskynēsis and the Gesture of the Kiss at Alexander's Court: The Creation of a New Élite', *Palamedes*, VIII (2013), pp. 75–85

——, 'Sending a Kiss to the King: The Achaemenid Proskynēsis between Explanations and Misunderstandings', *The Ancient World*, LXV (2014), pp. 122–33

Montefiore, Simon Sebag, *Voices of History: Speeches that Changed the World* (London, 2019)

Muccioli, Federicomaria, 'Classical Sources and *Proskynesis*: History of a Misunderstanding', in *Alexander's Legacy*, ed. France Landucci Gattioni (Rome, 2016), pp. 41–60

Müller, Sabine, *Alexander der Grosse: Eroberung, Politik, Rezeption* (Stuttgart, 2019)

——, 'Hephaistion: A Re-Assessment of His Career', in *Ancient Macedonians in Greek and Roman Sources: From History to Historiography*, ed. Timothy Howe and Frances Pownall (Swansea, 2018), pp. 77–102

——, 'In the Shadow of His Father: Alexander, Hermolaus, and the Legend of Philip', in *Philip II and Alexander the Great: Father and Son, Lives and Afterlives*, ed. Elizabeth Carney and Daniel Ogden (Oxford 2010), pp. 25–32

Naveh, Joseph, and Shaul Shaked, *Aramaic Documents from Ancient Bactria from the Khalili Collections* (London, 2012)

Nielsen, Inge, *Hellenistic Palaces: Tradition and Renewal* (Aarhus, 1994)

O'Brien, John M., *Alexander the Great: The Invisible Enemy* (London and New York, 1992)

Ogden, Daniel, 'Alexander's Sex Life', in *Alexander the Great: A New History*, ed. Waldemar Heckel and Lawrence A. Tritle (Oxford, 2009), pp. 203–17

Oldach, David W., et al., 'A Mysterious Death', *New England Journal of Medicine*, CCCXXXVIII/24 (1998), pp. 1764–9

O'Sullivan, Lara, 'Reinventing *Proskynesis*: Callisthenes and the Peripatetic School', *Historia*, LXIX/3 (2020), pp. 260–82

Perrot, Jean, 'Restoration, Reconstruction', in *The Palace of Darius I at Susa: The Great Royal Residence of Achaemenid Persia*, ed. Jean Perrot (London, 2013), pp. 209–39

Pietrykowski, Joseph, *Great Battles of the Hellenistic World* (Barnsley, 2009)

Pownall, Frances, 'Callisthenes in Africa: The Historian's Role at Siwah and in the *Proskynesis* Controversy', in *Alexander in Africa*, ed. Philip Bosman (Pretoria, 2014), pp. 56–71

Prandi, Luisa, 'New Evidence for the Dating of Cleitarchus (*Poxy* LXXXI. 4808)?', *Histos*, VI (2012), pp. 15–26

Rapoport, Amos, *The Meaning of the Built Environment: A Nonverbal Communication Approach* [1982] (Tuscon, AZ, 1990)

——, 'Systems of Activities and Systems of Settings', in *Domestic Architecture and the Use of Space*, ed. Susan Kent (Cambridge), pp. 9–20

Reames, Jeanne, 'An Atypical Affair? Alexander the Great, Hephaistion Amyntoros and the Nature of Their Relationship', *Ancient History Bulletin*, XIII/3 (1999), pp. 81–96

Rhodes, Peter J., and Robin Osborne, *Greek Historical Inscriptions, 404–323 BC* (Oxford, 2003)

Rollinger, Robert, and Julian Degen, 'Alexander the Great, the Indian Ocean, and the Borders of the World', in *Achemenet. Vingt ans après: Études offertes à Pierre Briant à l'occasion des vingt ans du Programme Achemenet*, ed. Damien Agut-Labordère et al. (Leuven, Paris, and Bristol, CT, 2021), pp. 321–42

——, and ——, eds, *The World of Alexander in Perspective: Contextualizing Arrian* (Wiesbaden, 2022)

Romm, James, *Ghost on the Throne: The Death of Alexander the Great and the Bloody Fight for His Empire* (New York, 2012)

Said, Edward W., *Orientalism* (Harmondsworth, 1978)

Sancisi-Weerdenburg, Heleen, 'Alexander and Persepolis', in *Alexander the Great: Reality and Myth*, ed. J. Carlsen et al. (Rome, 1993), pp. 177–88

——, and Amélie Kuhrt, eds, *The Greek Sources: Proceedings of the Groningen 1984 Achaemenid History Workshop* (Leiden, 1987)

Schachermeyr, Fritz, *Alexander der Grosse: Ingenium und Macht* (Graz, 1949)

——, *Alexander der Grosse: das Problem seiner Persönlichkeit und seines Wirkens* (Vienna, 1973)

Schmidt, Erich, *Persepolis I: Structures, Reliefs, Inscriptions* (Chicago, IL, 1953)

Scott, James C., *Domination and the Arts of Resistance: Hidden Transcripts* (New Haven, CT, 1990)

——, 'Everyday Forms of Resistance', *Copenhagen Papers*, IV (1989), pp. 33–62

——, *Weapons of the Weak: Everyday Forms of Peasant Resistance* (New Haven, CT, 1985)

Sekunda, Nicholas, 'Changes in Achaemenid Royal Dress', in *The World of Achaemenid Persia: History, Art and Society in Iran and the Ancient Near East*, ed. John Curtis and St. John Simpson (London, 2010), pp. 255–72

Smelik, Klaas, 'The "Omina Mortis" in the Histories of Alexander the Great', *Talenta*, X–XI (1978–9), pp. 92–111

Spawforth, Anthony, 'The Court of Alexander the Great between Europe and Asia', in *The Court and Court Society in Ancient Monarchies*, ed. Spawforth (Cambridge, 2007), pp. 82–120

Stadter, Philip, *Arrian of Nicomedia* (Chapel Hill, NC, 1980)

Tarn, William Woodthorpe, *Alexander the Great*, 2 vols (Cambridge, 1948)

——, *Alexander the Great and the Unity of Mankind* (London, 1933)

Tuplin, Christopher, 'The Great King, His God(s) and Intimations of Divinity: The Achaemenid Hinterland of Ruler Cult?', *Ancient History Bulletin*, XXXI (2017), pp. 92–111

——, 'Treacherous Hearts and Upright Tiaras: The Achaemenid King's Head-Dress', in *Persian Responses: Political and Cultural Interaction with(in) the Achaemenid Empire*, ed. Christopher Tuplin (Swansea, 2007), pp. 67–98

Vahman, Fereydun, ed., *Ardā Wirāz Nāmag: The Iranian 'Divina Commedia'* (London, 1986)

Waterfield, Robin, *Dividing the Spoils: The War for Alexander the Great's Empire* (Oxford, 2013)

Waters, Matt, *Ancient Persia: A Concise History of the Achaemenid Empire, 550–330 BCE* (New York, 2014)

Weiskopf, Michael, *The So-Called 'Great Satraps' Revolt', 366–360 BC: Concerning Local Instability in the Achaemenid Far West* (Stuttgart, 1989)

Wiesehöfer, Josef, 'The "Accursed" and the "Adventurer": Alexander the Great in Iranian Tradition', in *A Companion to Alexander Literature in the Middle Ages*, ed. Z. David Zuwiyya (Leiden, 2011), pp. 113–32

Worthington, Ian, *Alexander the Great: Man and God* (Harlow, 2004)

——, *Philip ii of Macedonia* (New Haven, ct, 2008)

ACKNOWLEDGEMENTS

I first properly encountered Alexander as an undergraduate student, when I chose to write about him for my dissertation. That thesis was supervised by Paul Cartledge, who had recently published his own biography of Alexander. Suffice to say that it was a real honour when Paul asked me to contribute to this series, and on Alexander no less. I am incredibly grateful to Paul for his guidance and support over the last fifteen years, and throughout the course of this book's development. I am indebted to all of the staff at Reaktion, who have guided me through the production process, and especially to Vivian Constantinopoulos, commissioning editor of the Great Lives of the Ancient World series, whose expertise and patience has saved this novice from many an error, and to Emma Devlin, who has expertly guided me through the final stages of publication. Matthew Coneys Wainwright and Pete Griffiths kindly read a draft of the whole thing, and their suggestions have enriched the final version no end. Talking about Alexander with Dylan James, my collaborator on another venture, has developed endless new insights; Lloyd Llewellyn-Jones generously put his extensive library of photographs of Iran at my disposal. Almost everything here has been presented in one form or another over the years to my students. Nothing makes it easier to spot a bad idea than frowns in the front row and I am incredibly grateful to my students for giving me the opportunity to work through so many of my ideas in a supportive environment. Those thanks extend to my colleagues at Swansea University, especially to the regulars of the HHC Lunch Club who heard more about Alexander than they would have wished and offered a vital escape from writing. My family, especially my mum and dad, nurtured and nourished my love of history and supported me in pursuing a career in a field that I love. But the biggest thanks of all go to Jennie, who has to hear all of my bad ideas so that some good ones end up on the page.

PHOTO ACKNOWLEDGEMENTS

The author and publishers wish to express their thanks to the sources listed below for illustrative material and/or permission to reproduce it. Some locations of artworks are also given below, in the interest of brevity:

© S. Ballard 2024: pp. 6–7, 36, 42, 66, 90, 112, 134; Dallas Museum of Art, TX: p. 63; From Edward S. Ellis and Charles F. Horne, *The Story of the Greatest Nations, from the Dawn of History to the Twentieth Century* (New York, *c.* 1906), vol. II, photo University of California Libraries: p. 147; Flickr: pp. 79 and 171 (photos Carole Raddato, CC BY-SA 2.0), 185 (photo George M. Groutas, CC BY-SA 2.0), 199 (photo Prince Roy, CC BY-SA 2.0); The J. Paul Getty Museum, Los Angeles: p. 174; courtesy Lloyd Llewellyn-Jones: pp. 100, 143; The Metropolitan Museum of Art, New York: pp. 46, 157, 200; National Gallery of Art, Washington, DC: pp. 18, 31; Rijksmuseum, Amsterdam: p. 97; Wikimedia Commons: pp. 14 (Ny Carlsberg Glyptotek, Copenhagen; photo Marie-Lan Nguyen, CC BY-SA 4.0), 51 (Museo Archeologico Nazionale, Naples; photo Berthold Werner, CC BY-SA 3.0), 53 (Château de Versailles), 71 (Musée du Louvre, Paris), 72 (The British Museum, London; photo Zunkir, CC BY-SA 4.0), 121 (CC BY-SA 1.0), 154 (photo dynamosquito, CC BY-SA 2.0); Yale University Art Gallery, New Haven, CT: pp. 23, 195.

INDEX